Praise for Jim Bagnola and
Becoming a Professional Human Being

"This is just the kind of book I want to read. It's an inspiration! Read it, employ it, and live longer, healthier, and happier. Jim Bagnola is funny and tells great stories, all of which are educational and enlightening while they entertain. Every few pages you'll discover a nugget and say, 'Of course, that's right. Why didn't I think of that?'"

Brian Rees, M.D.
Colonel, Medical Service Corps, U.S. Army Reserve
Command Surgeon, 63rd Regional Support Command

"Wow! Thank you for the intellectual feast of following your deep practical wisdom to become a PhB."

Dr. Fred Travis, Ph.D.
Director of the Center for Brain Research
Maharishi University of Management

"Jim Bagnola is an expert in getting to know the people in your business as well as getting to know your business. His experience with past business relationships helps him to be the best in his field in creating a marriage between 'the people' and the business. He is one of the best in one-on-one executive management development. His book, *Becoming a Professional Human Being,* will give you the feeling of that one-on-one coaching."

Jon Flora
Fry's Division President, The Kroger Company

"The practical knowledge that Jim shares in his book around finding our magic and the mind-body connection is the missing link for being on autopilot to becoming the architect of our destiny."

Adrian Ionescu
Services Delivery Sr. Manager
Dell Global Services Delivery, Dell Inc.

"Jim has truly left a legacy within the federal government that few have matched. His distinctive influence reflects great credit upon himself and the thousands of lives he has touched, especially mine. This book will touch innumerable more. This book will change your life by asking you, 'How are you investing your energy, creativity, and intelligence?'"

Earl R. Vialpando
Intelligence Program Manager, Department of Defense
The Pentagon

"For anyone wishing to become a Professional Human Being, Jim's book is a must-read. Jim Bagnola is a charismatic, entertaining, motivational speaker who lives what he preaches. His course on 'Becoming a Professional Human Being' has changed the lives of individuals and corporations worldwide. This book will do the same for the reader."

David Lee Sheng Tin, Ph.D.
Certified Holistic Health Coach
National Director, Maharishi Institute of Science and Technology
Trinidad and Tobago, West Indies

"I randomly opened the book, started reading, and found myself taking notes from it. This is Jim: a walking learning event. And this book in particular is a continuous source of learning opportunities. If you are a lifelong learner, open the book and prepare to be challenged."

Madalina Vintu
Co-Director of Leadership Training, Leaders Romania Foundation
Bucharest, Romania

"Jim activates the magic from within you and lets you spread this magic to others. Direction and purpose of life become clear. Most of all, Jim gives you the secrets to energize and evolve. The easiest and most rewarding degree to earn in life is the PhB; he imparts by example."

Dr. Suresh K. Chatrani
Managing Director, OmniSource, Inc.
Barbados, West Indies

"After reading this book I'm on my way to becoming a PhB. Everyone should have the chance to read this book—Can you imagine what our planet would look like afterwards? I'm a lucky person. Our company is a client of Jim Bagnola, and we have discovered that he has a gift to change you forever and so does this book. Do you know what kind of person can write such a book? Yes, only a PhB."

Mariana Sana
General Manager, MTC
Cluj-Napoca, Romania

Becoming a Professional Human Being

How to Enjoy **Stress-Free Work**
and **Personal Happiness**
Using the Mind/Body/Work
Connection

Jim Bagnola

Foreword by Veronica Butler, M.D.
Co-Author of *A Woman's Best Medicine*

GLOBAL THINKING
PRESS

Becoming a Professional Human Being

How to Enjoy Stress-Free Work and Personal Happiness
Using the Mind/Body/Work Connection

Jim Bagnola
© Jim Bagnola 2014
Tel: 512-419-4139

Published by Global Thinking Press

First Edition

ISBN: 978-0-9851964-0-0

Fifth Printing 2014

This book is dedicated to my parents,
Dominic and Beverly Bagnola.

Thank you for being who you are,
which taught me how to be.

To all of you who've attended my
Professional Human Being workshops:

I have learned so much from you.
This book is for you.

In memory of my mentor
Robert W. Larson
A true Professional Human Being
1919 - 2012

Contents

PART III — COMMENCEMENT

Foreword

Not a having and a resting, but a growing and
a becoming is the character of perfection.

— MATTHEW ARNOLD
British poet

Are you ready? In this book you will be inspired and challenged to take a giant evolutionary leap forward and become a Professional Human Being. Instead of just accepting the status quo, we all have the potential to live every moment in life to the fullest. A fast track for accelerated growth in every aspect of your life is available to you. Historically Homo sapiens have grown from hunting and gathering, to mastering machines in the industrial age, to using information and knowledge as an industry.

Next, we humans created a worldwide marketplace with the help of the Internet and computers. Then we turned inward and developed our self-awareness and personal consciousness to levels never before experienced on such a broad scale. With this book Jim Bagnola takes us to the next level by offering the world a vision and practical steps to actually do more, have more, give more, and be more than was previously thought possible.

The concept that our careers, minds, and bodies exist as separate entities is false and is limiting our experience of life. Our jobs, thoughts, and physical health are not isolated compartments, but different expressions of the oneness we call our "selves." Each interacts with and profoundly affects the other. Accordingly, we can't be fully effective at work unless we are healthy and happy. Our jobs should be instruments to heal ourselves and our world. True vitality is impossible unless we feel passionate about our vocations and relationships. The inner and outer rewards life has to offer are one and the same.

Jim clearly defines how a Professional Human Being thinks, acts, and contributes to society. The book begins with an inspiring story of Jim's chance meeting with a Professional Human Being who shines shoes for a living. My heart was touched by the beauty of this man's simple and successful life. Throughout the book, you'll find many stories, including several about the life and work of the world-famous magician and Professional Human Being, Doug Henning, that illustrate the power and wisdom of the point Jim is trying to teach us.

As a scientist, I appreciated the research that proved the veracity of the concepts presented. In Part II of this book, Jim provides practical "action ideas" to turn the information and knowledge into our own wisdom as we experience the power of each lesson.

For over a quarter century, Jim has shared his potent ideas and experiences with clients. Many of them are employers who were frustrated by escalating health-care costs. Data show that the average cost for an employee's health care in 2001 was $4,794; in 2010 it was $11,058. Organizations committed to the health and growth of their workforce have taken advantage of Jim's wisdom as he presented his win-win situations.

We are cheating ourselves, our loved ones, and society if we continue to play small. Now we all have access to the information previously reserved for the corporate world. The real possibility of turning our lives and the future of mankind around is exciting.

Whatever our current situation, we all can grow to new levels of abundance, passion, health, and fulfillment.

Get ready!

Veronica Butler, M.D.
Co-Author of *A Woman's Best Medicine*

Preface

Meet Leroy Grant, PhB

In this life we cannot do great things.
We can only do small things with great love.

— MOTHER TERESA
Catholic nun and winner of the 1979 Nobel Peace Prize

I walked into the Loews Anatole Hotel in Dallas, Texas. I was there to deliver a keynote address that evening to a group of engineers constructing the Dallas Area Rapid Transit system. Needing a shoeshine, I looked around the lobby and saw a shoe stand and a gentleman who seemed to be preparing to call it a day.

I hustled over and asked if he had time for one more shine. He was a tall, thin, African-American man with graying temples, and an infectious smile. He was wearing a crisp, white shirt and a bow tie.

"Of course," he answered warmly. "If you need a shine, I'll make time. Have a seat, son."

I sat down. He began to meticulously roll up the cuffs of my pants and lay out his tools of trade. I noticed that it was after six o'clock.

"When did you start your day?" I asked.

"Oh, around seven this morning."

"You've been here for nearly twelve hours? And you still look fresh!"

"I guess that's because I love my job."

"May I ask you how old you are?"

"Sure," he said. "I'm 72. And healthy and happy."

"And you worked twelve hours today?"

"Yes, I work twelve hours most days."

I was amazed.

He continued, "Well, to be honest, I do love my job, but my wife doesn't want me at home all day. You know how it is after many years of marriage." We laughed.

I introduced myself and he responded with a hearty handshake and his name: Leroy Grant.

"Well, how long have you been a shoe shiner, Leroy?"

He looked up at me with a serious look on his face and said, "Excuse me, but I am not a shoe shiner."

"Sorry," I said. "What *is* your profession?"

"I am a leather technician."

When he saw my confusion, he explained: "A shoe shiner is just a shoe shiner. A leather technician is an artist. I'm an artist. I'm going to give you the best shine you've ever had, and then I'm going to guarantee my work."

I've had my shoes shined all over the world but nobody had ever guaranteed their work.

"What does that mean?" I asked.

"I am gonna shine your shoes until you are happy. Then you should be able to buff them up to a nice, glossy shine for the next two weeks. If you can't do that, you come right back in here and I will shine them again, free. No charge. Now, if you walk through mud and puddles, you're on your own! My caring for your leather doesn't end until you are satisfied. That's my guarantee!"

"I got it, Leroy, and I'm impressed. You really do love your job, I can tell."

"Love my job?" he exclaimed. "Look at me! I don't have a boss looking over my shoulder. I am the boss! Look at my office!" He gestured to the large, fancy hotel lobby. "Look over there," he said, pointing at a nearby bank of public pay phones. "Those are my private phones. My wife and friends can call me. My kids call me. You know, I put all my kids through school doing this. If you come and I'm not here, you might meet one of them. My son is my vice president. He's a leather technician as well."

"How long have you been doing this?"

"Sixty years."

"Sixty years!" I exclaimed in disbelief. "You started when you were twelve?"

"I did," he nodded. "My father said that I had to work and help out— you know, it was around the Depression. He wanted me to sell newspapers. He felt that was the best way for a young boy to make money. But I wanted to shine shoes. When I would get my haircut at the barbershop, I would watch the shoe shiners in their shop and they always looked like they were having a lot of fun. I wanted to do that. I asked my dad and he said, 'You can't make money shining shoes. Sell the papers.' Since my father wouldn't let me do it, I figured out a way to sell newspapers and shine shoes, too.

"I asked the barbershop owner if he could teach me how to shine and to let me shine shoes part time if I worked for tips only. He said yes, and I was on my way. I had a little sign, 'Free Shine, Tips Only.' After a few months of doing this, I went to my dad with two piles of money. I pointed to one pile and said to my dad that this is how much money I had made from selling papers. I pointed to the bigger pile and said this is how much I had made shining shoes part time. My father looked at the piles and said, 'Son, time to shine shoes!'"

Leroy looked at me with a big smile. "I am lucky because I'm on my own and I don't worry about things. I also get to meet nice people all day long. I beautify the world a little bit every day. I am on a mission." Motioning with both hands towards the floor, he said, "I beautify the world down low!"

I was inspired.

But before I left I had one more question for him. I couldn't help myself; I just had to ask him, "Leroy, how do you manage to keep your shirt so white at the end of the day?"

I just knew he was going to tell me something about the careful technique of his shoe shining. Instead, he said, "Son, you change it at lunch!"

I laughed out loud. Leroy doesn't miss a beat. Great service down to the smallest detail!

After what I would call the best shine I have ever received, he offered me a discount card that was an offer for so many shines for $25—a half-price deal. I bought the card, not because I was going back to the hotel anytime soon, but because I wanted to support whatever he was doing. I also gave him a nice tip, which I'm betting all of his customers do.

Later, when I addressed the engineers, you can guess what I talked about. Yes, of course, Leroy Grant and how he transformed his shoe-shining job into something larger, into something he loved, into a profession and, indeed, an art form.

A few months later, I was back in Dallas working with another client, The Kroger Company, and of course I went out of my way to visit Leroy. He recognized me right away and said, "Hey, aren't you the fellow who gave a talk here and told everybody my story about the leather technician?"

I said, "That was me."

He grinned, "I'm telling you, son, I owe you some money."

"What money?" I was confused.

"Well, the day after you were here, I was swamped with business from those people at your talk. They all wanted a shine from the leather technician."

I responded, "You don't owe me any money, Leroy, but I've come for a shine and some inspiration."

I don't know about you but I want to do business with people like Leroy. In fact, I want to *be like* Leroy Grant. I want to view everything I do in a positive manner. I want to love what I'm doing and be happy with myself when I'm 72. Leroy seemed happy and healthy. He put his kids through school and supported his family for over sixty years doing a job he genuinely loved.

Leroy Grant is a Professional Human Being.

Introduction

Every artist was first an amateur.

— RALPH WALDO EMERSON
American poet

How many people do you know who approach their work like Leroy Grant? Do you approach your job with joy and purpose? Have you creatively transformed your job into an art form? Are you on a self-created mission? Do you enjoy your customers? Are you happy to be of service to those counting on your expertise? Do you guarantee your work? Are you delighted to be at work? Have you turned Pro like Leroy has?

If you can't answer yes to most of these questions, your health and the health of the organization you belong to might be at stake! The organization will never be what the individuals are not.

I educate executives, managers, and employees worldwide in business and government, to be peak performers in an uncertain, stressful, and unhealthy workplace. I've been doing this for more than twenty-five years for repeat clients that include Fortune 500 companies, federal and state agencies, and small privately held companies.

What sets me apart and appeals to audiences is my emphasis on the mind/body/work connection. Clients tell me this emphasis helps them switch gears and make the information stick. I will explain to you the mind/body/work connection in depth. You will discover how constructive thinking patterns produce the physiology to support success, the making of a Professional Human Being, and, at the same time, better health.

In my workshops, I link the consequences of thinking and actions at work not just to performance, but directly to health. I show people how their time at work should contribute to their health and rejuvenation and not, as is the norm, contribute to health problems and premature death. I tell them about my wise friend, Leroy Grant.

The advice I share with my audiences is this: *Make a living, not a dying.*

My approach resonates with a wide range of people who don't connect their jobs to their health and longevity. It's necessary to transform negative, self-defeating, disease-promoting thoughts into attitudes that generate creativity, productivity, fulfillment, and harmonious relationships. The result of this is better health for you and your organization. The fact is that the organization will never be what the individuals are not.

John Howard, Director of the National Institute for Occupational Safety and Health, recently said, "If we're going to keep improving productivity, we have to make sure that we keep workers healthy."

As an example of the crucial role health plays for both the individual and the organization, back in the late 1980s, my friend, Marci Shimoff (author of *Happy for No Reason* and *Love for No Reason*), and I were hired by General Motors to help educate employees in the art of managing stress. Why? They were then spending anywhere from $1500 to nearly $1800 right off the top of a car sale for health-care costs. Their present dire financial situation, with the government bailout, is in part due to the health of their employees and retirees. Health care will play a vital role in the viability of organizations going forward.

To me, keeping workers healthy goes far beyond the medical benefits an employer offers to employees. It goes, in fact, far beyond anything an employer does or doesn't do. It goes instead to what an individual at any level in the workplace—from the very top to the very bottom—does for himself or herself. If you don't care for your health, it doesn't matter which health-care system you have. None of them will work.

THE PROFESSIONAL HUMAN BEING

At more than 150 workshops yearly, I turn the thinking of the people in my audiences upside down and put them on the path (which I'm still on myself) to becoming Professional Human Beings—individuals you want to hire, promote, be members of your team, do business with, or otherwise be in relation with.

The book you have in your hands will help you gain what I call PhB status—becoming a Professional Human Being. It offers you the same holistic insights and action recommendations I give to my audiences, and it serves as a workplace guide for the well-being of both employee and employer.

For employees, I focus on *self-management*—the fundamental importance of the relationship we have with our own selves. Until you improve your relationship with yourself, you can't improve your ability to be hired, promoted, achieve goals, and enhance work relationships.

For employers and managers, these very same individual improvements contribute to organizational goals of increased capacity and productivity, along with decreased health-care costs.

In today's workplace, the common reality is just the opposite: decreased capacity and productivity and increased health-care costs.

The inspiration for my approach draws from Galileo's premise: "You cannot teach a man anything; you can only help him discover it within himself." Accordingly, I strive to turn people inward, then upside down, and awaken them to the reality of their own uniqueness, greatness, and capacity!

HOW THIS BOOK IS DIFFERENT

I've structured this book into three parts. The first part explains why we need to turn our thinking upside down from our Standard Operating Programs (StOP)—the habitual thinking patterns that undermine job fulfillment, happiness, and health—to Professional Human Being (PhB) thinking. In a nutshell, StOP thinking gets us stuck; PhB thinking moves us forward. What do I mean by that? Well, most self-help books focus on action, but what is action based on? Action is based on thinking. Before we can take action to change our lives, we must first change *how we think*. People want to improve, but they don't want to change. They remain stuck in StOP gear.

In the second part of the book, I lay out seven lessons for attaining, so to speak, a PhB degree—mind-shifting ideas that change the way we think. *When we change the way we think of things, the things we think of change.* Perspective changes everything. I conclude in the third part by introducing you to a Professional Human Being who is saving lives.

My job is not only to give you cutting-edge information and practical ideas but also to help you remember them. We're often human forgettings rather than human beings; we tend to forget more than we actually remember. What I learned from Doug Henning, the magician, is that we have to make it fun and entertaining in order for someone to remember. So what I do is wrap my principles in a charming story, a memorable anecdote, or a humorous vignette; if you remember my story, you'll remember my principles. The lessons are filled with personal stories, scientific research, and action ideas to inspire your own personal changes and move you from StOP to PhB. Moreover, I will introduce you to many of my friends and colleagues, whom I consider Professional Human Beings; I will recount their inspiring stories.

In this book, I link changes in thinking to improvements in individual health, and to health consequences if changes are not made. This reverberates to create a healthy organization. My audiences quickly understand and experience how PhB thinking makes them feel and function better compared to StOP thinking.

MIND/BODY/WORK CONNECTION

Many people regard personal computing and the Internet as the greatest discovery during the 20th century. I agree if you are considering only external life. When we include the internal frontiers of life, my proposition is that the most important happening of the last century is an internal discovery or re-discovery that *consciousness becomes reality*.

For example, when I laugh, I create health-producing endorphins and other uplifting chemicals in my body. If I serve a customer well I feel good about it—and myself. I create an inner biochemistry of satisfaction and success. If I'm angry, tense or dissatisfied, I create an entirely different biochemistry based on the destructive impact of stress hormones. Thus, my choices at all moments influence my body and my health. I am the first beneficiary of all those choices. Thinking becomes matter, for better or for worse. As you think, so you are, is an age-old truth.

In this book you will find fresh information that changes how we think about ourselves and how we can steer our emotions into a fulfilling and health-nurturing direction. The message aims to revolutionize your internal dialogue—the ongoing mental chatter at play in our minds.

Is this dialogue fulfilling or defeating?

Is it enhancing or damaging relationships?

Is it energy-reducing or energy-producing?

Does it create an inner biochemistry of success or failure?

I'll explain how self-talk affects the body, energy, behavior, relationships and how it sets us up for success or lack of success.

You'll also find ways that promote the inner change from victim, scarcity, and comfort-zone thinking to a mode of passion, abundance, and professionalism. That's what the PhB status is all about.

BE "SELFISH." THIS IS ABOUT YOU

You're about to embark on your journey towards becoming a Professional Human Being. If you'd like to become a bold creator of your own life, accomplish more, have meaning and fulfillment in your life, contribute to the welfare of others, and do it all with health, balance, and vitality, this book is for you!

Here's your syllabus.

The first thing you'll need to do is choose your major. Figure out what it is you're best at and what ignites your passion. Next you will discover why you should use your major, your magic, to serve others. Like every day in college life, you'll have to choose to stay on course based on the set of values you have chosen to follow. Envision your future. What and who do you want to be? Don't leave it up to chance. Plan it!

Of course, no set of studies comes without challenges but you'll find ways not to go out of your mind in dealing with them. Throughout this journey, you will need to take care of yourself, all the many aspects of yourself. You are here to examine your thinking. I'm going to push your buttons. I am going to provoke your thinking and challenge some of your beliefs. I'm going to lay out the consequences of continuing to do what has not been working but what you continue to do anyway. I'm going to propose some new ideas, supported by scientific research. I'm going to give you some options and suggest that you try something different.

That's *my* job. *Your* job begins when you turn this page. Grab a glass of water and an apple and get ready. You're about to be provoked and definitely inspired.

Jim Bagnola
January 12, 2012

PART I

PREREQUISITES

What a PhB Is
and
Why You Need It

1
Turn Your Thinking Upside Down

*The greatest revolution of my generation is the discovery that
individuals can change the outer aspect of their lives by
changing the inner attitudes of their minds.*
— WILLIAM JAMES, M.D.
one of the founders of modern psychology

How long do you want to live? What physical and mental shape do you want to be in during the last thirty years of your life? You may not have set these goals but it may be practical to reflect on them right now. I want to live to be 95. For the last thirty years of *my* life, I want to be flexible, strong for that age, able to walk briskly, be clear-minded, and continue to have useful wisdom for the people around me. What about you?

Research has identified five fundamentals for living a long and healthy life. They determine the length and quality of your life—or your life span and health span:

- How well rested you are: How much you sleep and whether you practice a meditation technique
- How well you eat and how much water you drink
- How physically active and flexible you are
- How moderate you are in what you do
- How you think

CLOSING THE KNOWING-DOING GAP

These fundamentals are critical to health. You know these things. You have heard them all your life—from the news, from doctors, from your mother. You know them. The problem is in doing them. My intention is to flip your thinking so that the gap between what you know and what you do disappears.

A diet emphasizing abundant fruit and vegetables contains natural compounds contributing to health. Do you get the recommended five servings a day? Probably not. Interestingly, 85 percent of us adults know that we should but research says that only 15 percent of us actually do. And water? Are you getting the recommended eight cups a day? I said water, not coffee, tea, or sodas. Many people drink two glasses of water at the most. Some don't drink any. Think of yourself at age 85. What do you want to have been eating: junk or healthy foods?

Are you physically active? You don't need to be a jogger or even join the gym to get the minimum of physical activity that experts say keeps your body functionally fit so you can carry out daily activities without huffing and puffing. For years we have been hearing endlessly how very important this is for health. Twenty years ago 20 percent of the population engaged in some form of regular exercise. How many do it today? Research tells us only 13 percent of the population exercises regularly. Looks like nobody is listening. We're getting fatter and less fit.

How much sleep do you get? We're supposed to get approximately eight hours a night. Yet half the adult population has insomnia and most of us have up to two weeks of sleep debt. That means if you fall asleep right now, sleep two weeks, you might catch up. Certainly, most of us are not rested.

What do you know about moderation? Probably nothing. I read a book recently by the comedian Bill Cosby called *I Am What I Ate…and I'm Frightened*!!! In the book, he's concerned about a good friend who's been drinking too much and says to him, "Why can't you drink in moderation?"

His buddy says back to him, "Why can't you eat in moderation?"

Cosby ponders, "What *do* I know about moderation?" So he dedicates chapter 15 to moderation—and it's completely blank!

I admit that it is hard to be moderate. Premature disease and accelerated aging are caused by a lifestyle to the left and right of moderation— not enough or too much, deficiency or excess. Moderation is the median point between deficiency and excess. And that's different in every person. They say drinking carrot juice is healthy. Nevertheless, too much too often can strain your liver. The hardest thing for us to know—and practice—is moderation.

Finally, what do you *think*? What occupies your mind space? Experts say that 78 percent of our daily thoughts are dysfunctional, counterproductive, and negative. This inhibits your ability to perform well in life and diminishes your capacity to achieve any of the previous four fundamentals necessary for a long and healthy life.

Notice how Leroy Grant viewed his job. Most people might consider Leroy's job somewhat on a lower level but this gentleman elevated his work to a supreme level, a totally professional level. By any standard, he turned his vocation into a successful and fulfilling endeavor. What some may think of as menial labor, he viewed as art. While some view shoe-shining as a throwaway task, he guaranteed his work. What some may consider as a spot tucked in the corner, he viewed as his corner office with a view of the entire hotel lobby. While some may view his work as hired help, he knew he was his own boss.

Leroy *turned his thinking upside down*. He took many negatives and turned them into positives simply by looking at them in a different way. In fact, they were never negatives to Leroy. There are many aspects of your life in which your thinking can be turned upside down.

Think upside down!

HUMAN BEINGS OR HUMAN THINKERS

Your *thinking* then is the real bottom line. It is what shapes your quality and quantity of life. And who else is responsible for your thinking except you? It's pretty much all in our own heads.

This book is primarily about how we think and, more specifically, about the way we *think in the workplace*. The principles spill over into the rest of our lives. And because how we think is the basis for action, and action is the basis for accomplishment, our thinking connects us directly to success, happiness, and productivity—or to the opposite.

You might not be aware of this, but every single thought we have is connected to our body and our health—or the lack of it. The body follows the mind. Every time we have a thought we create internal chemicals that are either toxic or friendly to our health. So, in every moment of life, our thoughts are activating unhealthy or healthy commands inside the body. Which direction are your thoughts taking you?

Research says that we generate about 60,000 thoughts a day. Essentially, not a second of your day goes by without your thinking a thought. And each of those thoughts is made up of words. People tell you to "think fast!" You already do! You think between 500 and 1,200 words a minute. That adds up to over a million words in a day! That's how fast we can think. But thank God we don't speak that fast! On average we speak about 150 words a minute, and that's only 15,000 to 25,000 words a day.

So think about that. If we *think* over a million words and *speak* only 15,000 to 25,000, whom are we talking to most of the time?

Obvious, eh? The chat line between me and myself, and you and yourself, is always busy. And all those thoughts and words—our mental operating programs—influence the actions and choices that affect how we work, relate with others, how healthy we are, the speed at which we age, and how long we live. Summed up, thoughts influence everything. What kind of thoughts are you thinking?

LEE TURNED HER THINKING UPSIDE DOWN

Let me introduce you to my friend, Lee Moczygemba.

At an age when most people begin thinking of retiring, Lee decided to take the bold step into a new career. She had been working for many years as an executive secretary at Exxon when, at age 50, she felt a burning desire to become a professional speaker and trainer. The fact that she had zero experience did not faze her! All her life she had been a natural "ham," becoming alive in front of an audience, holding their attention and making them laugh. Filled with blind confidence, she knew she could learn whatever else was needed to realize her dream!

However, going into business for herself proved to be more daunting and complex than she had imagined. She enrolled in a public relations night class where she met a young woman who professed to know most everything about the subject. Lee thought this was the missing link she needed to launch her career. Even though the fee for consulting was a huge blow to her budget, she agreed to pay $150 for the one-hour, private session in her home.

In preparing for this appointment, Lee carefully set out her course materials, everything she had prepared to begin her training and speaking business. She also painstakingly arranged the most professional items in her wardrobe so as to make a good impression.

Right on time Nancy arrived and after meticulously scrutinizing Lee's wardrobe and materials, she made a startling, bold declaration: "Let's see. You *don't* have the wardrobe. You *don't* have any experience. You *don't* have your act together. You *don't* know what you're doing, and you said you were very limited in funds. So I think the best thing for you to do is to *forget it.* That will be $150!"

Lee was dumbstruck. She literally felt the wind knocked out of her chest. Writing the check was excruciatingly painful. As she walked Nancy out to her car, she felt a tear creep down the side of her face. Desperately needing to defend herself, just as Nancy was about to drive off, Lee let her know how she felt: "You may be right—but you don't know me and you don't know what I will do when I have to!"

Nancy glanced back over her shoulder and with a big smirk and a wave called out: "Well, lots of luck, honey!"

Not surprisingly, Lee felt broken-hearted and broke. She went into the house and cried for the next three hours. Then she began to review the episode in a rational way. She talked to herself: *That woman doesn't believe in you. Do you still believe in yourself? Remember your promise to God and to yourself that if ever you were give a second chance, you would do whatever it took to master it—whatever talent*

God gave you! You know how persistent and resilient you are! You can do this! Remember, you have the determination of a Missouri mule!

You see, once before, Lee had let the chance of fulfilling a big dream pass by.

As a young woman, she believed talent came in finished form as a natural gift. She had been a fashion-design major in college and made A's in her art classes. However, she struggled hours on end to complete assignments while she saw her classmates whip out drawings quickly and "naturally." She considered herself not talented in this field. She thought, if she were talented, she would not have to work so hard. Talent was supposed to flow and make things easy. Right? This self-defeating thinking discouraged her to the point that she gave up her dream completely. She folded her hard-earned diploma and portfolio and put them away forever—never so much as lifting a paintbrush again. Instead, she took the practical approach and went to work in a major department store selling women's better clothing (that someone else had designed).

Many years later, someone casually mentioned to her that Beethoven rewrote his Fifth Symphony 31 times; in fact, he rewrote everything he ever produced many, many times. This struck Lee like a lightning bolt as she realized that even Beethoven *had to work hard.* She learned talent is given to various people in different levels, from rough and unpolished to absolute mastery (which we define as genius). It suddenly dawned on her it wasn't just the talent that made him successful; it was the hard work. *Talent plus hard work equals success.* Lee vowed if ever she were blessed again with the belief she had a gift (no matter how undeveloped), she would do whatever it took to become a master of her craft! She would never let another golden opportunity pass by!

That opportunity came when Lee was 50.

Coincidentally, she realized once again, this latent talent also came in rough and unpolished form. But this time Lee had a different mindset. By now, she could see things differently and was willing to turn her thinking upside down.

So she set to work—spending nights and weekends preparing. She never studied so hard. She never read so many books. She never lost so much sleep. She never before put so much energy into anything. She became alive! She admits she didn't just open her mouth and become a great speaker: "I had a miserable time getting my brain and mouth to work together. It was really hard, but I stuck with it and gradually it all came together. I made the long journey from apprentice to journeyman to master of my craft."

Fast-forward ten years. Lee had made her mark as an international professional speaker and trainer. Amazingly, this "late bloomer" worked another 8 successful years traveling the world, motivating and inspiring thousands of people. To top it off, she made an important contribution to her field by founding the first-ever local chapter of NSA (National Speakers Association), located in Houston, Texas. Today, she has transitioned from speaking and training into coaching and marketing speakers, creating her own bureau, Amazing Speakers and Trainers International. My friend Lee is now 87 years young. She has a clear mind, an energetic spirit, loves life, is hardworking, has boundless energy, laughs a lot, and thrives on the company of younger people. Above all, she maintains the attitude of gratitude—a most amazing woman!

In reflecting back over the years, Lee realized that in the process of becoming a professional speaker, she had gone through several metamorphoses. She had to shift her thinking in many different ways:

From "I can't" to "I can."

From thinking of talent as a gift in completed form to a gift that most often requires hard work to succeed.

From being skeptical of her talent to trusting and pursuing it to mastery level.

From thinking as an employee to thinking as a business owner.

From allowing someone to take away her power, her self-belief—and her dream—to reclaiming them forever.

Lee was preparing herself for what she does now. These shifts in her thinking have helped her in coaching others to shift their thinking in order to reach their highest level of success.

Lee plans to retire in about ten years!

Turn your thinking upside down! Think something different—the greatest revolution of William James' generation, as pointed out in the quote at the beginning of the chapter. To embark on the journey of becoming a Professional Human Being, the first step is that willingness to turn your thinking upside down—shift the inner attitude of your mind to change the outer aspect of your life.

2

What Is a Professional Human Being?

Try not to become a man of success,
but rather try to become a man of value.

— ALBERT EINSTEIN
1921 Physics Nobel Prize Winner

In February 2000, I suffered a great loss. My close friend, colleague, and former employer, Doug Henning, passed away. Doug was the world-famous, master magician who is credited with bringing magic to the mainstream in the late 1970s. For one thing, he was the first to do grand illusions in front of a live audience using a combination of colorful backdrops, story lines, choreographed dance routines, and magnificent music. He provided progressive family entertainment with an uplifting, positive mission.

I was fortunate to be in the middle of all of this for many years during the 1980s. I worked with Doug in various capacities, including his business manager as well as vice president of Doug Henning Magic. Working with Doug took me to many places around the world. For instance, we traveled on tours together across the United States and Canada, to South America, England, and India. Wow, those were exciting times. And you can imagine how thrilled we were when Doug was invited to give a command performance at the White House! I treasure this memory when I look at the photo hanging in my office of me standing next to President and Mrs. Reagan. Doug was honored to perform for the White House staff Christmas party in the East Wing. I spent almost as much time organizing that event as I did on Doug's wedding!

Doug is a great example of a Professional Human Being. Without doubt, he left a lasting impression on my life and that of many others. His generosity, creativity, and his ability to connect with people are what I think of when I remember him. Let me share with you several stories that demonstrate the PhB qualities he modeled.

One of the highlights of my years working with Doug was being involved with his magical musical *Merlin,* which played at the Mark Hellinger Theater on Broadway.

One day during the run of *Merlin,* I got a call from a woman who said Doug Henning was her son's hero. Her son was 11 years old and dying of cancer. "Would Doug possibly come to the hospital and see him?" I said I'd check.

Of course, Doug immediately agreed. "Absolutely. We'll perform some magic for him and bring some autographed pictures and photos of the tiger (from the show). We can spend a couple of hours with him." So he and his wife Debby then made plans to go to the hospital the following Monday, his one day off from performing.

Soon after finding out about our upcoming visit, the head nurse on the hospital ward contacted me with a request, "I heard Doug Henning is coming and we don't have just one kid here; we have 30 kids with cancer. Could he do some magic for all of them?"

Doug gave the go-ahead, "Sure. We'll just spend some time with the boy alone and then the whole group."

The next day our public relations agent called and said she had arranged for media coverage of the event. Specifically, newspaper and TV reporters would be there. She said the exposure would be great for Doug's career and for ticket sales, so I ran it by him.

Doug minced no words. "Tell her that if newspapers or TV are coming, I'm not coming." He was doing it, he said, for the kids and not for himself or his show.

So the newspaper and TV reporters were uninvited.

The event turned out to be a wonderful, intimate experience; Doug and Debby were thrilled to witness the excitement on the children's faces as they enjoyed their own private magic show. Then, the Hennings gave the boy's parents a generous cash gift to try an alternative cancer treatment. Sadly, the disease was too far progressed, but his mother said her son died happy, knowing that Doug Henning, his hero, had cared. I'll never forget the care Doug took to provide a wondrous experience for the children, letting them forget about their pain and troubles, if only for a short time.

Certainly, Doug knew his visit to the cancer ward would have been good press for him, and good press meant fame and money, but he wanted the focus to be on the kids rather than on him. For him, the delight in their eyes was his reward.

Doug had a soft spot in his heart for kids. I can still see him trying to make a phone call from an airport phone in between appearances with kids tugging at his jacket, begging for autographs. No matter how important the call, Doug would patiently tuck the phone between his chin and shoulder, and with a warm smile ask the child for his name, and sign the paper, ticket, or napkin. Doug was very generous with his time and displayed extraordinary caring for his fans.

WHO IS A PROFESSIONAL HUMAN BEING, ANYWAY?

If I ask you to describe the qualities of a Professional Human Being, what would they be? In my Professional Human Being workshops, I invite participants to write down what they feel are the qualities of a Professional Human Being. I ask them to consider how they would describe a Professional Human Being both in the context of their personal lives and in the workplace.

How would you identify a PhB? What qualities would you look for?

I get a wide range of qualities as you would see in the next few pages but perhaps the most insightful answer I ever received is this one: *A Professional Human Being is a positive role model I would like to emulate.*

Here is a sampling of what participants have written.

YOU MIGHT BE A PROFESSIONAL HUMAN BEING IF YOU ...

Show Common Courtesies and Social Etiquette

- ✓ *Stand up to show respect*
- ✓ *Hold doors open for others*
- ✓ *Use good manners with everyone*
- ✓ *Shake hands and smile*
- ✓ *Thank the receptionist and say "goodbye" on the way out*
- ✓ *Use the words "please" and "thank you" generously*
- ✓ *Don't use offensive language; if you do, you apologize*
- ✓ *Offer associates a refreshment when they visit your office*
- ✓ *Say "good night" to all on leaving for the day*
- ✓ *Don't interrupt*
- ✓ *Don't put your briefcase on the client's desk*
- ✓ *Help someone put a bag in the overhead compartment on the plane*
- ✓ *Offer to assist people with heavy items*
- ✓ *Thank and praise associates for a good job*

Are Happy and Content

- ✓ *Look like you are enjoying your day*
- ✓ *Trust people*
- ✓ *Are open-minded*
- ✓ *Don't dwell on the negative or mistakes*
- ✓ *Have a spiritual orientation to life*
- ✓ *Are nice and very upbeat: engage, interact, have fun, are energetic*
- ✓ *Smile*
- ✓ *Make friends*
- ✓ *Don't get angry with a waiter because the food is cold or with a gate agent because your flight was cancelled*
- ✓ *Don't complain*

Treat Everyone with Kindness and Respect

- ✓ *Are sensitive to the needs of others*
- ✓ *Respect everyone: respect others' feelings and opinions*
- ✓ *Greet and talk to everyone regardless of their status*
- ✓ *Don't consider anyone a little person*
- ✓ *Treat others like you would like to be treated*
- ✓ *Deal with delicate issues face-to-face, not by e-mail*
- ✓ *Know (or learn) peoples' names*
- ✓ *Are willing to help*
- ✓ *Assist elders*
- ✓ *Are generous*
- ✓ *Are gracious and courteous*

Are Organized and Professional

- ✓ *Return every call every day*
- ✓ *Stick to the facts; don't make emotional decisions*
- ✓ *Have a clear easy-to-read business card*
- ✓ *Leave all personal problems at the door*
- ✓ *Call ahead and make an appointment; don't show up unannounced*
- ✓ *Leave short and to-the-point messages on voice mail*
- ✓ *Dress appropriately and professionally*
- ✓ *Don't try to impress*
- ✓ *Are fair and consistent*

Support, Coach, and Mentor

- ✓ *Respond to the needs of associates*
- ✓ *Encourage associates*
- ✓ *Look for the positives in associates as well as opportunities to improve*
- ✓ *Engage everyone, associates and customers, in a positive manner*
- ✓ *Speak well of others*
- ✓ *Understand your associates; have a sincere relationship*

- ✓ *Compliment the competition*
- ✓ *Make people feel important*
- ✓ *Ask dumb and interesting questions*
- ✓ *Listen with the intent to learn*
- ✓ *Recognize and truly celebrate success with enthusiasm*
- ✓ *Do not chastise others in front of coworkers*
- ✓ *Aren't afraid to say "I don't know"*

Value People and Have Good Work Ethics

- ✓ *Care, respect others, and demand high standards*
- ✓ *Consider each associate a valuable member of the team*
- ✓ *Know that every job counts*
- ✓ *Are genuinely interested and sincerely care for others—coworkers, customers*
- ✓ *Ask associates how they are and what their interests are*
- ✓ *Are ethical and have integrity*
- ✓ *Ask "How can I help you today?"*
- ✓ *Ask about any challenges*
- ✓ *Reward good performance*
- ✓ *Have an open-door policy*

Are Personally and Socially Responsible

- ✓ *Hold yourself accountable*
- ✓ *Give and share responsibility with others*
- ✓ *Volunteer in the community*
- ✓ *Are physically fit*
- ✓ *Are punctual*
- ✓ *Keep commitments*
- ✓ *Don't name drop*
- ✓ *Turn off cell phones in meetings*
- ✓ *Are open-minded*
- ✓ *Don't gossip*

Have Good Communication and Relationship Skills

- ✓ *Communicate goals clearly*
- ✓ *Are approachable*
- ✓ *Are polite and cooperative*
- ✓ *Listen more than you talk*
- ✓ *Do not raise your voice with others*
- ✓ *Are assertive and say what you mean*
- ✓ *Are assertive but not aggressive*
- ✓ *Remain calm in the face of challenge*
- ✓ *Don't always attempt to be right*
- ✓ *Look associates in the eyes when you interact*
- ✓ *Don't make enemies*
- ✓ *Are respectful, caring, and demanding*
- ✓ *Appreciate objections or different points of view*
- ✓ *Give honest and helpful feedback*
- ✓ *Interact with class*

Now, those are a lot of qualities of a PhB! From this panoramic view painted by my workshop participants, I will focus on deeper, more subtle aspects of what makes a Professional Human Being. I will also make that *critical connection between work and health*, the essence of this book.

To zoom into these finer levels and help you form a clearer picture, I will identify five key fundamentals. I call these five principles the *Five PhB Laws*. These key distinctions will help guide your thinking and actions and keep you focused on how to become a Professional Human Being. To earn the degree, I invite you to adopt these laws as the operating guidelines for your life.

THE FIVE PhB LAWS

LAW 1

P Primary Beneficiary — *I am the main and first beneficiary of everything I think, do, and say.* When I sow positivity, I harvest growth and good health. When I sow negativity, I harvest the undesirable effects of that thinking and behavior, which may include a lack of good health.

LAW 2

R Relationship — *The most important relationship I have is the one I have with myself.* This relationship is created by the manner in which I relate or talk to myself. It forms the basis for all other relationships and has a profound influence on my health, success, happiness, and capacity to lead.

LAW 3

O Outcomes — *Every choice has physiological outcomes.* Every choice I make has physiological outcomes: either health-producing or disease-producing. Every choice has consequences.

LAW 4

H Help — *I cannot help another without helping myself.* Accordingly, I cannot possibly harm another without harming myself. I will always experience what I desire for others.

LAW 5

B Body — *Body follows mind.* Everything I think, do, and say causes a physiological response within myself. I do things primarily for this response within myself, not for the response it has in others.

Essentially, the most important impact of all my behavior is not so much the influence it has on others, although obviously that is important, but the effect it has on myself. When I pay attention to my thoughts and behavior and to the effects they create *within myself* I will naturally behave like a Professional Human Being.

DOUG HENNING, PhB

Doug dramatically altered the world of magic. The magic programming you see today on stage and screen has Doug's signature all over it. His revolutionary formula was magic plus theater equals art. He was first to incorporate theater into the performance of magic.

His mode of operating was "thinking backwards." With his "think tank" of a half dozen or so experts, including a magic historian, a physicist, a choreographer, illusion experts, and a musician, he would start with the result he wanted and then they would figure out how to get him there. For example, Doug would say, "I want to walk through a wall." Then he'd ask his think tank what they knew from history, from physics, from chemistry, and from the use of optical illusion. "How can we choreograph it? How can we put it on the stage?" They would all think backwards from there and create the illusion.

One day, after a meeting of the think tank I received a call from one of our experts. He told me his wallet had just been stolen and asked if he could borrow some money. Although I didn't know him well, I knew he was part of the think tank, so I gave him the money from my own account. The next day at work, I mentioned to Doug about his buddy losing his wallet on the subway. Doug looked at me knowingly, "You didn't give him any money, did you?"

I admitted I had. Doug chuckled and said, "You won't believe how many times that guy's lost his wallet on the subway." The guy evidently had some kind of problem. I told Doug not to worry about it and let it go.

In the envelope with my next paycheck I found an extra three-hundred-dollar check from Doug's personal account. This care for others was just one of his PhB qualities.

Whenever I talk about Doug, I'm also talking about his wife Debby, who was just as generous. One summer, Doug, Debby, and I were in India working on a project. We took a break and went to downtown New Delhi. In one of the stores, I was attracted to a sacred Hindu artifact that I immediately fell in love with. But it was expensive and heavy, and it would have cost too much to ship home. So I just let it go and forgot about it. Six months later, I was living at Doug and Debby's house in Brentwood, California. I was renting their house while they were away. It was Christmas Eve and I got a call from them. They instructed me to go downstairs and look in a certain cabinet, where I would find something covered with an orange silk cloth. I had no idea what they were talking about but I followed their directions. I found the something, took the cloth off, and—wow!— there was the artifact! They had bought it, shipped it home, and at some point hidden it there in the cabinet, for me. That was just how they were. They were PhBs.

YOUR PhB DEGREE

Are you a Professional Human Being? (What? Not yet?) Follow me through this book and turn your usual, self-defeating, unhealthy thought patterns upside down. Now is the time to put yourself on the path to becoming a Professional Human Being.

Do you have a B.A., M.A., an M.B.A., or Ph.D.? These are obviously important credentials in the workplace. However, the corporate and government clients who keep asking me to talk to their executives, managers, and employees seem equally interested in the PhB qualities of themselves and their employees. You may be surprised to learn that your boss places more value on your personal qualities than on your résumé. In this book, we're focusing, not on your credentials, but on your becoming a Professional Human Being—getting your PhB. Are you ready to have your thinking turned upside down?

Employers today do not hire or advance people who are just smart. Increasingly, they want people with the right human skills. Describing the criteria for hiring personnel from baggage handlers to pilots, one airline executive told me, "We look for five things—listening, smiling, saying 'thank you,' caring, and being warm."

Clearly, a lot of people are smart and can ably do a job. What often gets in their way, and makes them sick in the process, is their lack of those other human elements.

A Professional Human Being balances achieving goals and building relationships with increasing productivity while reducing stress.

I AM RESPONSIBLE AND ACCOUNTABLE TO MYSELF

Accordingly, when you adopt these five PhB Laws as your operating program in life, you will naturally behave as a PhB. Instead of a vicious cycle of behavior, you will create an uplifting cycle of behavior. If you treat yourself as a Professional Human Being, you can't help but treat others the same way. In the process, you contribute to your own good health. Remember PhB Law 5: *Body follows mind.*

This is not a new understanding. The same natural laws exist everywhere. In philosophy: As you sow so shall you reap. In physics: Every action has an equal and opposite reaction. And in business: What goes around comes around. You are responsible and accountable to yourself.

The Professional Human Being approaches life knowing that every thought, word, and action has a health and physiological consequence. This knowledge provides enough reason to hold ourselves responsible and accountable, no matter what the situation.

While the idea of outward consequences for your actions is not new, what might be new to our awareness is that every thought, word, and action has a health consequence, a physiological consequence that can be either positive or negative, a consequence that never leaves the body. This is the mind/body connection.

It is a new awakening to the real reason for self-accountability and self-responsibility. We may have lost sight of why we do things the way we do. Organizations have tried almost every kind of training and development and, even though each has something significant to offer, problems in the workplace continue. The information you are about to discover ahead may not totally eliminate those problems but it will wake up individuals and organizations to what may be contributing to absenteeism, lower productivity, lack of passion, gossip, accidents, high health-care costs, and the list goes on.

I hope this book inspires you to reevaluate many parts of your life and that you are open to making necessary changes for yourself. Because only you can! Remember the title of this chapter: What Is a Professional Human Being? Here is your chance to become one.

3

Waves of Change—From Outer to Inner

If you don't like change,
you're going to like irrelevance even less.

— GENERAL ERIC SHINSEKI
former Chief of Staff of the Army

Since time immemorial, we have strived to be Professional Human Beings. This effort is an evolutionary process, and evolution is change. As we evolve through these waves of change, we find ourselves being taken to the internal frontiers.

The first five waves that humans have gone through have started to shift the focus from external to internal to reach the crest of the sixth wave—which we are currently in—where the focus is on individual thinking patterns and the effects of those thinking patterns on mind and body.

The foremost discovery during the 20th century is this internal discovery or re-discovery that *consciousness becomes reality.* Our thinking and emotions create a specific physiology and this specific psychophysiology supports health or the lack of it, success or the lack of it, happiness or the lack of it, and finally leadership capacity or the lack of it.

Looking from a historical point of view, this connection is not only the biggest occurrence of the last century but also the central issue: the science of the mind/body connection. Alvin Toffler and other social scientists have marked human transition dating back 6,000 to 10,000 years. We can talk about these transitions as waves of change.

See how the changes start from the outside and move inward.

THE WAVES OF CHANGE

Approximately 6,000 years ago we experienced our first wave of change. We shifted from a nomadic existence of hunting and gathering to farming. As farmers, we learned we could stay put and live without constantly moving from one location to another in search of food.

The second wave ushered in the industrial age. This occurred approximately 300 years ago. We created mass production and factories and learned we were capable of more than just surviving and subsisting on the family farm. This wave was characterized by a large movement of people from farms to factories.

The third wave that swept the planet was the information and knowledge explosion. More of us now earn a living as knowledge workers than as factory hands. Peter Drucker, father of business management and arguably one of its leading experts, observed that knowledge is now our primary industry. The guesstimate is that the sum total of all knowledge is currently doubling every few years.

The fourth wave was the communication revolution. Personal computing and the Internet have pushed forward the concept of a global marketplace. The Internet brings the world to our doorstep in a matter of mini-seconds.

These first four waves focused on an external dimension, the outer world; that is, not on ourselves.

The fifth wave turns us inward—from external back to the internal—the self. We could designate this wave as the Age of Brainware or the Age of Mind. Many of the breakthroughs in this century will be centered on the development of self-awareness and individual consciousness.

Why? Because all information and knowledge exist *out there*, external, if you will; and the brain, the mind, must take it in, understand it, assimilate it, and then put it to use. The shift must be internal to where the burden is: on the human hardware, the brain. We are challenged to adapt to and capitalize on the myriad of ever-changing external forces of the 21st century. Arie De Gues, the Royal Dutch executive who created the Learning Company (later called The Learning Organization), put it this way, "The ability to learn faster than your competitors may be the only sustainable competitive advantage."

NOW THE SIXTH WAVE

My proposition is we have now gone even further—to a sixth wave. Scientists such as Candace Pert and Michael Ruff give us good reason to call it the Age of the Mind/Body. They, and other researchers, have shown that every time we have a thought or feeling every cell of our body produces combinations of amino acids called neuropeptides, which directly affect the operating mechanics of the body. It is part of a wondrous internal pharmacy that responds to our thinking and attitudes and leads us in positive or negative directions.

I suggest further that all the major breakthroughs during this sixth wave will be internal: increasing brain capacity, physiological capacity, and mind/brain or mind/body capacity. Our capacity to change, adapt, unlearn, and relearn is connected to the condition of our brain and nervous system— the processor of information. The information is only meaningful if our processor is capable of taking it in and making sense of it so we can translate and convert it into success. MIT's David Birch characterizes this by stating, "We are working ourselves out of the manufacturing business and into the thinking business." We have the opportunity now to examine and upgrade both the hardware (the brain and nervous system) and the software (our mental models, the kinds of thoughts we choose to entertain).

The sixth wave, like a tsunami, has smashed aside convention and turned everything upside down. The adaptations we have to make are all-encompassing.

The sixth wave is about self-responsibility and accountability for one's own thinking and actions. As George Bernard Shaw said, "The reasonable man adapts himself to the world; the unreasonable man persists in trying to adapt the world to himself. Therefore, all progress depends on the reasonable man." It is a responsibility thrust on us by the need of the time. This premise is supported by scientific findings which cannot be ignored.

In September 1992, *Scientific American* published a special issue called "Mind and Brain." It contains a summary of the research examining this relationship at the close of the last century. These studies bring to light the biological and physiological foundations of how we sense the world, think, remember, and use language. The research looks at where in the brain we store memories and how we relate one thought to another. It was clearly demonstrated that the functioning of the mind/body is responsible for the following: vision, memory, learning, language, disorders, development, and consciousness.

Gerald Fischbach, a neurobiologist at Harvard Medical School, has described the brain as "the most complex structure in the known universe. Genes and experience have jointly shaped its machinery; its design is the result of millions of years of evolution. Our survival depends on a deeper understanding of the marvelous biochemical happening that arises from it: the mind."

This new knowledge is a fundamental science that reveals a mind/body approach to life: to success, health, happiness, managing self and others, and the capacity to lead. Like all great discoveries, it promises new technologies to enhance the development of mind and body. It is time to examine our own thinking patterns, time to think about how we think, what we think, and how this affects the body.

THE *INVOLUTION* OF BUSINESS THINKING

The social evolution has gone from external to internal, from the external elements of what we do and how we do it, to the internal aspects of thinking based on emotional stability and self-responsibility. Business has taken a similar turn.

Stephen Covey's 1989 book, *The Seven Habits of Highly Effective People,* separates the thinking realm from the acting realm. It differentiates becoming independent from acting interdependently.

Become Independent	Act Interdependently
Habit 1: Be Proactive **Habit 2:** First Things First **Habit 3:** Begin With the End in Mind	**Habit 4:** Think Win/Win **Habit 5:** Seek First to Understand, Then to Be Understood **Habit 6:** Synergize

These thinking habits lead us to Habit 7, which is Sharpen the Saw. It guides us back to the self, reminding us that taking care of ourselves mentally, physically, and spiritually is the basis for the success of the other six habits. This book is an exposé of changing our internal thinking habits in order to change external acting, ending in self-responsibility.

Peter Senge's 1990 book, *The Fifth Discipline: The Art & Practice of The Learning Organization,* proposes five thinking technologies to assist individuals and organizations to negotiate change more effectively and create opportunities for growth:

1. Mental Models
2. Systems Thinking
3. Building Shared Vision
4. Team Learning

Finally, back to self-responsibility:

5. Personal Mastery

These technologies take us beneath action to what creates action: thinking, paradigms, learning, and vision.

In 1995, Daniel Goleman introduced another kind of intelligence in his book *Emotional Intelligence*. The traditional intelligence quotient (IQ) alone too narrowly defines a person's potential. Goleman's "emotional quotient" (EQ) expands the definition of both intelligence and potential. People with higher EQ are more successful in all areas of life, especially at work, than those with higher IQ.

In 1998, Doc Childre and Bruce Cryer gave us *From Chaos to Coherence: Advancing Emotional and Organizational Intelligence Through Inner Quality Management*, a landmark book based on thirty years of study and the discovery that the human heart "plays a demonstrable role in human emotional response and intelligence." It showed that the better we are at operating our internal systems, by managing the data pouring into us, the more effective we become at managing stress, being effective decision makers and maintaining positive emotions. They called it "inner leadership."

All these books and ideas are helping us become reasonable men and women who adapt to the world—the people who George Bernard Shaw deemed capable of ushering in progress. The sixth wave is upon us.

4

Is Your Workplace Stuck in StOP Gear?

While we are free to choose our actions,
we are not free to choose the consequences of our actions.

— MAHATMA GANDHI
prominent figure in India's Independence

I had just graduated from The University of Akron and was thrilled to get my first professional job at the university's Student Financial Aid office. I was familiar with this office, having frequented its door for four years; in order to maintain my scholarship, I had to have my grades checked every quarter by the director, Bob Larson.

My title was Assistant Director of Student Financial Aid and my boss was none other than Bob Larson; I had grown to admire this man greatly and still consider him my mentor. Mr. Larson, the other assistant director, and I served over 19,000 students. Daily, I was faced with a steady stream of students needing help as well as a tall stack of work on my desk. It was overwhelming, but I reveled in the position.

In the midst of all this busyness, the phone would ring with more help requests. I treated them as interruptions of my work. The phone took time away from dealing face-to-face with the students and papers in front of me. Every time the phone rang, I became irritated. I would grab the phone and pointedly say, "Yeah?" I was not customer conscious—I didn't even know what that was. I was abrupt and not very polite. Every day, I left the office exhausted.

One day my best friend Warren was in the office waiting for me to finish my work. He observed me in action. After I finished a phone call, he gave me a funny look and asked, "Jim, why were you mad? That was your *job* calling."

"My job? What do you mean my job calling?" I asked, perplexed.

"Do you think those students or faculty need your help, too?"

"Well, yeah."

"That's part of your job. So why would you get upset?"

I thought about that for a moment, pondering the idea, but brushed it off. Warren's words, however, lingered in my mind the rest of the day. He was right. I needed to change my mindset.

The next morning when the phone rang, I yelled out to everyone in the office, "Excuse me, everybody. That's my job calling." I answered the phone, "Hello, this is Jim. How can I *help* you?"

I had needed to make a mind shift. I had to realize I was there to serve all the customers. They were the reason I had a job. With this shift my days were much less stressful.

Sir Winston Churchill said it aptly: "The empires of the future are the empires of the mind."

CHANGE YOUR MIND TO CHANGE YOUR FUTURE

In the workplace, how you think influences your health, your satisfaction, your level of success and effectiveness, and your ability to manage and lead other people on the job. Even if you're not a manager, you still have to manage your boss and your coworkers; and, above all, you have to manage yourself. With this ability, you can make the critical transitions that are more and more valued in today's changing workplace. I call them "global transitions"; these are changes that influence how we work and how we work with others to reach goals.

Standard Operating Program (StOP) thinking is the old mode. This is programming that has been guiding our thinking up till now. This thinking has to be replaced by a new operating program. In this book we will call the old thinking "StOP" and the new "PhB." We change our thinking upside down in the Professional Human Being (PhB) mode.

I was inspired by a presentation given by Denis Waitley, speaker and author of the best-selling book, *Empires of the Mind*, in which he describes this evolutionary shift toward new, internal frontiers. In this chapter we look at the paradigm shift articulated by Waitley: "What worked yesterday won't work today." We will put the differentiations Waitley made into our StOP versus PhB model. Here is what the shift looks like on an organizational and societal level today. You will notice that this description is also organized from external to internal, culminating in personal responsibility and accountability.

StOP THINKING	PhB THINKING
Hierarchy was the model.	*Synergy is the new model.*

Hierarchy at work used to matter the most. Now, synergy—working together—is more valued. We're all working on one team and are all paid by our real bosses, the customers! From them we get our money to pay for our mortgage, our cars, our food, and our clothes. Without customers, there is no money and no company. We serve the customer and the customer pays us, regardless of the corporate ladder rung we occupy. We cannot do this alone; it takes our entire team.

While waiting for an appointment with Sam Goodner, the CEO of Catapult Systems, at their headquarters in Austin, I once saw an amazing PhB in action—the receptionist. As I watched, Robin handled a dozen calls with great charm and sincerity and, in a similar manner, attended to the concerns of two employees. I suddenly realized what an important role the receptionist served as a liaison between the company and the customer. I was impressed enough to mention it to Sam, who thanked me and explained that was why her title was the Director of First Impressions. Hierarchy should be turned upside down. The most important people on the organizational team really are the ones closest to the customer.

StOP THINKING	PhB THINKING
Managers commanded, controlled, demanded respect.	*Mangers facilitate, encourage self-respect, gain followers.*
They overpowered	*They empower*

When managers run the Standard Operating Program of command and control thinking they may be successful in the short term but fail in the long term. Under the old model, managers felt they were due respect and followership based on their title alone. However, employees don't follow titles; they follow those who are competent, caring, and trustworthy. In the old model the culture seemed to be organized around management satisfaction, not customer satisfaction. The new model—PhB thinking—suggests that the organization should be focused on employee and customer satisfaction.

"Radically new approaches are needed: approaches to analysis, synthesis and control of work; to job structure, work relationships, and the structure of rewards and power relations; to making workers responsible. We do know that we have to move, from managing personnel as a cost center and a problem, to the leadership of people." Peter Drucker writes in his book, *Management*.

StOP THINKING	PhB THINKING
Production determined availability.	*Quality determines demand.*

The best example of this new way of thinking is Apple with the iPod, iTouch, iPhone, iTunes, and iPad. I stood in line for hours—it was in Honolulu so I didn't mind—waiting to get my iPhone. Apple creates high quality, user-friendly, absolutely ingenious products. Demand chases quality.

StOP THINKING	PhB THINKING
Value was extra.	*Value is everything.*

To observe this shift take a look at how the sales process has been revolutionized. Simple transactional selling didn't change much for 100 years, but now it has shifted to what author, Ram Charan, in his book, *What the Customer Wants You to Know: How Everybody Needs to Think Differently About Sales*, calls "value creation selling." Salespeople used to be order takers when the number of suppliers was low and suppliers were in power. Now that there is a glut of suppliers and because of the Internet, the customer has greater choice and access.

The customer is now in power. Walmart is the prime example. Walmart knows that customers want more bang for their buck. Selling organizations now must deliver value in terms of intense focus on the prosperity of their customer. Measuring success means measuring the success of your customer. This means adding greater value by spending large amounts of time and energy to learn their business, and building a network and partnership with them. If you want to offer deeper value, learn about your customer's customer: their wants, problems, and thinking.

StOP THINKING	PhB THINKING
Capital resource was power.	*Human resource is power.*

Capital resource used to be the almighty power. Of course, financial assets are required to fuel activity and allow us to perform our jobs. But capital alone can't succeed without human creativity, ingenuity, and energy. An organization is organized around people, strategy, operations, a budget, and a product or service. The people create the strategy, run operations, monitor the budget, and create and deliver the product or service. People are the power behind the organization. Their creativity and capacity is the resource behind their success.

The glass ceilings will be shattered even further. The new organization will be dominated by female resource power. Research cited by Richard Donkin, in his book, *The Future of Work,* shows that "Fortune 500 companies with the highest representation of women in their top management teams significantly outperformed those with the lowest averages."

StOP THINKING	PhB THINKING
Shareholder clout	*Customer clout*

Shareholders don't make a dime unless the enterprise has, keeps, and grows the customer base. The enduring corporation is customer centered.

StOP THINKING	PhB THINKING
Making a living	*Making a difference*

Too many people have killed themselves in the process of making a paycheck. Now it's about making a difference and handling your job so that it contributes to your life span and health span. Our work is our most important tool for self-development. We grow through making a difference for our customer and those we serve. Zig Ziglar said it like this: "You can have everything in life you want, if you will just help enough other people get what they want."

StOP THINKING	PhB THINKING
Having a job	*Acting self-employed*

Instead of working for an organization until retirement, the new perspective is "I'm the CEO of me, running myself." Me, Inc. This amounts to a new social contract. The relationship between employer and employee endures as long as we both agree to the relationship. The contract with me and the customer who counts on me, never expires.

StOP THINKING	PhB THINKING
Natural resources defined power.	*Knowledge is power.*

Natural resources held power in the past. Now it's about how the mind accesses, assimilates, integrates, and utilizes knowledge to mold natural resources into something useful.

StOP THINKING	PhB THINKING
Hired hands mattered in a material world.	*Mind matters in a mental world.*

In a world dominated by physical labor, we used to call ourselves hired hands based on the practice of "Don't think; just do what I say." Now it's more about the mind. The boss/organization rents your mind for eight hours and puts it to use. The contemporary workplace increasingly involves mental rather than physical and material activity—from manual workers to knowledge workers. The prized commodities are trained minds operating creatively with energy and enthusiasm. Employers are now realizing that you can't just hire hands; you must hire the entire mind/body.

StOP THINKING	PhB THINKING
Changing others	*Changing self*

Have you ever attempted to change someone else? In case you haven't noticed, it's hopeless. At my job at the financial aid office, I had to change myself and the way I viewed the "interruptions" in my day.

Managers get behaviors from their employees that they model, reinforce, or tolerate. If a manager wants to change the behavior of her employees, she can't. She can change only the way she models, reinforces, and tolerates their behavior. Mahatma Gandhi said, "Be the change you want to see."

StOP THINKING	PhB THINKING
Quality of life based on outer circumstances	*Quality of life: taking control of your own feelings, thoughts, and responses*

Most people tend to think the quality of their life is determined by the quality of outer circumstances beyond their control. This suggests a victim mentality. It's the kind of thinking that says, "Well, I can't help it. That's the way it goes. There's nothing I can do." The reality, however, is that your quality of life is determined by your quality of thinking about your circumstances; that is, how you interpret those circumstances. The saying is, "The world is as I am." There's a critical shift needed: from outer control and trying to change people and circumstances, to inner control and taking command of your own thoughts and feelings. In your life, what is the only thing you have some control over? There is one correct answer: your own thinking. This implies four things:

- Where you place your attention
- What your intentions are
- How you interpret things
- How you respond

As you see, the frontiers have moved from external to internal, from hierarchy and outer circumstances, to you and your thinking, feelings, and responses. It's not what comes to you; it's how you come to it. It's not how it comes to you; it's what you do with it. It is the "I am responsible" principle. If you want to make a change, change your thoughts: the subject of the next chapter.

5

Is Your Mind Stuck in StOP Gear?

When we are no longer able to change a situation,
we are challenged to change ourselves.

— VIKTOR FRANKL
founder of Logotherapy

During the mid-80s I was living in Pacific Palisades, California. One hot Friday afternoon driving home from work, I was sitting in a massive traffic jam on Wilshire Boulevard, when I saw an elderly gentleman hitchhiking. He was dressed in a dark brown suit and tie and had on a little hat. I noticed the pleasant look on his face as the cars in front of me crawled past him and I felt unusually drawn to him.

As I approached, I thought, *I'd like to help that guy.* I maneuvered into the right lane and rolled down my window. He took his hat off, tipped his head down, and in his limited English explained that he was headed to the corner of Fairfax and Wilshire. I offered him a ride.

When he got in, I asked, "Where are you from?"

"Romania."

I looked at him and he was weathered and frail. I couldn't help asking him how old he was.

"Seventy-eight," he replied.

"And why are you hitchhiking?"

He replied that he had missed his bus and was going to the synagogue. "I have seen other people hitchhiking so I thought it was safe. The only way I will make my appointment is if I get a ride."

He told me that he lived in the Los Angeles Jewish home for the aging and that he went to the synagogue every day to make minyan (minyan is a ten-men quorum needed to conduct Jewish religious services), for which he was paid $35.00 a week.

So I wondered aloud, "Why do you do that?"

"Well, I'm not allowed to work here. I am a rabbi. I used to be the rabbi in the oldest synagogue in Romania. It was in a city called Iasi."

"Why can't you work here as a rabbi?"

He furrowed his eyebrows and looked directly at me, "Are you from the government?"

"No," I responded, "I'm not from the government. I'm in the entertainment business. Why do you ask that?"

"Well, I'm an illegal alien," he said. He continued by explaining that Nicolae Ceausescu, the president of Romania at the time, was a dictator who was persecuting the Jews. Then he added, "Back in my country, in the synagogue they made me talk about the government and the state for 25 minutes and about God for only five. So I escaped from Romania."

I introduced myself. "By the way, I'm Jim, what's your name?"

"My name is Rabbi Yehudi." He said that Jewish organizations had smuggled him out of Romania, first to Israel then to California.

"Is your family here, too?" I asked.

"No," he replied.

"Are they in Romania?"

"No."

We talked about a couple of other things and all the time this gentleman had a smile on his face. He was 78 years old, by himself in a foreign country, spoke English poorly, and earned only $35.00 a week. I wondered how he was managing. "Rabbi, none of your family is here? I mean, where is your family?"

Rabbi Yehudi turned his head away from me and looked out of the window for a moment. He turned back to me and said softly, "I tell you this and only once. I don't usually talk about this. But I will tell you. You seem to be a nice and understanding boy. My family was eliminated in Romania."

He took a breath and continued, "I don't like to put my attention on that, because I miss them. I am the only person remaining of my family, and luckily I escaped. Jim, there's a reason I don't talk about my family."

And then he looked at me with his very bright eyes, and said, *"The past is in the hands of God. Leave it there."*

This has stuck with me. I live with this now. I realized then the car ride was not just for him. This was a huge lesson for me. Now as we drove towards the synagogue, I had made a new friend, a very enlightened friend. When we reached the synagogue, I gave Rabbi Yehudi some money and my card. He thanked me and kissed me on the forehead. Driving away, I looked back to see the little old man in a suit and hat, smiling and waving. My heart soared. I was high on my way home.

Several weeks later, I received a call from the rabbi. He said he was very ill and asked if I could give him money to buy his medication. "Absolutely. How much do you need?" I was delighted to send him what he needed.

Every few days following that I received a message on my answering machine which said, "Good morning, Jim. This is Rabbi Yehudi. I want you to know that I'm praying for you today, Jim, and thank you for the money."

This went on for some time, and then the calls stopped. I called the home and found out that he had passed. But I will never forget this Rabbi and the powerful lesson that he taught me about the past.

Interestingly, though he was the first Romanian I'd ever met, I have since grown to have a close relationship with the warm and welcoming Romanian people through my work with my clients in Romania. In fact, in the summer of 2008, while I was doing work with Ecolab, a client in Romania, and AIESEC, an international student organization, I stayed in the city of Iasi. I was able to visit Rabbi Yehudi's synagogue and pay my respects to the memory of my old friend. My fondest memory is hearing him say that he couldn't change the past so he chose to accept it and live his life in the present.

Rabbi Yehudi perfectly exemplifies the essence of this chapter: Shifting our focus from StOP thinking—common, negative thinking patterns that stymie our aspirations, daily performance, and good health to PhB thinking—attitudes that support health and enthusiasm. It sets the stage for the mind-shifting lessons in Part II of the book that will take you from StOP to PhB, from Standard Operating Program thinking to Professional Human Being thinking.

The mind is a living chat room, only it is us talking to ourselves in a self-talk marathon of more than a million words a day. This inner conversation helps us explain our world to ourselves. Author and psychologist, Martin Seligman, calls it an explanatory style. We constantly relate our feelings and perceptions to ourselves, and, based on this experience, create an operating template for life.

Research shows that we follow and get stuck in repetitive thought patterns. Nearly 80 percent of our inner chatter is negative, self-defeating, and counterproductive. Constantly, we misuse our imagination, think ill of others, fret about what others think of us, worry needlessly, doubt ourselves, and create failure fantasies—all useless, repetitious, and frequently harmful—a waste of precious mental resources. We traffic in negativity that fails to serve our goals, our business at hand, and the health of our bodies. Such negativity clearly fails to serve the new direction of business trends, which increasingly emphasize the great untapped potential of individual creativity and responsibility.

StOP VS. PhB THINKING

Let's now look at a dozen common mindsets and see how they fit into StOP or PhB mode. Notice the difference between dysfunctional thinking (StOP) and what I call the psychological antidotal thinking (PhB). Dysfunctional thinking causes a physiological response that can cause disease and aging. During each of the following experiences, we make split-second decisions that will be either health-producing or disease-producing.

1. Anger/Hostility

Do not allow anyone to occupy your mind space—rent-free. In other words, the anger you demonstrate toward another is actually damaging you.

The StOP thinker makes a habit of anger/hostility and uses it as a way to punish the other person.	The PhB understands that anger triggers more damage to himself than the intended recipient.

When you are angry, it's like drinking poison and hoping the other person dies. This is sad, but true, once you understand the mind/body connection and what chemicals we create when we are angry. The person to whom you direct your anger may also feel uncomfortable, but not as uncomfortable as your own physiology.

A great thought from Buddha: Holding on to anger is like grasping a hot coal with the intent of throwing it at someone else; you are the one who gets burned.

This story is also told: Late one afternoon the Buddha was sitting under a banyan tree meditating. He heard some rumbling and concluded it was the sound of a horse's hooves coming toward him. The horse approached closer and closer until he stood right over the meditating Buddha. Buddha opened his eyes. There, sitting on a great white horse, was the king, his face red with anger. "You sit here all day with your eyes closed doing nothing!" He shouted at the Buddha, "This doesn't help the kingdom at all! And now you have many, many young men sitting in the morning and the afternoon with their eyes closed as well, doing nothing."

Buddha slowly looked up and said, "King, you must have had a long ride. You are probably tired. Please come down from the horse and I will get you a cool drink and some sweet fruits. Please rest for a moment."

The king looked at the Buddha, astonished. "Buddha, didn't you hear me insulting you? Why are you not upset with me?"

Buddha answered, "King, if someone offers you a gift, and you do not accept it, who has that gift?"

"The giver, of course," responded the king.

The lesson is that the anger remained with the king and was not transferred to the Buddha. If someone brings anger to us, there's no need to accept it. Ralph Waldo Emerson reminds us: "For every minute you are angry, you lose sixty seconds of happiness."

Mind/Body Connection

When we become angry our body launches its fight-or-flight response to prepare for danger. The sympathetic nervous system is put on full alert. Stress hormones pour into the bloodstream. Heart rate and blood pressure surge upward, the blood tends to clot more rapidly and the immune system is temporarily crippled.

Chronically hostile people seem to be especially vulnerable. In the 1960s, cardiologists Meyer Friedman, M.D., and Ray Rosenman, M.D., popularized the term "Type A behavior" to describe a combination of overdrive behavior—constant hurriedness, hostility, and intense competitiveness—that seemed to characterize many of their patients with heart disease. Over the years, researchers learned that hurriedness and competitiveness are less damaging to the heart than hostility. People prone to hostility have an increased risk of hypertension and coronary heart disease. According to Brian Seaward in his book, *Managing Stress*, "hostility and aggression are thought to be the most important factors with regard to heart disease, rather than the Type A behaviors as a whole."

Many medical studies have shown that laughing causes an opposite effect. There is more oxygenation of the blood, relaxation of the arteries and heart, decreased blood pressure, all of which have a positive—and even lifesaving—effect on the cardiovascular system, as well as increasing immune system function.

Our response to any given situation is our choice. Create a cooling-off period: a gap between stimulus and response. Laugh at yourself. Practice empathy and forgiveness. There is a stark contrast between the physiology of anger and the physiology of laughter. If we don't take ourselves so seriously, we will be able to laugh at the situations we find ourselves in.

We have a choice to be sovereign over the moment or prisoner of it. Getting angry, and becoming hostile, is becoming a prisoner. By laughing and staying centered, you become the sovereign of your domain.

You can make a choice that will increase quality and quantity of life span. The choice should be clear if you use a mind/body yardstick.

Real freedom is the ability to pause between stimulus and response and in that pause choose.

— ROLLO MAY

I call this pause the most important 1/10th of a second in your life.

This reminds me of a great Chinese proverb: Beware, the fire you kindle to burn your enemy may also consume you.

2. Acceptance

The StOP thinker expects the world to change to accommodate his needs.	The PhB adapts to what the world offers.

A benevolent king in ancient India had great empathy for his subjects and strived to ease their hardships. One day he decided to allow the people of the land to approach him with any problem. Many of them complained about the roughness of the harsh, uneven terrain under their bare feet. They entreated the king to lay carpet across the breadth of the land. He contemplated their request for some time, knowing that it would be a massive undertaking. He turned to his advisor, the Raj Guru.

The guru counseled, "It is easier to change oneself than it is to change the world. Why don't you tell them to put the carpet on their own feet rather than over the whole land?"

"Great idea," said the king. Thus, the shoe was born.

Take responsibility for changing yourself. We create our own reality!

3. The Past

The StOP thinker assigns great importance to past events.	The PhB focuses on the positive past since it has a positive effect on the nervous system, but does not focus on the negative, unless the focus is to change the interpretation, and create a better future.

An old Buddhist saying advises, "Do not regret the past. Do not dread or be afraid of the future. The wise one dwells peacefully and happily in the present moment. Peace is in every step."

The PhB knows there is no reason to look back. Why? You're not headed that way. Psychologists have said we spend 78 percent of our time in the past, 15 percent in the future, and only 7 percent of the time we actually live here, now, in the present. If you're not in the present, how could you possibly enjoy it? We spend a lot of time thinking about our childhood and how we were raised and how that affects us.

Ken Keyes, Jr., the personal growth guru, put it succinctly and correctly when he said, "You are not responsible for the programming you picked up in childhood. However, as adults, you are 100 percent responsible for fixing it."

Create a better future and leave the past in the hands of God. So put your mind in forward gear—PhB gear. StOP gear doesn't work. Past is blame oriented. Looking forward to the future is solution oriented.

Never let yesterday use up too much of today.

— WILL ROGERS
Humorist

4. Forgiveness

The StOP thinker does not forgive easily; he cherishes his grudges in order to punish others.	The PhB forgives others easily; and knows that forgiveness is a selfish act that frees himself.

Two Buddhist monks were walking through a forest. The elder monk was the younger monk's teacher. They came upon a riverbank and noticed the rickety bridge over the flooded river. A young woman stood by the river and approached the two monks. She said she was afraid to cross and needed help. The monks had taken a vow of celibacy, which meant they were not allowed even to touch a woman. Seeing her distress, the elder monk said, "I will help you across." He carried her across on his back and placed her at the other side of the river.

The monks continued on their path. After some time, the younger monk could no longer contain himself and burst out, "We're not supposed to touch women, yet you did! How am I supposed to follow you as a teacher if you break the rules? How do you think that makes me feel?"

After a few moments, the elder monk replied, "It is you who should tell me how it feels. I put the woman down at the edge of the river; you, however, are still carrying her."

This is a common Buddhist story that talks about what we carry in our minds. The stories we hold in our minds are most likely heavier than anything we could haul on our backs. The questions you should ask yourself are, "What am I carrying in my mind that I should let go of? Is there someone I should forgive? What patterns of thinking am I playing back on the disc of my mind?"

I'm not talking about saying a quick, "Sure, I forgive you." Instant forgiveness is usually shallow. It takes steps to really forgive. Unless we forgive *with intent*, the process of forgiveness never really begins. It never begins because it never started. Once we understand that carrying around a lack of forgiveness affects our physiology, increases our blood pressure, and produces stress we can start to shift our mindset.

Forgiveness is letting go of the hope for a better past.

— SUDHARMA LAMA

Mind/Body Connection

People who have generally forgiving natures tend to have lower blood pressure readings, compared to people who are not as forgiving. In a study at Florida Hospital in Orlando, researchers found that people who learned effective ways to forgive actually lowered their blood pressure. Dick Tibbits, Ph.D., explained that by the end of the eight-week study, "over 80 percent of those who entered the program with high levels of anger had lowered their blood pressure to the normal range."

Chronic high blood pressure is a risk factor for stroke and heart attacks.

The ultimate destination of forgiveness is in *self*-forgiveness. Ask yourself: Can I forgive myself for all the judgments I have been carrying? Can I release the judgments?

A great example of this is in the movie, *Antwone Fisher*, which is based on a true story. Denzel Washington plays a naval psychiatrist and Derek Luke plays Antwone Fisher, a troubled soldier who has a violent outburst against a fellow crewman. During the course of treatment, Antwone reveals his painful childhood. The doctor discovers that because Antwone's parents had abandoned him when he was very young, he still carries a lot of anger toward them.

The doctor instructs him to find his parents and forgive them. Antwone responds, "Why do I need to find them and forgive them? I have you. I don't need them."

And the doctor replies, "You need to find them and forgive them, so that you can free yourself."

The PhB guards his peace, understanding it is better to be free than to be weighted down by any judgments in his mind; he knows that holding onto the judgments poisons his physiology.

5. Love

A StOP thinker figures that when he gives love to others they become obligated to him.	A PhB knows the love he gives to others springs from inside himself and nurtures his own heart first.

The German writer, Johann Wolfgang von Goethe, summed it up best, "If I love you, what business is it of yours?"

His quote perfectly indicates where loving comes from and where it ends up. It starts from within us. We feel it; we just assign it to someone else. In the dramatic final scene of the 1990 movie *Ghost*, Sam finally tells his girlfriend Molly that he loves her. And then, as the light shines for him to depart, he realizes out loud, "The love inside—you take it with you."

You may say, "I'm in love." And yes, you can have an outside stimulus, an object of that affection which allows you to feel the love. But whose love are you really feeling? Answer: your own. Have you ever experienced feeling love, just for love's sake, without it being reciprocated? All of us have.

The StOP thinker withholds love to punish people. The PhB understands that he punishes himself by withholding his love.

Self-love and self-forgiveness are two of the most powerful practices of the PhB. I call them slayers of all demons. *I like myself, and I also forgive myself for any and all transgressions against myself and all others.* This is a powerful concept practiced by the PhB.

I spend a lot of time in airports. I vividly remember waiting at the gate years ago as passengers disembarked from a flight. In an age before 9/11, airport security was much looser than it is today; we were allowed to stand at the gate, even if we didn't have a ticket, and wait for passengers. When soldiers or airmen were coming home from the war, their families would be there to greet them at the gate. It was a sight I witnessed many times.

I watched as soldiers and airmen came off the plane after the 1991 Gulf War. One soldier emerged and entered the gate area. His family and friends rushed forward. More soldiers deplaned and were received with a lot of crying and hugging and kissing by loved ones.

As I watched from a distance, my heart expanded with love for these people. Tears welled up in my eyes and trickled down my face. I was in love, and these people had no idea I existed. Did it matter that they didn't know I existed? No, I was feeling my own love. They were the stimulus. I was the first beneficiary of my loving, filling my body with endorphins, the most powerful self-healing molecules in the nervous system. My love was and is a gift to myself. This is reflected in the U2 song "Luminous Times" as Bono sings, "I love you because I need to, not because I need you."

In summary, whatever you do or intend to do to others affects you first. It affects your body chemistry. Your thinking can either create molecules of disease or well-being. You are simply designed to have chemical reactions from life's experiences. The body follows the mind.

6. Gossip

A StOP thinker talks about people and is overly concerned with what others say about him.	A PhB talks to people and knows that his life is lived based on his own values, not the opinions of others.

It's none of our business what others say about us. What we say is our responsibility; what others say is their responsibility. In the same way, if people speak negatively of us, that's their responsibility. My responsibility is to speak well of others. While we may prefer others to speak positively about us, we are not in control of that. Fritz Perls, the founder of Gestalt Therapy, put it like this: "I do my thing and you do your thing. I am not in this world to live up to your expectations, and you are not in this world to live up to mine."

Somehow, we imagine if we are thinking negatively of someone else, it damages that person. However, this negative thinking damages our own body. Remember the first Law of the PhB: *I am the primary beneficiary of everything I think, do, and say.*

In other words, I am in control of only my thoughts; what I *say to myself.* This is what affects my physiology. Thinking positively of others allows me to live with myself in a more comfortable way. This honors PhB Law 2: *The most important relationship I have is the one I have with myself.*

> *To be nobody but yourself, in a world which is doing its best, night and day,*
> *to make you just like everybody else, means to fight the greatest battle*
> *there is to fight—never stop fighting.*

> — E.E. CUMMINGS
> American poet

Life is not a popularity contest. The object of our behavior is to fulfill our personal mission, and not to worry about pleasing everyone.

7. Criticism

The StOP thinker fears criticism.	The PhB welcomes all criticism and is able to discern that which is useful.

Elbert Hubbard, an American author, said, "To avoid criticism, do nothing, say nothing, be nothing." And, I might add, if you do that, someone will still criticize you for it.

"You seem to be having a bad hair day."

"You never take out the garbage unless I ask you six times!"

"Your report makes no sense."

"This place is a mess."

"How did you get us so lost? Do you even know where you're going?"

Do these sound familiar? Now, take a look at each criticism. Notice each one criticizes something you have *done.* Notice they do not criticize *you.* The you

47

that you know. You were created perfectly by the Creator. You can change your behavior. When you are asked to change your behavior remember that you are not your behavior.

For sure, nothing you do will ever be to everyone's satisfaction. We will always be criticized so you must simply prepare yourself for it and consider it as "for-your-information" only. A person's criticism of you is just his or her perception of you. There is no reality, only perception.

Consider the criticism. If it has relevance to you, act on it; if it has no relevance to you, let it go.

8. Negativity

A StOP thinker wallows in negativity.	A PhB makes a conscious decision to focus on the positive.

Norman Vincent Peale talked about positive thinking for about half a century before he died at age 95. You can imagine why he lived so long. During his time, there wasn't the scientific research there is today on negative versus positive thinking. It turns out he was correct when he connected positive thinking to good health.

I once said to a pessimistic friend, "Why don't you try to be positive for once? Then maybe things will change in your life."

He responded, "I tried that once. It didn't work."

StOP thinking for sure.

The assumption is that if you think positively, then you promote the desired outcome, and that the opposite is true for thinking negatively.

Thinking negatively does predispose us to a lack of success or achievement. Despite that, it doesn't necessarily guarantee we won't achieve our goal. During the process, however, it exposes our physiology to a disease-producing biochemistry.

Mind/Body Connection

Negativity breeds toxicity in the body and depresses and weakens the immune system. A researcher at Zurich University in Switzerland determined that negative thoughts or feelings could depress the immune system for several hours.

On the other hand, thinking positively does not guarantee we will achieve our goal. What it does do is predispose us to getting what we want, and, more importantly, expose us to a health-producing biochemistry.

When we become aware of the influence of negative versus positive thinking on our physiology, then we begin to understand the outcome is not the most important element.

The positive journey is more important than the positive destination. This is the most important aspect concerning negative versus positive thinking.

There is an old Cherokee legend in which a chief is teaching his grandson about life. "A fight is going on inside me," he said to the boy. "It is a terrible fight and it is between two wolves. One is evil—he is anger, envy, sorrow, regret, greed, arrogance, self-pity, guilt, resentment, inferiority, lies, false pride, superiority, and ego. The other wolf is good—he is joy, peace, love, hope, serenity, humility, kindness, benevolence, empathy, generosity, truth, compassion, and faith. This same fight is going on inside you and inside every other person too."

The grandson thought about it for a minute and then asked his grandfather, "Which wolf will win?"

The old chief simply replied, "The one we feed."

Be careful what you put your attention on because it will grow! Your attention is like sunlight, when you place it on something, it grows. If you take your attention away from it, it withers. Focus your attention on what you want.

Put your attention on positive, it grows; put your attention on negative, it grows, and at the same time, has a weakening effect on your physiology.

9. Obstacles

A StOP thinker sees obstacles.	A PhB sees challenges as there to instruct, not to obstruct.

Many years ago, I was working in Singapore. One Sunday I visited a Buddhist monastery, witnessed the Buddhist ceremonies, and then had a great vegetarian lunch. One of the monks talked to me about my stay in Singapore. I was explaining to him how difficult it was to work with the Singaporean government and do business because the system was so strict and rigid. He looked at me and said, "You cannot reach your destination by traveling on sunny days only." I then realized, in order to get where I was going, I would have to travel on some rainy days. Obstacles are part of the path. They don't block the path. They exercise us. They make us stronger.

10. Worry

A StOP thinker constantly worries about what might go wrong.	A PhB chooses to think about what he wants to happen.

Think about what your options are, not about what you don't want to happen. Worry is the setting of negative goals and a misuse of the imagination. Why? Worry is imagining things going wrong or having negative outcomes. This is counter-productive. Worry tends to be a negative future fantasy; meaning, as we fantasize about bad things, we imagine ourselves in a losing position. This creates anxiety in the nervous system. If you choose to fantasize, why not be the winner and have a positive outcome?

The destructive quality of worry is indicated in the origin of the word *worry*. It is derived from an old Anglo-Saxon word meaning *to choke*. When we feel fear and worry about the future, we choke the nervous system. Worry is a subtle and destructive human disease. It feeds agitation and disturbance inside of you. Unsurprisingly, "choking" is the term applied to an athlete who becomes so overwhelmed with worry and anxiety that he becomes dysfunctional and loses his nerve and the game or match.

When I look back on all these worries, I remember the story of the old man who said on his deathbed that he had had a lot of trouble in his life, most of which had never happened.

— WINSTON CHURCHILL

Research shows that worry is indeed wasted thought power.
- Forty percent of what you worry about never happens.
- Thirty percent of worries relate to things that happened in the past.
- Twelve percent are needless health worries.
- Ten percent are petty worries.
- Eight percent are actually substantial. Only half of these (four percent of all worries) are worthwhile, substantial, and within the control of the person doing the worrying.

We are wasting thought power. After reading research that confirmed forgetfulness was caused by what was called *congestive brain theory*, I came up with the analogy of a disc. If there is too much on the disc, short-term memory is not good. Long-term memory is good, so what has been in there you won't forget. But, if the disc is full, we can't add more to short-term memory.

For example: I enter a room and, once I am in the room, I forget why I came. The disc is full, in this case, with a *lot of irrelevancy*. Worry is irrelevant thinking taking up space that could be used for creative thought.

Since this habit constricts creativity and stresses the nervous system, how can you counter worry? One technique is to allow yourself to feel the physiological discomfort when you first become aware that you are worrying. Then, go to the next step. If you can think one thought, you can replace it with its opposite. So here are some questions to ask yourself at that moment: What is the worst thing that could possibly happen, if the thing I'm worried about came true? Then, what would I need to do right now so that this worst possible outcome would never happen? What action can I then take?

Mind/Body Connection

Worry creates the physiology of fear and anxiety. Blood is diverted from organs to muscles. Tension builds. Breathing becomes shallow and less effective. Carbon dioxide increases in the bloodstream. The greater the fear, the more powerful is the fight-or-flight response. Chemicals, such as cortisol, adrenaline, and noradrenaline course through the body. High levels of these stress chemicals cause damage to the arteries and brain cells and weaken bone structure.

Negative emotions—worry, anger and hopelessness—reduce the number and activity of disease-fighting white blood cells, major players in the immune system.

On the other hand, positive thoughts strengthen and enhance the immune system through the release of endorphins into the bloodstream. This enables the body to resist disease and recover more quickly from illness. Endorphins are the body's natural painkillers and mood elevators. Among other effects, they stimulate dilation of the blood vessels, which allows the heart to do its pumping job with less strain.

In the moment, another technique is to switch from the negative emotion of worry to a positive emotion such as gratitude. Or, imagine what you want to occur, instead of what you don't want to occur. This shifts the whole physiology. If you think a positive thought, then you'll have a positive emotion. This all sounds easy, right? However, we all know that, in reality, it's not so easy. But it's really important to put this into practice.

After one of my classes, a participant handed me a piece of paper with these words scribbled on it: *If you can change it, why worry? If you can't change it, why worry?* Fear is worry magnified. Let's look at the letters magnified:

F - False
E - Evidence
A - Appearing
R - Real

The less you know about a subject, the more fear you will have embarking on something new. A PhB is a learner, and learning eliminates fear.

Do the thing you fear most and the death of fear is certain.

— MARK TWAIN

11. Doubt

A StOP thinker doubts and doubts and doesn't do.	A PhB feels the doubt and does it anyway.

Doubts keep you in the comfort zone—the StOP gear. Doubts are not the product of accurate thinking, but habitual thinking. Doubts do damage so don't give them any mental space. If you must doubt something, doubt your limitations. "Our doubts are traitors and make us lose the good we oft might win, by fearing to attempt," wrote Shakespeare, in *Measure for Measure*.

12. Failure

A StOP thinker fears mistakes because of the fear of being a failure.	A PhB sees mistakes as essential to success. Falling is followed by getting right back up. Course corrects. Feels free to make mistakes.

Becoming a Professional Human Being

Failure is never fatal, failure to change might be.

— JOHN WOODEN
Basketball coach

I once heard a story of a Japanese samurai warrior and a Zen monk that I think summarizes this chapter.

The tough samurai warrior approaches the Zen monk and confronts him in a disrespectful way. "You're a monk and you should be smart enough to tell me the difference between heaven and hell," he says rudely. "What is the difference?"

The monk looks at him condescendingly and says, "I don't discuss things like that with imbeciles. They don't understand even if I tell them."

The samurai angrily pulls out his sword and threatens the monk. "You can't talk to me like that. I could cut your head off right now."

"Hold it," the monk says. "That's hell."

The samurai hesitates. His anger disappears. He puts his sword away.

"Yes, I understand now," he says. "Thank you for the lesson."

The monk smiles and, as he walks away, says, "And that's heaven."

What is the lesson of this simple story? You don't have to wait until life ends to get a certificate to go to heaven or hell: You create it right here. And only you create it. Furthermore, like the samurai, you create it all the time, every moment of the day, with every thought and decision you make. John Milton, the English poet, puts it like this: "The mind is its own place, and in itself can make a heaven of hell and a hell of a heaven."

Modern science validates the samurai and monk story. The mind/body connection is real and relevant to everyday life. In my work, I apply it to the way people handle their jobs, which is also a snapshot of how they handle their lives in general. Let's find out more.

6

Are You Making a Living or a Dying?

Every stress leaves an indelible scar,
and the organism pays for its survival after a stressful situation by
becoming a little older.

— HANS SELYE, M.D.
the father of stress medicine

I met Susan in graduate school at the University of Santa Monica. At that time she was teaching high-school algebra and geometry in Southern California but was unhappy and frustrated with her job. After fifteen years, she felt she was no longer making a contribution to her profession. She still loved and cared for the kids, but she said she couldn't seem to reach them. Their behavior was out of control and she couldn't cope with the demands of the administration, the parents, or the kids. She felt horrible and miserable; I could tell how much pain she was in. She said her physical heart literally hurt.

I believe this is the connection research talks about, that our cardiovascular system is hurt when we are not happy and not enjoying life. There is a lot of heart value taken away at that time, and Susan expressed it explicitly. She was ready to quit. Luckily she didn't.

Fast-forward a year when I saw her again, Susan had a different story to tell. She was now enjoying her work and looked forward to teaching every day. I was curious. Susan explained that she had to learn a different way of teaching and a different way of looking at teaching.

She also had to throw out a lot of the teaching methods she had been taught. She introduced entertaining methods to keep her students' interest and empowered them to take responsibility for what they wanted to learn. She said she completely released the pressure off herself. She changed. She gave them the responsibility of telling her how they wanted to learn and things shifted dramatically.

She explained, "I needed to just treat them with a higher regard and love them more. When my attitude changed, I changed. Work became a joy again. The kids began to bond with me. They didn't feel I was judging them anymore. I wasn't. I actually have more kids doing more work now than ever before.

I changed myself inside and the students began to change and relate to me differently. It was amazing."

I wanted to find out what triggered this transformation. So one day during lunch I sat with her to hear her story. She told me that it all began one day when she was driving onto the high-school campus and saw a student leaving who had often been in trouble. She had run-ins with him in the past and he was always very defiant. This time, she decided to try a different approach. She stopped her car and asked him where he was going and he said, "I'm going to get a doughnut." She reminded him that he was on probation and would be suspended if he got caught leaving.

He insisted, "But I'm hungry."

So she said to him, "Look, I've got some carrots and peanut butter. I know that sounds odd, but I think you'll like it. I'll give you my food and I'll even give you a pass to class."

He grudgingly agreed—it was free food, after all. She parked her car and as they began walking back to campus, they both noticed a beautiful feather lying on the ground. She said, "Look! A feather means an angel has been here. That must be why I saw you. An angel is taking care of you." He laughed and they went into her classroom, where he ate the peanut butter and carrots.

"Boy, I love this stuff!" he exclaimed.

One morning, a few days later, Susan walked into her classroom and he was sitting in her chair, spinning around, kind of feeling it out.

Susan didn't let anyone sit on her chair; she would tell the kids that there's a force field around it. But there he was. She asked him what he was doing sitting on her chair.

He answered, "Well, maybe I want to be a teacher."

Susan hid the gigantic smile she wanted to let out and simply said, "That sounds pretty good to me. If that's what's going through your head, I hope someday you do become a teacher."

He got up from her chair and walked to his seat. She looked down and noticed that there was a feather lying on the floor by the chair. She looked up at him and he looked at her and grinned, and she knew that he had left that feather there. She said it was one of the most beautiful things she had ever seen—the feather, the look on his face, and the hope that he had in his eyes about someday becoming a teacher. Right then, she felt her passion for teaching coming back. Under the ashes she had found a burning ember that began to light the flame again for her love for teaching.

Susan's experience shows that the change you have to make is internal. It's not the job; it's how you look at the job. By the end of that year, Susan felt that she had become a very good teacher. She had changed herself, and that changed her relationship with her students. She credited a lot of her changes to the amazing work we were doing at the University of Santa Monica (USM). I will tell you more about this, but I strongly recommend you go to the USM's website and take a look at this program. I certainly saw it change Susan, myself, and many others, by giving us some very powerful life skills.

You can't always change your job. But fortunately, you can always change your perspective and approach to your job. In the U2 song "Rejoice," Bono says it like this: "I can't change the world, but I can change the world in me."

Fall in love with your work!

GENETICS VERSUS LIFE CHOICES

In a 1996 study conducted by Yale University and the MacArthur Foundation, researchers found that *the way people age is mostly a matter of how they live*. Surprisingly, only about 30 percent of the factors of aging are genetically based. Current research reduces that number to 25 percent. In other words, you have control over the rest—about three times that much!

So what makes up *the rest* of the story? I suggest that since we spend about 60 percent of our waking hours on the job (managers spend even more, an estimated 70 percent), a big chunk of *the rest* involves work. So our approach to work (and the time spent doing it) is really crucial to how well we age—to our quality and quantity of life.

The fact is most of us have to work to make a living. Even if we take all our sick leave and vacation days, we still must show up for work most of the year.

Now, here's the thing: If your job doesn't match your talents, you will not be happy at work. You will complain about how bad the job is, how bad management is, and how bad the place is. Statistics indicate that up to 78 percent of workers are dissatisfied with their jobs and 60 percent say they plan to leave their jobs for other pursuits within two years. Job fulfillment comes from doing what you love to do. You have to perform your magic: make the job something you love or get out before it affects your health and shortens your life. That's why I always ask the people in my audiences, "*Are you making a living or a dying?*" It gets them thinking.

KAROSHI: MADE NOT JUST IN JAPAN

Have you ever said, "My work is killing me"? You may have been kidding, but work-related stress is no joke. It is certainly serious business in Japan where they even have a word for it: karoshi. It means *early death from overwork*, usually caused by heart attack or stroke.

The first reported case was in 1969. Since then, some 10,000 deaths yearly have been attributed to karoshi, and several lawsuits have been won by relatives of workers who literally worked themselves to death.

Research indicates there are six major factors involved in karoshi:
- Extremely long work hours
- Night work interfering with rest patterns
- Working without holidays or breaks
- High-pressure work without breaks
- Extremely demanding physical work
- Continually stressful work

Some of us experience all of these factors, but most of us experience factor number six. I doubt if more than a few people in the U.S. are familiar with the word karoshi. Still it's happening big time. In 1999 a U.S. government report found the number of hours worked increased 8 percent in one generation to an average 47 hours a week. American workers put in more hours on the job than the labor force of any other industrial nation. Japan had the previous record until around 1995 but Americans, according to the report, work almost a month more than the Japanese and three months more than Germans.

STRESS SHORTENS LIFE

In 1983, a *Time* magazine cover article named stress "The Epidemic of the Eighties," referring to it as our leading health problem. Today, more than a quarter century later, the situation is much worse and yet most people, including doctors, trivialize stress and do not realize the degree to which it spoils and shortens life.

"Numerous surveys indicate that adult Americans regard themselves under much more stress than a decade or two ago," says Paul J. Rosch, M.D., Ph.D., president of the American Institute of Stress. "An estimated 75-90 percent of all visits to primary care physicians are for stress-related problems. Still, most people don't realize the high degree of damage stress inflicts on their personal health. They simply brush off or underestimate the stress in their lives.

'I'm just a little stressed,' they'll say, as if chronic stress equates to caffeinated edginess. They are fooling themselves. Stress actually is a killer that destroys and shortens life."

Dr. Rosch has listed some of the many ways in which stress kills and maims:
- The leading cause of sudden death, insomnia, and depression
- Can cause heart attacks in people with no evidence of coronary artery blockage or disease
- The leading cause of memory loss now common in people in their thirties and forties
- Promotes the deposition of deep abdominal fat and the development of insulin resistance and diabetes
- Promotes weight gain by causing overeating, especially sweet, salty, and fatty foods
- Elevates cholesterol far more than increased consumption of fatty foods
- Elevates blood pressure and increases risk of hypertension and stroke
- Promotes chronic but silent inflammation now thought to be the prime cause of arterial disease
- Increases the frequency and severity of colds
- Turns asymptomatic HIV infection into AIDS
- Causes recurrent herpes and reduces resistance to other viruses and certain cancers
- Aggravates allergic responses such as hay fever, hives, rashes, and itching
- Contributes to autoimmune diseases such as rheumatoid arthritis, lupus, and multiple sclerosis

- Aggravates or leads to Parkinson's, Alzheimer's, and other neurodegenerative diseases
- Delays wound healing and recovery from surgery
- Is a major source of both tension headaches and migraine
- Is a major cause of low-back pain and neck discomfort due to muscle spasm
- Accelerates osteoporosis and other types of biological aging
- Causes erectile dysfunction in men and lack of libido in both men and women
- Worsens pain, bloating, other menstrual complaints, and menopausal symptoms
- Makes people smoke and drink more and suffer from substance abuse
- Causes impulse disorders such as compulsive shopping, gambling, and kleptomania

"Stress is the overlooked root cause—the first cause—of many of the most prevalent disorders we have today," Dr. Rosch says. "It is a hydra-headed assassin of well-being. It is the clandestine cause—not fat or cholesterol—of heart attacks and coronary disease. It can abruptly end your life by exploding an arterial plaque, or by triggering a lethal disturbance in the rhythm of the heart. It is the leading cause of sudden death. Stress drains the immune system and opens the door to the common cold and the latest flu bug. It is difficult to name any disorder in which stress cannot exert a causal and/or aggravating effect, yet this connection often goes unrecognized."

Did you know that your doctor's treatment of a stress-related problem can cause more stress? Dr. Rosch writes, "Most physicians have scant training in recognizing stress or treating it, other than to prescribe a tranquilizer, anti-depressant, sleeping pill—or perhaps all three—depending on a patient's complaints. Such "bandaid" approaches rarely solve problems. Conversely, they cause additional stress."

For more information on stress, check out Dr. Rosch's highly informative website at www.stress.org.

JOB-RELATED STRESS—THE LEADING FORM OF STRESS

According to Dr. Rosch and other experts, job-related stress perennially tops the stress chart. It is more strongly associated with health complaints than financial or family problems. The National Institute for Occupational Safety and Health (NIOSH) describes it as "the harmful physical and emotional responses that occur when the requirements of the job do not match the capabilities, resources, or needs of the worker. Job stress can lead to poor health and even injury."

NIOSH tells us that health-care expenditures are nearly 50 percent greater for workers who report high levels of stress, and that psychologically demanding jobs that allow employees little control over the work process can increase the risk of cardiovascular disease.

A 2000 Gallup survey of attitudes in the American workplace found that 80 percent of workers feel stress on the job. Nearly half say they need help in learning how to manage stress; 42 percent say their coworkers need such help; 14 percent felt like striking a coworker in the past year, but hadn't; 25 percent felt like screaming or shouting because of job stress; 10 percent were concerned about an individual at work they feared could become violent; 9 percent were aware of an assault or violent act in their workplace; and 18 percent had experienced some sort of threat or verbal intimidation in the previous year.

Sounds more like a war zone than a work zone!

STRESS SURVEY

How much job-related stress do you have? The American Institute of Stress has developed this survey designed to help you learn more about your own job stress level. Keep score for each question.

Strongly Disagree			**Agree Somewhat**				**Strongly Agree**		
1	2	3	4	5	6	7	8	9	10

_____ I can't honestly say what I really think, or get things off my chest, at work.

_____ My job has a lot of responsibility, but I don't have very much authority.

_____ I could usually do a much better job if I were given more time.

_____ I seldom receive adequate acknowledgment when my work is really good.

_____ In general, I am not particularly proud or satisfied with my job.

_____ I have the impression that I am repeatedly picked on or discriminated against at work.

_____ My workplace environment is not very pleasant or particularly safe.

_____ My job often interferes with my family, social obligations, or personal needs.

_____ I tend to have frequent arguments with superiors, coworkers, or customers.

_____ Most of the time, I feel I have very little control over my life at work.

Add up your responses to each question for your total job stress score and check your results against the scores on the next page to find out how you handle stress.

10-30 You handle stress on your job well.

40-60 You handle stress on your job moderately well.

70-100 You're encountering problems that need to be addressed and resolved.

Stress costs U.S. business an estimated $300 billion a year. This results in lower productivity and higher health-care costs.

A World Health Organization report has called job stress a *global epidemic.* According to the European Agency for Safety and Health at Work, nearly one in four European workers is affected by it, and studies suggest that between 50 and 60 percent of all lost working days are related to it. "Stress at work can affect anyone at any level," the agency says, and "in any sector and in any size of organization. Stress affects the health and safety of individuals, but also the health of organizations and national economies."

Looking ahead, the agency predicted that the number of people suffering from stress-related conditions caused or made worse by work is likely to increase. "The changing world of work is making increased demands on workers, through downsizing and outsourcing, the greater need for flexibility in terms of function and skills, increasing use of temporary contracts, increased job insecurity and work intensification (with higher workload and more pressure), and poor work-life balance."

None of this is new, of course. What's new is that experts are screaming more loudly for remedies to solve the problem, and more and more companies are trying to implement workplace solutions.

Our forefathers, Dr. Rosch points out, were often farmers and craftsmen who took pride in their work, labored under a more controlled and predictable pace, and were much more likely to see the benefits and pleasure it provided for others. They did something which they enjoyed and could see benefited others. This experience produced powerful satisfaction that many workers rarely experience today. This pride of accomplishment is a powerful stress buster.

Today too many of us are merely cogs in some giant technocratic venture, rarely having any control over the finished product or having enough time to use our talents effectively.

YOU ARE THE SOLUTION

Politicians talk about having a health-care system that provides for everyone. But providing for health has to start with the individual. That's where the ultimate responsibility resides: with you! Not with your government or insurance plan. And definitely not with your doctor.

"American manufacturers are losing their ability to compete in the global marketplace in large measure because of the crushing burden of health-care costs," GM CEO Rick Wagoner has said, while calling on corporate and government leaders to find *some serious medicine* for the nation's ailing health system.

In a 2007 *Time* magazine article on stress, Sheldon Cohen, a psychology professor at Carnegie, Mellon University, commented that current evidence "was enough to start asking whether reductions of stress would reduce disease outcomes," but that "people have not been asking this question."

In the same article, Daniel Brotman, director of the Hospitalist Program at Johns Hopkins Hospital and an expert in the stress response, said many doctors don't have the time to ask. "It's ironic that as we're getting a broader picture of how important stress levels are to physical health, we're simultaneously cramming appointments into shorter and shorter periods of time."

Doctors tend to blow off emotional triggers. "Traditional western medicine has really endeavored to think of the body as a machine, and disease as how the machine breaks down. [Doctors can be] reluctant to think of the mind and body as being part of that same machine."

The message is clear: You had better start taking care of yourself because the system isn't going to do it. Your self-interest is the best system. And prevention is your best tool. YOU are the best person to take care of your own health.

It all starts with how you think. Mental events exert harmful or beneficial effects on the brain and are transmitted to the body. In reality, everything is created within the self and directed back to the self.

The new-age understanding—and the way the Professional Human Being approaches life—is that every thought, word, and action has a health and physiological consequence. An understanding that gives all the more reason to hold ourselves responsible and accountable, no matter what the situation.

We know that dysfunctional thinking undermines successful action, but what is it doing to us on the inside?

Let's find out.

7

Meet Your Internal Pharmacist

We are all aware of the bias built into the Western idea
that the mind is totally in the head, a function of the brain.
But your body is not there just to carry around your head.

— CANDACE PERT
internationally recognized pharmacologist

The most powerful pharmacy in the world is right inside your skin. It fills prescriptions immediately. No waiting. Your every thought produces a chemical response that can lead you in the direction of health or sickness. But did you know that your pharmacy is busy responding to your thought process at work just as it does while you're at home or on vacation?

A lot of fascinating mind/body/work research has been conducted in recent years. It shows quite conclusively how workplace thinking and stress—heavy on worry, anxiety, fear, doubt, anger, and frustration—can produce bad health. Meanwhile, workplace thinking involving service, fulfillment, and creativity will support and enhance an opposite, healthy effect.

One of my favorite researchers in the area of *thought chemistry* is Georgetown University's Candace Pert, who found that *we are the only species that can change our internal biochemistry by changing our thinking.* Our thoughts and emotions produce specific molecules in the body. They either sustain health or promote disease. I'll bet you've never considered your thoughts as molecules.

Pert, in her groundbreaking book, *Molecules of Emotion*, explains how this works. She describes how thoughts and emotions can manifest as molecules in the nervous system. For example, bouts of laughter can help the body synthesize endorphins. Endorphins are health-producing molecules.

KEEPING MY BIOCHEMISTRY IN CHECK

One day during the summer before my sophomore year of high school, I was going home from August football practice. Central Catholic, my high school, was about ten miles from my home. It was a hot day and I had missed my ride so I had to hitchhike. I put my thumb out and began walking, as the cars whizzed by. After a while I started to get a little disheartened. Football practices were tough and held twice daily, early morning and late afternoon, because of the heat. I wanted to get home to eat, then go to bed early. The next day it would start all over again.

After I had trudged up the road for ten minutes, a car approached. I watched it stop about fifty yards ahead of me. I was excited. I ran toward the car and, just as I reached it, it suddenly pulled away. I saw a car full of guys laughing.

And as it sped away, I laughed too. I thought it was pretty funny! You guys made me run all this way and you took off. It was funny. I just laughed. I didn't get angry. I didn't get upset, probably because I was too tired to get upset, not because I was any kind of a budding psychologist.

Five minutes later, the same car pulled up with the same guys and stopped alongside me. I got in and they began apologizing.

"Sorry, man! We had a girl in the car and no room for you. We just dropped her off. You were a good sport, so we had to come back and get you. Where are you headed?" I told them and they took me all the way home. To top it off, they were football players from the neighboring rival, Perry High School!

I'm glad I kept my cool in that moment. I had chosen to *interpret their actions* as playful and not spiteful. And this helped me to keep my inner balance. I kept my internal biochemistry in check. You too can maintain your sovereignty over the moment and not become its prisoner. The key is striving to alter your interpretation of the event. You can choose your *interpretation of the stimulus* in each moment. Recognizing you have this choice creates a gap between the stimulus—whatever is happening in the environment—and your response to it. In that gap lies freedom, freedom to be who you want to be.

THE MIND/BODY CONNECTION

Does the name Ivan Pavlov ring a bell? This Russian scientist did not set out to discover laws of behavior when he was studying digestion. His groundbreaking experiments with dogs were one of the world's most famous demonstrations of the mind/body connection. Pavlov later received a Nobel Prize in Medicine for discovering what he called "conditional reflexes." To his annoyance, the dogs in his experiments would salivate before they were able to smell or see the meat he put down before them. He would ring the bell and they would salivate thinking about the meat to come. "Psychic secretions," he called them; I call it a strong example of mind/body behavior.

In the East, the mind/body concept is well understood. For thousands of years the sages of India and China have known that thoughts and feelings cannot be separated from the physical effects they create; the body transmutes consciousness into matter.

The West has been slow to accept such notions. In the late 1980s, medical science conceded that illness is connected to a person's emotions, beliefs, and expectations. Yet this concept is something that mainstream medicine tends to ignore in its reductionist, pharmaceutical, and surgical approaches to illness. Some doctors seem to forget that the whole body is connected. In 1990, a newsletter of the American Medical Association (AMA) queried its members and found that only 10 percent believed in the mind/body connection. In response, one physician asked the question, "How do the other 90 percent of the doctors think they wiggle their toes?"

ARE YOU PROTECTING YOUR DELICATE MACHINERY?

The autonomic nervous system (ANS) is the highly sophisticated machinery running much of the show. The ANS is a network of nerves that travel from the brain, down the spine, out to the muscles and the glands of your internal organs, and on to the skin and blood vessels. The nerves carry messages that activate one of the two most important reflexes you have: *fight-or-flight reflex* or *restful-alertness (rejuvenation) reflex*. This system controls about 90 percent of the body's inner workings and functions. The name refers to its involuntary or automatic functioning.

Within this hardwire setup are two divisions: the sympathetic and parasympathetic nervous systems. The sympathetic system activates the body toward the stress response—fight-or-flight. The parasympathetic system creates a calm and tranquil state. I refer to this as rejuvenation response because of its restful and restorative nature. Most stress-management techniques, including meditation and biofeedback, aim to induce a positive parasympathetic state by calming down a nervous system constantly in sympathetic overdrive.

THE FIGHT-OR-FLIGHT or STRESS RESPONSE

As you know, the fight-or-flight response is the body's internal response to a threat or perceived threat. When this occurs, the nervous system is flooded with more than a thousand different biochemicals that over time can be toxic to brain cells, artery walls, and bone tissue, and cause premature aging and a lack of emotional and physical vitality. We need small amounts of these chemicals for proper functioning, not a flood—and certainly not kicking in all the time.

Among the excesses are stress hormones that trigger a cascade of events priming a person to flee or fight or freeze. This type of mechanism served well for the survival of the cavemen facing saber-toothed tigers. Most of the threats we face today, however, tend to be psychological and cannot be handled by fighting or fleeing (as much as we might want to).

In 1930, the great Canadian researcher and physician, Hans Selye, coined the term *stress response*. He demonstrated that the body reacts to modern-day stresses as though it were still facing the tiger. The response has been studied vigorously ever since Dr. Selye's groundbreaking work. It has also been called the body's *emergency response* and *amygdala hijacking*, a reference to the part of the brain (the limbic area) that signals an emergency and then garners, or *hijacks*, most of the body's resources to defend itself by fleeing, fighting, or freezing in place.

Whatever name we use, it remains one of the most important reflexes in the repertoire of our mind/body responses. It is our evolutionary heritage. We have this built-in instinct to instantly respond to a threat or perceived threat. Whether the threat is physiological or psychological, we respond in the same way; the body mobilizes for defensive or offensive action. Heart rate, respiration, muscle tension, and blood pressure all increase, as well as blood flow to the extremities—our arms and legs—to assist in running or fighting.

When the limbic system is excited, it stimulates the production of three powerful chemicals—cortisol, epinephrine, and norepinephrine—which are useful when you encounter danger or need special focus. These, nevertheless, can compromise the immune system, and can weaken our bodies in general, even aging us, if they remain chronically present in the bloodstream at elevated levels. An overcharged sympathetic nervous system promotes poor immune function.

The consequences of this range from the common cold, to cancer, bone disease, and musculoskeletal disorders. From a cardiovascular perspective, the introduction of these chemicals produces very negative changes in blood texture, blood pressure, and arterial function that result in heart attacks, stroke, and premature death. Under chronic stress—such as an unfulfilling job—the stress hormones can promote arterial constriction, rise of blood pressure, and increased heart rate. They also may cause the blood to clot more. This is beneficial for a soldier exposed to constant life-and-death situations. Should you become wounded, you want more clotting to slow down or plug up blood loss. However, the equivalent of daily conflict or dissatisfaction in the office generates a similar process in the body. The blood becomes thick and sticky. The thicker and stickier your blood becomes, the greater your risk for cardiovascular problems.

My good friend and writer, Martin Zucker, has coauthored a great book with Stephen Sinatra and James Roberts, two holistic cardiologists. The book, *Reverse Heart Disease Now*, brings a good deal of attention to the connection between the heart and emotions. Doctors point out that accountants die from heart attacks more during tax season because their oxidized cholesterol goes way up due to the stress. They also point out—and this is very revealing—that the single biggest incidence of heart attacks (28 percent) occurs on Monday morning. And, according to a Japanese study they cited, many workers suffer a spike in blood pressure as they return to the office after the weekend.

MONDAY-MORNING SYNDROME

"We cardiologists call this phenomenon the Monday-Morning Syndrome," Drs. Sinatra and Roberts wrote. "For many, going to work on Monday is like going into battle, so no wonder heart attacks occur en masse at this time."

Looking at stroke, Israeli researchers reported in 2004 on a study of 200 consecutive patients who had experienced a mini-stroke (transient ischemic attack or TIA). Their investigation showed that anger and intense negative emotions could increase the risk of stroke by as much as 14 times. And, in 2002, Swiss doctors found mental stress causes the inner layer of the blood vessels to constrict, which may increase the risk of a heart attack or stroke. Their study provided the first evidence that mental stress induces dysfunction in this very sensitive and critical arterial tissue.

In the February 2007 issue of Dr. Sinatra's *Heart, Health & Nutrition* newsletter, the Connecticut cardiologist brought up his concern about stress in a very personal way. "I'm always asking my heart patients how they handle stress," he wrote. "It's a big deal for me, probably stemming from the time I was thirteen years old and my grandmother died from a massive stroke. I remember asking my father what had caused the stroke. He explained that the oil burner in my grandmother's house had started smoking and she became emotionally upset about it. Within a few minutes she became confused. Then she collapsed to the floor.

"When people get fired up emotionally, anything can happen. They light a fuse inside their bodies that can cause an immediate and deadly explosion, like a heart attack or my grandmother's stroke, or trigger a cascade of harmful chemical changes that becomes deadly over time. I've seen anger, chronic stress, depression and social isolation take a big toll on patients. These constitute hidden risk factors not usually addressed by doctors.

If you can recognize your emotional issues, and deal with them, you become less prone to angina, irregular heartbeat, heart attack, stroke, and high blood pressure."

THE CALMING EFFECT

We all like to think of ourselves as cool, calm, and collected. And, if that's true, we are functioning more in the mode of the parasympathetic nervous system. However, because of the emphasis on disease and malfunction in our society and in research, this system doesn't get nearly as much attention as it deserves.

The parasympathetic system is the set of nerves responsible for a calming, restful, rejuvenating response. I call it the *regeneration response*. It fosters a state of the mind/body that is regenerative and health-producing. It assists us in healing from stress. During this state your heart beats more slowly and less forcefully. Oxygen consumption is reduced. Your trillions of cells get to work taking care of internal repair and restoration. Your brain and endocrine systems have geared down from overdrive.

When I think of parasympathetic function, my mind conjures up images of sitting in the shade with a cool fruit drink after a long, hot day of yard-work in the sun; or better yet, meditating, which I have been doing regularly for the last forty years.

SELYE, MAHARISHI, WALLACE—AND STRESS

In July 1972, I was working at the University of Akron and decided to take one month off to attend a course on the Science of Creative Intelligence (development of consciousness) offered by Maharishi Mahesh Yogi, the founder of Transcendental Meditation (TM), at Queen's University in Kingston, Ontario. During that month, I met three men who would shape my thinking on stress, health, and self-development.

Maharishi was there. Hans Selye, the father of stress medicine, was there. And so was a young physiologist from UCLA, named Robert Keith Wallace.

Maharishi popularized meditation in the West. He inspired repeated scientific studies showing that meditation was not merely an esoteric practice for Himalayan recluses, but a relevant self-development booster for all of modern society. Before I met Maharishi, I had read his first book, *The Science of Being and Art of Living: Transcendental Meditation.* From Maharishi, I came to understand that science-based meditation is one of the most effective, natural ways for not just reducing stress and anxiety, but for simultaneously improving health, learning ability, brain coherence, productivity, creativity, and relationships. In a very real sense, meditation enables one to grab a bigger chunk of one's potential in life!

I had earlier read Dr. Selye's book, *The Stress of Life,* and knew he was considered the "Einstein of medicine." He defined stress as an overload on the system, a chemical response caused by a perception of physical or psychological threat accompanied by a negative emotional arousal. From his lectures, I gained a clear understanding of the harmful effects of stress and its profound, negative influence on health and longevity.

At the time, Dr. Selye was attempting to find a way to medicate stress. He was concerned with a pharmaceutical intervention, which, as current research tells us, can actually cause an increase of stress on the system. Maharishi was saying there was a natural means to overcome stress and maximize self-development. We experience this when we align our individual awareness with the healing source of universal consciousness within each and every one of us—real mind/body medicine with no negative side effects.

Dr. Wallace's landmark report in a 1970 issue of *Scientific American* shows that Transcendental Meditation opens the door to a completely unique state of psychophysiology in the mind/body of the meditator. He calls this state *restful alertness*: the body rests deeper than deep sleep while the mind remains extremely alert. This state is the opposite of stress. In fact, it is the antidote to stress and it is something that can be achieved by meditation. Later in this book I will show how this effect increases productivity, creativity, intelligence, and workplace harmony—among other things.

I came away from that conference with a totally different perspective on the human condition. These experts made it simple for me. Dr. Selye taught me about chronic stress, an enemy that silently works within to shorten our lives. Maharishi taught me how to reach the silence beneath my own active consciousness to counteract that stress and help me realize my full potential. Dr. Wallace taught me that the mind/body experience of restful alertness—the opposite state of the *stress response*—was not just some mystical concept but a scientifically measurable phenomenon.

HOW ARE YOU TREATING YOUR INTERNAL SECURITY AND DEPART-MENT OF TRANSPORTATION?

We have examined in brief our two most important reflexes—stress and calm. These two reflexes profoundly affect what I call our internal "security system" and "transportation system." The "security system" is my way of describing the immune system and the "transportation system" refers to the circulatory system. The smooth functioning of these two systems is vitally important to our health and longevity.

In any situation, weak security makes for vulnerability. You become an easy target. In the body, such vulnerability can give rise to infections, cancer, arthritis, and other forms of disease. Stress can severely weaken your security.

The immune system is made up of an army of billions of free-floating cells and chemical agents in search of abnormalities such as viruses and bacteria. These entities go by such names as B cells, T cells, and killer cells. The system is also comprised of stationary sentinels, including lymph nodes, the thymus gland, bone marrow, and the spleen. All working in concert, they protect us against disease. I won't get into the biochemistry of all this. It's way too complex (even for me).

On the transportation side, when your blood vessels become damaged and aged, you put yourself severely at risk for cardiovascular disease. Your arteries are the highways that carry oxygen and nutrients to every cell of your body, including your heart and brain. This system also includes the veins, which carry waste products and deoxygenated blood from your muscles and organs back to the heart and lungs.

Over-activation—inappropriate reactions to our environment— causes problems to these two systems as well as the autonomic nervous system (ANS). These systems can either be strengthened or suppressed according to how we think and act.

When we consider the ANS, we must understand the word *autonomous* is somewhat misleading because the system is not exclusively involuntary. By our actions, we can ignite either the fight-or-flight response, and all of the chemical concoction it creates; or the rejuvenation response and its more calming biochemistry.

A CHOICE EVERY MOMENT

As an example, you may have been working very long and hard on a project and have grown very attached to seeing it through to completion. Your boss comes into your office and asks, "How's that project coming?"

You answer, "It will probably take another week to complete."

Her response, "Unfortunately I have to take you off that project. We urgently need you on something else. I am reassigning that to another coworker."

You could argue that the boss could have handled this a little differently. Let's assume, because of a time-sensitive emergency, this is the best she can do. The important question for you is, *what will be your response?*

Within a split second you make a decision about how you are going to interpret this situation and, based on that evaluation, you respond. The response can be internal or external, but it is there. It can be one of anger or one of flexible acceptance. It's your choice—and you do have a choice. You are in control! Our inclination is to feel our response is due to the stimulus and not due to our evaluation of the situation, or what is called our *explanatory style* (how we explain the world to ourselves).

What if you were able to activate your sense of humor in the same situation? I believe having a sense of humor on the job—and in life in general—is vital. The *American Journal of Medicine* reports laughter increases secretions that improve oxygenation of the blood, relaxes the arteries, and decreases blood pressure. Laughter has a positive effect on all cardiovascular and respiratory ailments and increases the overall immune system response as well.

This choice may be the most important routine in your life. Why? Because you are faced with a choice at *every single moment* of change! Have you developed a process to handle these moments? Or do you mishandle them on a regular basis? Are you a slave to your bad habits?

MANAGING YOUR INTERNAL PHARMACY MOMENT-BY-MOMENT

Here's your choice: You can be a prisoner of the moment or have sovereignty over it. How you manage your moments, how you manage your life, results in what prescriptions you write for your internal pharmacist. You can either handle the moments or be handled *by* them. Each experience you have is an opportunity for you to respond in a way that invokes one of two reflexes—the stress response or the rejuvenation response.

If you invoke the emergency response chronically, you create a *disease-producing biochemistry*. If you invoke the rejuvenation response habitually, you create a *health-producing* biochemistry. If we get the mind right, the body will follow. And, in turn, if you get the body right, the mind will follow.

What you don't pay attention to, and what this book presents, is your physiological response *because of* the interpretation of the event or situation. This is the manner in which your body physically reacts to your thinking about life's circumstances. Life is all the moments put together. Let's split each moment into three components:

1. **THE SITUATION**: The actual external event or circumstance you're experiencing.

2. **YOUR INTERPRETATION**: Your internal evaluation of the event; how you explain the event to yourself; your internal dialogue. Evaluate the good or bad of the event, the rightness or wrongness, the fairness or lack of fairness, and whether the event threatens you in any way.

3. **YOUR RESPONSE**: How you choose to react, whether in a fit of anger or with calmness or with joy.

By developing appropriate moment management, you can rise to the level of a PhB, poised and ready to handle and take advantage of the moment. The PhB prepares ahead of time with proper rest and mental rehearsal even before encountering the stimulus: a disgruntled coworker, an angry boss, or an irritating customer. Moment Management provides the foundation for the psychophysiology of success, happiness, health, and the capacity to lead.

One of the major challenges we face when we activate our fight-or-flight reflex is realizing the perceived emergency is really not an emergency to begin with, or realizing the emergency is over and we must call off the troops (stress hormones). Sometimes we forget to retreat. Research indicates unresolved stress causes a multiple downer: loss of blood flow to the higher centers of the brain, resulting in reduced efficiency, articulation, and problem-solving ability; and a mental shift downward to a superficial, simplistic, and unoriginal style of thinking. Anxiety and depression are common byproducts.

As we have seen, it takes a split second to decide which branch of your nervous system you want to activate: the sympathetic (the fight-or-flight response) or the parasympathetic (the rejuvenation response). It's your *choice.* We may have an immediate, instinctive reaction. But, in the long run, it's your choice.

8

Muscle Test Your Inner Dialogue— Is It Harming or Helping You?

Your body doesn't lie.

— JOHN DIAMOND, M.D.
psychiatrist and alternative medicine advocate

One of my clients is TAROM, the national airline of Romania. For my first assignment with them many years ago, they provided me with a business-class ticket to fly to Bucharest from Chicago, where I had just completed a full-day workshop for another client. I boarded the plane and sat down in my seat, exhausted from the day's work. I closed my eyes to meditate and then, as soon the plane reached cruising altitude, I heard click, click, click, click, click. What was that? And then—sniff, sniff—smoke!?!?! I was shocked. All around me, lighters were being lit. By then, all U.S. airlines had banned smoking on domestic flights and my usual carrier, American Airlines, had already banned it on international flights. However, apparently, the Romanian airline had not.

In any event, I'm a non-smoker. I mean a real NON-smoker (like a fanatic)! I immediately pushed the flight-attendant call button. "Is there a non-smoking area?" I asked.

"No," she responded. "This is a totally smoking flight."

"But I'm allergic to smoke!" I replied, stunned.

She asked, "Are you going to die?"

"Maybe!! I'm not going to die, but I'm going to feel very bad by the end of this nine-hour flight."

She asked if I would like her to ask all the people in business class not to smoke.

"What were they told before they got on the flight?" I asked.

"That they could smoke."

I joked, "Then YOU will die!"

We both laughed. I told her I'd figure out a way to handle it and for her not to worry. She apologized and left.

About 45 minutes later she tapped me on the shoulder. At that time, my eyes were closed. I was attempting to disappear in sleep. "Mr. Bagnola," she whispered, "would you gather your things and come with me, please?"

I was wondering where they were going to put me; my seat was already in business class. She took me forward to the cockpit.

She looked at me and said, "You were very kind to me. I thought I was going to have to ask everyone in business class to stop smoking and that would have been difficult. When I told the pilots, they said, 'Bring him up! We're not smoking.'"

I was in disbelief as she knocked on the cockpit door.

I sat in one of the two seats behind the pilots and looked around. The cockpit was a sea of lights and gauges. But the flickering lights inside the cockpit paled in comparison to the panorama outside. Talk about a bird's-eye view! The pilots explained to me that the shortest route for our flight path would take us completely north. Once over the North Pole, I experienced the treat of a lifetime, the Northern Lights. The Aurora Borealis started playing in the sky, and it is something that cannot truly be described in words. It was a magical experience. I was mystified by the dancing lights. I felt awed and humbled by nature's grand light show. What a ride!

Imagine how this experience might have been different had I shown anger toward the flight attendant. I did feel upset inside, but I kept a cool exterior when talking to her.

A Japanese proverb says that we should keep our misfortunes for three years for they may turn out to be gifts.

VISIBLE THOUGHTS: THE SQUID AND THE POLYGRAPH

If you are a fan of Animal Planet or National Geographic Channel, like I am, you have probably seen documentaries on the squid, a truly fascinating creature. It is highly intelligent and has a large brain. Besides having eight arms and two tentacles, which allow for multi-tasking, the squid also has quite an extensive multi-media communication ability.

Just as we have elaborate writing systems, squid have elaborate color-coding systems through which they communicate with each other. They change the colors of their own bodies to send each other messages. A squid can even change the two different sides of its body to relate separate messages to other squid on each side. When a squid becomes aggressive, he flashes one color or releases an inky substance. When he becomes amorous, he changes colors and flashes to attract. He flashes colors indicating how he wants to hunt and attack his prey. His dual-layer skin allows him to communicate via polarized light.

It is amazing to watch the flashing and luminescent displays which obviously serve for survival, courtship, and hunting applications. His sophisticated control of his physiology allows him to contract, expand, and change his color. The changes are absolutely clear and visible.

One big difference with humans, however, is that we cannot vividly see the changes in our physiology based on the changes in our thoughts, like the squid. Some researchers have used the squid model to learn more about how the human nervous system works. While squid are transparent literally (the skin is see-through) and figuratively (we can see what they're thinking), human beings are more complex and express their thoughts and feelings in various ways: specifically by saying or telling, by showing or demonstrating through facial expressions or gestures, and lastly by changing internal physiology.

The first two methods are discernable by sight, sound, or touch, but the last is measurable only through tests.

Obviously, there are some telltale signs when our feelings are unconsciously exposed externally, such as a blush, a gulp, and some microexpressions. A microexpression is a brief, involuntary expression of the emotion that you are trying to hide. Recently, the field of reading microexpressions has become more prominent with the popularity of TV shows such as *Lie to Me*. The problem with relying on this type of signal, however, is that few people know enough about how to read them accurately.

Expressions and microexpressions are *visible* displays of the emotions and reactions to what you're thinking. There are also a few empirical ways proven to decipher the *physiological* responses to the thoughts of your mind. The two tests commonly used are the polygraph test and the manual muscle test.

TWO WAYS TO TEST THOUGHTS

This is where the polygraph, better known as the lie detector test, comes to our assistance. I call this a demonstration of the "mind shaking hands with the body." This test is often associated with determining whether someone may have committed a crime, but it has also proven useful in some job interviews (e.g., FBI, CIA, and Secret Service). The polygraph is a machine which records (graphs) multiple (poly) signals from sensors placed on the body. The sensors usually record several physiological indicators: breath rate, pulse, blood pressure, muscle movements, and perspiration (galvanic skin response).

First, the well-trained examiner establishes a baseline, then asks the subject some basic questions to determine the norms for that person's signals. What the examiner looks for are fluctuations such as higher blood pressure, increased heart rate, faster pulse rate, or increased perspiration measured by the galvanic skin response.

I'm sure, we've all seen the polygraph test as it charts the physiological changes based on the subject's responses. With every thought and response, the physiology changes. The polygraph test suggests on paper what is displayed in the flashing brilliance of the squid's colorful communication—the fine coordination between what is going on in the mind and what the physiological effects are. The body follows the mind.

It is agreed, that the polygraph is not 100 percent accurate. Some people may fail an exam just because of nervousness. Experts also agree that the term *lie detector* is a misnomer. The instrument doesn't detect lies; it monitors a person's physiological reactions. It can detect only whether deceptive behavior is being displayed.

Back in the 1980s, my friend and colleague, Marci Shimoff, and I were hired by General Motors to help educate employees in the art of managing stress, because the company was concerned about the performance of their employees. At the time, the company was spending a good portion of their revenue on employee health-care costs.

After spending time with several groups of employees, Marci and I found that they were experiencing high levels of stress and this appeared to be affecting their jobs. In our workshops, we discussed with the employees the several factors relating to their stress—bad diet, overwork, lack of rest, and the lack of any practical method to release the accumulation of stress. But our main message to them was that this stress was caused by the way they were *approaching* their work. The faulty approach was both physical and mental, and the mental approach was the most crucial. This is because the majority of our stress is caused by our own thinking, by our interpretation of and our response to the situations we are faced with at work and at home.

People talk mostly to themselves, and 90 percent of this self-talk is repeated day after day. Marci and I conjectured that the GM employees were filling their minds with *negative* self-talk. We had to come up with a method to demonstrate to them the body's response to this negative self-talk. After all, as Dr. Diamond says in the quote at the beginning of this chapter, "The body doesn't lie." We asked ourselves how we could illustrate this dramatically enough to cause a paradigm shift and make an impression on our audiences.

We could have talked all day and people's eyes would have glazed over. How could we be interactive? How could we get them to really understand how the body follows the mind? How could we get them to be cognizant of the self-talk of worry, a useless and damaging form of fantasy, and to see the value of something on the opposite side of the thinking coin, like humor?

My job back then and now is to make my audiences acutely aware of this fork in the road—choosing between positive and negative self-talk—and how the sum total of these experiences during a day, a month, a year ultimately translates into the creation of good health or bad health.

At GM, I initially thought about utilizing a polygraph device to dramatize the message. But it wasn't practical. Too bulky to carry around, for one thing, and you could hook up only one person at a time, while everybody else would be standing around. You would lose the audience. Moreover, some people might be intimidated because of the device's association with police work. We also couldn't bring in a whole medical laboratory to draw blood or do EKGs—hardly practical or even legal.

Instead, we decided to use the technique called muscle testing, widely used by health professionals, particularly in the field of alternative medicine, to determine tolerance to specific foods and supplements. It proved to be exactly what was needed—very simple to apply.

Later on in this chapter, I'll walk you through the test step-by-step and you will see how you can test your thoughts and statements with the muscle testing technique.

ABOUT MUSCLE TESTING

According to appliedkinesiology.com, "Applied kinesiology is a form of diagnosis using muscle testing as a primary feedback mechanism to examine how a person's body is functioning."

In a lecture I attended some years ago, I learned that muscle testing may have begun thousands of years in the past. Egyptian and Greek healers would have patients put a certain food in their mouths and then attempt to lift a bucket of water to test their strength. The patient's ability to lift the water indicated whether the food was good for the patient (or not).

Similarly, in his 2002 book, *Power vs. Force: The Hidden Determinants of Human Behavior*, psychiatrist David R. Hawkins, M.D., Ph.D., describes the work of George Goodheart, the father of applied kinesiology. Goodheart tested a patient with functional hypoglycemia. When sugar was placed on the man's tongue, testing indicated that the deltoid muscle (the one usually used as an indicator) instantly went weak. Conversely, it was discovered that, when substances that were therapeutic to the body were placed on the patient's tongue, the muscles did not lose strength.

This is the most striking finding of applied kinesiology: when the body is exposed to harmful stimuli—including thoughts—muscles are instantly weakened.

In the early 1970s, research on manual muscle testing or applied kinesiology was done to determine if the technique could be used to accurately detect allergies, nutritional disorders, and responses to medications and supplements.

You may be surprised to learn that, with muscle testing, you don't even have to taste or swallow the substances! You can hold them in your hand or place the object against your body.

Psychiatrist John Diamond, M.D., described this phenomenon in great detail in his 1971 book, *Your Body Doesn't Lie*. In this book, he uses muscle testing to demonstrate the powerful impact—beneficial and adverse—of physical and psychological stimuli such as music, art forms, facial expressions, voice modulation, and emotional stress.

You may never have seen a squid perform its magical light show demonstrating its instinct/body connection or undergone a polygraph test yourself, but I'll teach you how to use your deltoid muscle to experience how the body responds to health-producing or disease-producing stimuli.

In my workshops, I ask people if they have heard of muscle testing. Most haven't. I demonstrate for them the simple sequence I use. When I teach them in minutes how to perform this dramatic test, they leave astonished and eager to go home and practice the technique on friends and family members.

I first demonstrate the muscle testing technique with a volunteer from the audience and then have people pair off and practice on each other. As an example, when you say, "I can," your arm resistance is invariably strong, as compared to when you say, "I can't." Similar reactions occur when you say, "I will have the report ready next Monday," as compared to "I'll try to have the report ready next Monday."

At a workshop for the Shell Corporation some years ago, I used this technique with a group of very skeptical company engineers. We conducted several tests to determine the pounds of pressure being used by the tester. In our research, if there are negative or harmful stimuli, less than four pounds of pressure was enough to bring the arm down. However, in some cases when the test subject made a positive statement, the muscle withstood up to forty pounds of pressure.

(Author's note: To see an example of what I'm describing, go to my website jimbagnola.com and click on the link "Watch Video." For those of you who are curious about the research behind this feedback system, you can do a web search for "On the reliability and validity of manual muscle testing: a literature review." You will find several scholarly articles. For those of you who are experimenters and would be interested in a detailed description of how this process works and how I use it, please read on.)

HOW TO PERFORM THE MUSCLE TEST

This is a two-person exercise—the tester and the subject. Check to ensure that the subject does not have a shoulder injury or some other physical condition that could distort the outcome of the test or cause discomfort to the subject.

Test One: Establish a "Resistance" Baseline

The tester applies pressure firmly and evenly but not hard, just enough to test the spring and bounce in the arm, not so hard that the subject's muscle becomes fatigued. The tester will feel the subject's level of strength. The tester presses and the subject resists. The subject actually feels his own level of strength and the ability to resist. It is not a question of who is stronger, but of whether the muscle can *lock* the shoulder joint against the pressure applied.

1. The subject and tester stand facing each other.
2. The subject extends his dominant arm (right arm if right-handed) straight out, parallel to the floor, with thumb pointing down. *This is*

the ready position. This locks the elbow in place and isolates the deltoid muscle. If the subject allows his thumb to move from that downward position, the elbow will bend; this creates leverage at the elbow and the tester will get a false reading.

3.   The tester places two fingers on the subject's wrist. The tester asks the subject to resist and then he applies slight pressure with his two fingers. A subject in normal condition will be able to hold his arm up, parallel to the ground, resisting the pressure.

Test Two: Establish a "Weak" Baseline

This position imbalances the body structurally and energetically so that the subject and the tester feel the arm give way under the pressure. Both subject and tester will know the difference between testing strong and testing weak.

1.   The subject and tester stand facing each other.
2.   The subject extends his arm in the ready position.
3.   The subject places the back of his other hand on his forehead in almost a salute fashion or, as I call it, the "woe is me" position.
4.   The tester places his fingers on the subject's wrist and tells him to resist the pressure. The tester then applies downward pressure. You will notice that it goes weak. The deltoid collapses. The muscle cannot *lock* the shoulder joint against the push.

Test Three: Muscle-Test Your Own Speech

Now let's experiment with the simple phrases below to experience the impact of each phrase (your *speech*) on the physiology. The subject will say phrases out loud. (In my early days of muscle testing in the late seventies, I would allow the subject to say the phrases silently, but this skewed the results because the subject would often repeat something else to himself.)

1.   The subject and tester stand facing each other.
2.   The subject extends his arm in the ready position.
3.   The tester places two fingers on the subject's wrist.
4.   The tester says one of the empowering-language phrases out loud and asks the subject to repeat it out loud.

5. Immediately following, the tester says, "Resist"; then he applies downward pressure on the wrist with two fingers. A subject in normal condition will be able to hold his arm up, parallel to the ground, resisting the pressure.

6. Repeat the test using a disempowering-language phrase.

7. Now have the subject say out loud his own empowering- and disempowering-language phrases as the tester applies pressure.

Disempowering Language	Empowering Language
I'll try to have the report by Monday.	I'll have the report by Monday.
Why does this always happen to me?	I am in control of my life.
He makes me so mad.	I control my own feelings.
I can't do that.	Let's look at some possibilities.
There's nothing I can do.	Let's look at some alternatives.
That's just the way I am.	I can choose a different approach.
I have to …	I choose to…

You will find that the subject's use of empowering language, such as "I am in charge of my own life," results in strong resistance—the arm will remain locked. Conversely, negative statements made by the subject will cause the muscle to test weak. A phrase I often use here is, "She makes me so mad"; although you are pushing down no harder than before, the subject will not be able to resist the pressure and his arm will fall to the side.

So far, we have tested how the subject's own thinking and speech affect his physiology. Now let's take a look at how others' thinking and speech influence the subject's physiology.

Test Four: Muscle-Test the Speech of Others on You

As you perform this section of the experiment, be thinking of how you speak with your children, coworkers, direct reports, or spouse. You may be surprised.

Take a look at the phrases below. The tester will say the phrases out loud; the subject will not repeat.

Disabling Language	Enabling Language
Who did that?	What action should we take now?
Don't you know better than that?	What will it take to have it work?
Who made that decision?	What would work here?
Why did you do that?	What are the benefits of achieving that objective?
What's your problem?	What kind of support do you need to assure success?
Why are you behind schedule?	What will it take to move closer to our objective?
Why are you so far behind the other team?	What key things need to happen to achieve our objectives in a timely manner?

1. The subject and tester stand facing each other.
2. The subject extends his arm in the ready position.
3. The tester places two fingers on the subject's wrist.
4. The tester says one of the enabling-language phrases out loud to the subject, looking directly at him.

5. Immediately following, the tester says, "Resist"; then he applies downward pressure. A subject in normal condition will be able to hold his arm up, parallel to the ground, resisting the pressure.
6. Repeat the test using a disabling-language phrase.

Notice that the negative stimuli (disabling) cause the subject to be weak. The positive stimuli (enabling) allow the subject to test strong. This exercise gives us powerful insight into how we enable or disable someone by the language we use.

Test Five: Muscle-Test Your Own Thinking

Repeat steps 1 – 3 as above.

Now have the subject just *think* of someone he is fond of or loves. Apply the usual downward pressure on the wrist. You should find that the subject is very strong. Next, test the subject as he thinks of someone he fears, hates, or resents. The normal subject will go very weak and will not be able to resist the pressure. If the subject is having trouble visualizing someone, use a picture of someone he loves (strong), versus an image of the Twin Towers burning in New York City (weak).

Test Six: Muscle-Test Food and Other Objects

Just for fun, you might like to use this technique to see how you test with some tangible stimuli—such as food. I use this test in my stress-management sessions to show how stressful some foods may indeed be on an individual's physiology. (There are over 6 billion different bodies and each person's physiology may react differently to any substance. To confirm any result, please see a physician or certified nutritionist.)

Repeat steps 1 – 3 as above.

With the subject's other hand, he holds a food item against his body just above the navel, the area referred to as the solar plexus. Try it with artificial sweeteners, refined processed white sugar, a small bottle of alcohol, a bottle of water, a can of soda, an apple, an organic tomato, conventional tomato, etc. You may be surprised with the results! The body is extremely intelligent and will not lie about what has a positive influence on it and what does not.

Now try the test with small quantities of the same items placed in an envelope. Don't let the subject see what is in each envelope. I usually use packets of refined sugar, raw sugar, and other sweeteners in packets because they all feel the same in a closed envelope. Have the subject hold one envelope at a time next to the solar plexus and see what the results are. Your body knows.

If you want to know more about muscle testing, go to www. icakusa.com or read *Applied Kinesiology* by George Goodheart.

By now you will have figured out that we are continually creating our physiological states by everything we say, think, and do. The muscle test demonstrates this link between the body and mind, just as the polygraph test does. When we are asked questions by a licensed polygraph examiner, our body naturally creates a physiology from our mental state—calm or agitated—which can be described as health-producing or disease-producing. In other words, based on our thoughts and feelings, our internal pharmacist churns out specific molecules which directly affect our bodies. The body metabolizes everything through all five senses and it responds electrochemically—just like the squid.

PART II

THE CURRICULUM

How to Get a PhB

9

Lesson 1: Perform Your Magic

Do what you are.

— PAUL D. TIEGER
and BARBARA BARRON-TIEGER
personality experts

I am a professional speaker. Speaking is my job but I wouldn't call it a job. I've done a lot of other work in my life, but I've come to realize that speaking is where I perform my magic. In fact, speaking performs magic on *me*.

Some years ago on a trip to Trinidad and Tobago, I fell extremely ill. I suffered with high fever, joint pain, and a crushing headache. I didn't know if I had contracted dengue fever or the West Nile virus, since both were rampant at the time. My biggest concern was that I was scheduled to give a keynote address in Los Angeles a week later. It was a major conference, and missing it was not an option. I flew to L.A. still under the weather.

The morning of my address, after my sleepless and uncomfortable night, I had a meeting with the conference organizer and she noticed that I was perspiring excessively and didn't seem well. With a worried look on her face, she reminded me that they were counting on me to come through as the closing speaker. I assured her that I wouldn't pass out—but wasn't convinced myself.

Later on when she introduced me, I still wasn't feeling a whole lot better. I felt weak and wondered how I would pull it off. I walked to the front of the room, held on to the podium to steady myself, looked out at the audience, took a deep breath, and began my presentation. By the time I'd finished my first anecdote, I noticed I was sweating less. The more I talked, the better I felt. And by the end of the speech, I had forgotten that I had ever been sick!

This has happened to me several times and I'm always surprised by the experience. I start off not feeling well or feeling tired and, by the end of the presentation, I feel exhilarated. Speaking is not only my magic but also my medicine.

To me, there's nothing more satisfying than giving a presentation and then having people come up afterwards and tell me how they benefited from what they heard, how well prepared I was, how well delivered the speech was, and how inspired they were to see somebody doing something which he really loved to do. There is no better high than this. I thank God every day that I have the opportunity to perform my magic.

WHAT MAKES A JOB MAGIC?

What kind of job is *magical*? It is work that is rewarding and satisfying while accessing your strengths and creativity—work that you get lost in, so when you're doing it, you wouldn't call it *work*. That's what I call magic! Often, workaholics, myself included, love what they do. We gain great satisfaction from what we do and consider it a gift. We understand that our work is our primary tool for *developing ourselves*, while serving other people. And, when we are performing our magic, it truly is magical.

There's an old saying, "If you love the work you do, you'll never work a day in your life." That describes my job.

It also describes the job of Frances Hesselbein.

A few years ago, I had the pleasure of visiting the Drucker Foundation in New York City, and I was honored to meet Frances Hesselbein. Talk about loving one's job! Frances is *in love with* service. A prolific author, she has written several books including *Hesselbein on Leadership,* one of my favorite books on the topic. She changed the thinking in her industry.

Ms. Hesselbein started as a volunteer in the Girl Scouts organization and rose to become the CEO, navigating the organization through very tough times. Peter Drucker, father of business management, was so impressed by her leadership skills that he's quoted as saying she "could manage any company in America."

She's the chairperson and founding president of the Drucker Foundation and recipient of the Presidential Medal of Freedom, which is America's highest civilian honor. Ms. Hesselbein is still educating the world on leadership at her young-at-heart age. Last week I spoke to a close mutual friend and was delighted to find out that she had just boarded an international flight on her way to make a presentation.

Mind/Body Connection

A study cited in *The Extraordinary Healing Power of Ordinary Things: Fourteen Natural Steps to Health and Happiness* by Larry Dossey, M.D., found that married, middle-aged American working women "had better health than did housewives, provided they had positive attitudes toward their jobs."

Can you imagine loving your current job so much that you choose to keep doing it at the age of 95? That's exactly what Antonio Mancinelli is doing. Partner in the Antonio and Pasquale Barber Shop in Newburg, New York, Mancinelli began cutting hair in 1924. He was cited in the 2009 edition of *Guinness World Records* as the world's oldest barber at 98. Even at his advanced age, Antonio is still passionate and extraordinary, according to his customers, and still comes in to cut hair at least once a week. He says, "You know, there's no law against working. I'm going to keep on barbering until I just can't do it anymore—and I still can do it."

Antonio was in pretty good health when the news media swooped down on him after being recognized by *Guinness*. He enjoys the interaction with his customers. It's his love of people that has kept him working at a job that's not a job. We know of many others like Antonio and Frances: Lena

Horne, Norman Vincent Peale, comedians Bob Hope and George Burns, Peter Drucker, W. Edwards Deming, Kitty Carlisle, and Linus Pauling. All were able to keep working at their "jobs" into their 90s.

DOUG HENNING'S MAGIC

One night after a performance of Doug's Broadway show *Merlin*, a friend and successful entrepreneur named Lincoln Norton and his wife June visited us backstage.

Before Doug joined us in the dressing room, Lincoln and I were chatting about Doug's mission—to recreate the wonder we all felt as children. We were both impressed at how much Doug loved his work. Lincoln then said something that resonated with me. He said that when people perform their magic—the one that they were made for, the one that's in their heart—everything comes to them through that work.

"Do you think that happened to Doug?" he asked.

At that moment, Doug entered the room and we posed the question to him. "Absolutely," he said. "I got everything through magic—my friends, money, new and exciting places to live, satisfaction, and happiness. I even got my wife through magic! Magic is what I'm supposed to do."

I thought about that conversation with Doug and realized that each of us must perform our own individual kind of "magic." I've had a much similar experience; I've also received everything through my magic of speaking. I've gotten to travel the world, build lifelong friendships, and make a living. And, funnily enough, I also met my wife through my work—Sais attended one of my workshops in Trinidad and Tobago.

We can all excel at something. For me, it's speaking and helping others find their own path. For Antonio Mancinelli, it was barbering and interacting with people. For Leroy Grant, it was becoming the best leather technician who guaranteed his work. For these two men and for Doug, fulfillment was reflected in their work, as is mine. Each one of us found his niche. We all need to find our niche—our magic—not only because we'll get everything through it but for our own good health, as you discovered in the first section of this book.

I'm not unrealistically optimistic. I'm no Pollyanna. As I say this, I understand that no one loves 100 percent of his job. In most jobs, about 20 percent of what we do is routine, but necessary, and we have to trudge our way through it. For me, that part is the travel. While I treasure the opportunity I've had visiting over 80 countries, the part I don't enjoy is the drudgery of it. Packing, early morning flights, driving to airports, lugging suitcases, going through security, airplane food (the lack of!), picking up rental cars, navigating through new cities, managing my stuff in hotel rooms, sleeping while lying down on strange beds and sitting up in airplane seats, searching for healthy food every day—you get the picture.

I find this to be the toughest part of my job. I don't like it. There are hard parts to everybody's job, but enjoying 80 percent of it, I would say, is an absolute requirement. In my case, that 80 percent more than makes up for any hardships I experience traveling. What about you?

Charles Allen, a Methodist minister and newspaper columnist in Atlanta, once wrote, "Remember that you are needed. There's at least one important work to be done that will not be done unless you do it."

I believe nobody was created as an *extra*. Embedded in each of our souls is a seed for our work, our duty, our way of serving. In Lesson Six we will explore this topic further.

Often, you will have a hint of your calling as a child.

Larry King, the famous TV interviewer, used to ask questions all the time when he was a kid. At the age of five he would ask bus drivers, "Why do you do that? Why do you drive?" He would ask teachers, "Why do you teach this instead of that?"

King has said, "I was the most curious little boy growing up." He's been performing his magic for nearly 50 years now, and you know how famous and rich he has become through asking others questions. I'm one of the lucky ones, I guess, like Antonio, King, and so many others, I found my magic early on.

DIFFERENT STROKES FOR RELATED FOLKS

In a play in second grade, I was *the wind*. Imagine my mom's reaction when I told her I had to look like the wind and she had to make my costume! After having practiced my lines over and over, I walked on stage wearing the grey, hooded cape that my mom had made. I stood there waiting to say my lines and noticed the sea of faces familiar and unfamiliar. Then came my cue. I looked straight out into the audience and boldly said my lines, then went back to flapping my arms as the wind. After the play, my mother told me that she could hear my words clearly and that she liked how I spoke to the entire audience, not just one person. And my father was totally amazed because he didn't like to speak in public at all.

My mom is smart! She tells me now that it was at that moment she knew that I could find success through public speaking. "Whatever you do for a living," she told me, "use your mouth." I have to admit I do like to share knowledge and I do like to talk to and interact with groups of people. It invigorates and nourishes me. It feeds my soul.

A similar thing happened to Doug Henning. When Doug was seven years old, he wanted to be a magician so his parents bought him a magic kit for his birthday with an assortment of illusions. He tried them over and over again but he couldn't get them to work so he just threw the kit away.

His mother came to check on him and took it out of the trash. She scolded him, "No. I bought this for you, and you will learn it." She took it out of the trash many times. Finally, he mastered one of the illusions. Triumphant, he performed the illusion for his dad, who was astonished and asked Doug to show him again. Doug did it again and his father still couldn't see how he was doing it. He fooled his dad. Then he finally blew his dad away. Doug got hooked on astonishing people. He'd found his magic. Literally!

Many years ago, my brother John helped me find a summer job in Youngstown, Ohio. I was to fill in as an accountant and payroll clerk for three weeks. During the first week, I was being trained. By Monday of the second week, I was in absolute misery. Then, and for the following two weeks, I started developing some of the signs and symptoms that experts label as job stress. The last thing in the world I was meant to be was an accountant. It was awful. I couldn't wait for the three weeks to be over.

By contrast, my brother Dean is a certified public accountant and owns an accounting firm plus two other businesses. That's his magic. He knows numbers and he knows business. He's an excellent accountant. I call him Midas because whatever business he touches it turns to gold. Thankfully, I've never had to do my taxes because of Dean.

My brother John has another area of magic. He is extremely creative, and a diligent and extraordinary teacher. He teaches Interactive Media at the Trumbull Career and Technical Center in Warren, Ohio. He has taught and coached over 300 students during the past 10 years. John also has a second profession. He owns an independent television production company.

His school competes in the Business Professionals of America's (BPA) National Leadership Conference annually. They present student-produced projects. John's students compete regionally, and if they place 1st or 2nd they move on to statewide competition and then the national competition if they win. More than 30 of his students have moved to the national level during the last ten years. Two students have won national first places and two students have won second places in the nation.

Seventeen of his students are in the Wall of Fame in the school. That means they either placed first in the state or first or second nationally. Remarkably, for 10 years in a row, John has had students who ranked top 10 in the nation or better. Of the 52,000 members of BPA, 6,000 compete at the national level. This is a prestigious accomplishment for John and the school, and is significant for the student's résumé.

John is quite proud of his students and I'm quite proud of him, as you can tell. He loves his work, his students, and his field of television production and marketing. He displays the magic of the ultimate in teaching.

My sister Theresa, who is one of the most patient and intuitive people I know, is a university administrator. She's incredible with people in general but is extraordinary with students. Theresa's daughter Angela reads endlessly and is an especially gifted writer. She loves stories. One time, at the end of a presentation I had given to Angela's sixth-grade class, her teacher, Ms. Hall, pulled me aside to show me Angela's work. We began talking about how bright Angela was and I told her I knew that Angela was intelligent, athletic, creative, very sweet, and was always writing.

Ms. Hall said, "She is all those things and more. For example, once I assigned the class an assignment to write a 10-page story." Then, holding up a thick, 68-page document, she said, "This is what Angela turned in!" She said it was so interesting she couldn't put it down.

Angela's love of fascinating stories has led her into the field of ancient studies, Greek, and writing. That's her magic.

My nephew Dino, an outgoing, articulate, influential leader is a successful senior sales executive at a Chicago based firm called Acquirent. On the other end of the spectrum of magic and life work is Aaron my intelligent, focused, caring nephew who is interested in relieving pain and suffering in the world. He is a pharmacist and cardiology resident at The Ohio State University Medical Center.

Transcending the entire spectrum is my bright, creative daughter Julia, who has a masters degree in Vedic Science and is a certified instructor of the Transcendental Meditation Program. She is also a yoga instructor and passionate about teaching. Her total focus is her own spiritual development and assisting others in theirs.

This is the microcosm of all our families and represents the tapestry of the many forms of magic and intelligence expressed in the world.

The magic for Eric Liddell was his running. One of my favorite movies is *Chariots of Fire*, the 1981 British film that tells the true story of two Olympic athletes in 1924. The two runners raced for different causes; the Scottish Christian, Eric Liddell, ran for the glory of God, and the English Jew, Harold Abrahams, ran to overcome prejudice. In one of the final scenes of the movie, Eric Liddell, played by Ian Charleson, was running his final race and, as he sprinted ahead of the pack, his thoughts were audible: "God made me for a purpose but He also made me fast, and when I run I feel His pleasure." Liddell won a gold medal in that race. Love of what you do must be your driving force and you will feel His pleasure.

By now, you must surely know I love what I do for a living! When I do it, like Liddell, I feel connected to a greater presence. I also enjoy dealing with people who love what they do. Just think of a world where everybody is doing exactly what he or she wants to do for a living! This may never happen for everyone but it can happen for you. As you go through your career, you are building and developing yourself. It is magic to find your magic!

WHY LOVE YOUR JOB?

> **Mind/Body Connection**
>
> According to a report by the Massachusetts Department of Health published in the *New England Journal of Medicine*, the primary reason for the 1.5 million heart attacks annually in America is stress. The biggest source of stress is job dissatisfaction. The secondary reason named is a low score on the self-happiness scale.

The link between performing our magic and our good health is unmistakable. The fallout from not doing our magic is, as we have seen, pretty grim. Heart disease causes the most fatalities in the Western world. And the number-one cause of heart disease is—well, it's not the cholesterol in your body, high blood pressure, smoking, or lack of exercise. All contribute in one way or another to heart attacks, but the number one reason, at least in the U.S., is actually stress.
It's all interconnected. Work has a lot to do with how our happiness is going, and our happiness has a lot to do with how our work is going.

As I mentioned earlier, the most concentrated incidence of heart attacks occur on Monday mornings between 6:00 and 9:00—right when most of us return to work from the weekend. Just over 28 percent of heart attacks occur then!

I find this fascinating. As far as I know, humans are the only species that succumb to a specific disease at a specific time slot. Dogs do not go "paws up" on Tuesdays around two o'clock. There's no specific canine check-out time.

The difference obviously is that we humans work. Our work and health are intricately interwoven. If Monday has the most heart attacks, guess which day has the least. Friday it is. We almost say to researchers, "If you think I am going to have a heart attack before the weekend you're crazy. I'm waiting till Monday."

Mind/Body Connection

The Monday-morning heart-attack spike is preceded on Sunday night with *anticipatory anxiety*. We start to think, "Oh Lord, I have to go to work in the morning. My weekend is over." It starts then. The blood pressure starts rising and the attack hits in the morning.

It's interesting to note that Saturday has the second-highest incidence of heart attacks with 14 percent occurring on this day. Stress is behind this as well: a combat zone at home.

Clearly, our health and our job are tied to our heart. I like the phrases "My heart's in it" and "My heart's not in it." If your heart isn't in it, your heart will be affected adversely by that fact. And, in that case, you have two choices: keep your job or change jobs. If you decide to keep your job, you have two new choices to make: continue to hate it or change your approach and love it.

Here are some warning signs that your job is taking its toll. Be alert to these symptoms. This selection of symptoms of job dissatisfaction comes from a piece in *High Technology Careers Magazine*, written by Tami Anastasia.

- Mental signs include poor concentration, boredom, lack of confidence, forgetfulness, no stimulation, a feeling of loss of control, and a generally negative attitude.

- Emotional signs include distress, depression, irritability, anxiety, impatience, frustration, incessant worry, and feelings of being helpless, lonely, near tears, or failing.
- Physical signs involve restless sleep or insomnia, weight gain or loss, ongoing fatigue, headaches, recurrent colds, flu, infections and tightness in the jaw, shoulders and neck.

Once you've ruled out all other sources for these symptoms, you may discover that the source is your job.

Mind/Body Connection

A study of health-care workers found that, when employees work for a boss they dislike, they develop significantly higher blood pressure, which puts them at greater risk to develop cardiovascular disease and also increases the risk of stroke by 33 percent. If you are unable to manage the relationship with your boss, move on.

— Dr. George Fieldman, University of London

LOVE THE JOB YOU HAVE

There is a book called *Take This Job and Love It: How to Change Your Work Without Changing Your Job*, by Dennis T. Jaffe and Cynthia D. Scott. The title is right on. You are in charge of transforming your job into one you like. Fall in love with what you do for a living or fall in love with why you're doing it. To fall in love with *why* you're doing it, focus on the reason for your work, for example, providing for your family or buying a new car. When you are trudging through that 20 percent of routine work, think about the skiing vacation or the new furniture the job will afford you to buy.

To fall in love with *what* you're doing, you will need to change the way you work and begin to enjoy the work you're doing. Like my teacher-friend, Susan, you might need an attitude adjustment.

It is very important to honor yourself for what you do for a living. Refer to my favorite saying: *Make a living, not a dying.* I strongly recommend you examine whether or not you are making a living or a dying. Everyone has a bad day and everyone has a bad week, but when it slides over into a month, two months, three months, then you should take stock of what you are doing.

In the *High Technology Careers Magazine* article, Tami Anastasia goes on to summarize ways to manage a dissatisfying job:

1. Find meaning and value in your work. Make your work meaningful to you regardless of what others think.
2. Concentrate on working to your full potential. Don't compare yourself or your work to others.
3. Give to yourself what you don't get from others. Acknowledge your own achievements, praise your work, and reward yourself for a job well done. Don't wait for others to give you credit for what you've accomplished.
4. Hold people accountable for their own actions. Remember that they are responsible, not you.
5. Pay attention to what is predictable. Develop strategic interactions that won't hook you into negative situations.
6. Think before you act and don't act out of haste. Always ask yourself if your choices are in your best interest.
7. Don't take what others say and do personally.
8. When frustrated or angry, turn the situation around by asking, what can I learn from this and how can I apply it?

Sometimes we find that we cannot manage in the job we have and we have the opportunity to change the work we're doing.

FIND A JOB YOU LOVE

There can be magic in the change, as comes across in the following e-mails I exchanged with Bob Whitmer, who had attended one of my workshops.

Dear Jim,

We first met during a Leadership Seminar for the new Department of Defense Managers in Denver, Colorado. I believe it was 1998. We bumped into each other a year or so later at the Pentagon where I recognized you in the hallway and gave you a quick tour of the Pentagon Press Briefing Room, which I managed at the time.

I have never forgotten what you taught and still use the muscle test (arms out, you standing in front trying to pull the arm down) with friends and family to illustrate the power of the mind-body connection.

At the time of the seminar, I was very unhappy in my job and was looking for fulfillment in a new career, which, as it turns out, was a long ways away. I remember a quote you used, "If you love what you do for a living, you'll never work a day in your life." I knew you were right at the time, but your words ring true every day now.

After surviving 9/11 and enduring the post 9/11 days at the Pentagon, I resigned in 2005 and moved to Hilton Head Island, South Carolina. Now, my wife owns a Pilates studio and I am a commercial pilot and flight instructor. Talk about never working a day in my life!

If you ever find yourself in Hilton Head Island, I'd love to buy you dinner and talk about the possibility of doing some workshops down here. The people here, despite their incredible wealth, could really use your help.

All the best,
Bob Whitmer

I then sent a message back to Bob:

Great to hear from you, Bob! I am writing a chapter in my book on Performing Your Magic and I'd like to have your permission to reprint your great letter in my book. Hope to visit you sometime in the future, maybe summer. You can sell me a lesson in the air.

Thanks, Bob,
Jim

Then from Bob:

By all means print my letter, you've earned it. The career is moving forward. I write this from Houston, Texas. I am doing some corporate flying and today flew from Savannah, Georgia, to Houston. Back to Savannah tomorrow morning. Having fun, loving life, and not working a day in my life.

All the best, my friend,
Bob

Then my answer to Bob:

Thanks, Bob. You have earned the right to be an inspiration to those who are in your position and need to take the leap. You did it. You are an inspiration to me, as you will be to my readers. We will meet somewhere down the line.

Jim

And the final note from Bob:

Jim, your book is very necessary now for a lot of people and I can't wait to read it. Taking the leap took a lot of courage, as you can well imagine. Things haven't been easy. If this were an easy process, you wouldn't have to write your book. My wife made the same leap at the same time. We paid a dear price in some ways, but there hasn't been a day since we left Washington that we would go back, even if they tripled our previous salaries.

Bob

Bob and his wife are heroes to me—Professional Human Beings. They understood PhB Law 5: *Body follows mind.* They realized that their health was a priority and chose not to remain in a comfort zone of high perks while sacrificing their happiness. They saw that being in jobs they didn't like was affecting their health and they knew they would be happier in the new jobs they chose. It takes a leap of faith and a lot of guts to do what they did.

You want to find your magic. The question is, *how*?

FINDING YOUR MAGIC

Here are six different ways to help you discover your magic. Choose the ones that work best for you.

1. Complete the Magic Discovery Checklist

Self-reflection is an effective way to pause in your life and figure things out. Take some time to ponder these questions. The answers will reveal clues to what your magic is. Take out a sheet of paper and write down your answers. Don't overthink it. Just write what first comes to you.

- What are five things you're especially good at?
- What are three things your friends have told you you're good at?
- Which two of the ideas you've written down so far can you become especially good at?
- What three activities were you drawn to when you were young?
- What is one thing you like to read about, learn about, and talk about?
- In school, what subjects did you enjoy most? What subjects did you get the best grades in?
- What activities do you find yourself completely absorbed in, to the point of losing track of time (besides computer solitaire, Internet, and TV)?
- What three things do you do that satisfy you and heighten your self-esteem when you're done?
- If you won the lottery today, what work would you do?
- If you had extra time, what kind of volunteer work would you do?
- Which of your talents can make a difference in other people's lives and your own?
- What skills have you used that have made you successful thus far?

On your list you should now have some great ideas about yourself. Let it all simmer. You may need to take some time away and come back tomorrow to your list. You may want to revise your list. Now, which three things stand out to you? You should have a new picture of your talents.

2. Put the Question Out There

Here's my secret. This is a simple technique that has worked for me and may work for you. Reflect on this thought when you arise and before you go to sleep at night so that it is etched into the fiber of your mind. The intention is to allow Nature to provide you with the answers.

What is my magic? Please, let my magic be revealed to me. How can I use my magic in service of others? I am ready to perform my magic in the service of others. I want to make a difference in the lives of others and in my own life. How can I become financially self-sufficient in the process?

3. Help Others Find Their Magic

One of the fastest ways to discover your magic is to help others discover theirs. When you meet someone new, seek out his or her magic. Learn about that interesting part of everyone. I still like to do this; when I first meet someone, I like to find out what his or her magic is. What makes that person special? What can I learn from him/her? What can he/she teach me today?

See everyone as a teacher sent to you with some information or lesson you need. Become impressed with the experience and knowledge of others. Everyone you meet is interesting. Emerson said it this way, "Every person I meet is superior to me in some way and in that I learn of him." It's amazing how much spice and interest that attitude puts into your daily life. Every person you meet or deal with is a potential discovery for you. Look for the magic in other people.

How significant is this technique of "finding the magic"? Recently, while visiting Fairfield, Iowa, where about twenty years ago I facilitated a workshop on the topic of this book, a gentleman approached me on the street and introduced himself as a participant in that workshop. Dr. James Farkas, D.C., a very successful local chiropractor, told me that the most powerful tool that he had learned from that workshop was "finding the magic." He continues to utilize the technique and finds it very powerful
110

both in his practice and his personal life. Impressed and appreciative, I was reminded that not only is performing your magic crucial to becoming a PhB but also that it is equally important to look for and find the magic in others.

4. Ponder These Three Questions

Here is a different angle to discovering what work you could perform. Ask yourself these three questions. Where your answers converge should give you a clue as to your calling or *your dharma* (purpose).

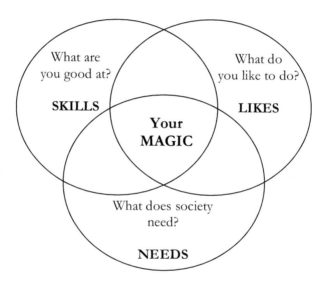

5. Take These Assessments

- Get tested at Johnson O'Connor Research Foundation if you are unsure about your natural abilities and talents. www. jocrf.org
- Check out the *Career Passion Test* developed by Catherine Jewell, a specialist in mid-life career changes. Through her test, you identify your key passions or the roles you play in work situations. With knowledge you can strategize a powerful career move, find a new job, and gain a sense of purpose for your life. See: www.careerpassioncoach.com

- Read *The Passion Test, The Effortless Path to Discovering Your Life Purpose* by Janet and Chris Attwood. The Passion Test is a simple yet profound tool and the perfect way to align yourself with those things that you are most passionate about so that you can share your special gifts. www.thepassiontest.com
- Seek a better understanding of your talent through an assessment with Talent Plus, Inc., the premier global human resources consulting firm with more than 200 world-class, quality, growth-oriented clients. www.talentplus.com

6. Read These Books

- *What Color Is Your Parachute?* by Richard Nelson Bolles.
- *The Professional Job Changing System* by Robert J. Gerberg.
- *Now, Discover Your Strengths* by Marcus Buckingham and Donald O. Clifton, Ph.D. Based on research by the Gallup Organization, this book will give you important insights into your five "*signature strengths.*"
- *Go Put Your Strengths to Work: 6 Powerful Steps to Achieve Outstanding Performance* by Marcus Buckingham. This book addresses "why your strengths aren't 'what you're good at' and your weaknesses aren't 'what you're bad at.'" It also helps you to identify personal strengths and offers "simple steps you can take to push your time at work toward those activities that strengthen you and away from those that don't."
- *MOJO: How to Get It, How to Keep It, How to Get It Back If You Lose It* by Marshall Goldsmith with Mark Reiter. Mojo is the moment when we feel we're *on a roll*, "firing on all cylinders *and* everyone in the room senses it." It's when we're "moving forward, making progress, achieving goals, clearing hurdles, passing the competition—and doing so with increasing ease. Sports people call this being 'in the zone.' Others describe it… 'flow.'" Marshall describes mojo as "that positive spirit toward what we are doing now that starts from the inside and radiates to the outside."

Once you've discovered the treasure chest of your magic, this is your next challenge, and here is the crux of it: how you incorporate your talents into your job.

Thought Provokers

- *Throw your heart over the wall and your body will follow.*
  – Plaxico Burress, American football wide receiver, when asked how the underdog could win the Super Bowl

- *I get from the soil and spirit of Texas the feeling that I, as an individual, can accomplish whatever I want to, and that there are no limits, that you can just keep going, just keep soaring. I like that spirit.*
  – Barbara Jordan, first Southern African-American woman to be elected to the U.S. House of Representatives

- *Go confidently in the direction of your dreams. Live the life you've imagined.*
  – Henry David Thoreau, American author

- Reflect on your work. Ask yourself, "How do I add value daily?" All wealth and success come from serving a customer and adding value. You may be stuck in a box, but you can color inside the box.

- You are not what you think you are; rather WHAT YOU THINK → YOU ARE.

Action Ideas

- Donate some time utilizing your gifts and knowledge. The more you teach, the more you learn. For example, if you like art, teach a class on art. Coach a team, give a speech, or be a visiting speaker at a school.

- Every year, create a wish list of what you'd like to accomplish. Look at your list once a month. Take a step towards accomplishing each one.

- Read *Happy for No Reason: 7 Steps to Being Happy from the Inside Out* by Marci Shimoff and Carol Kline, and *Love For No Reason: 7 Steps to Creating a Life of Unconditional Love* by Marci Shimoff, Marianne Williamson, and Carol Kline.

- After attending a meeting, seminar, course, or workshop, resist the urge to let that information fade in you; instead, find ways to share what you learned. You become what you teach.

- Create an Intelligence Network—a collection of people whose intelligence you can draw from to multiply your own. Don't become a hermit crab; you'll always need people in your life.

Spotlight
LLOYD ROGERS, BORN TO BE A FIREMAN

Have you ever wondered whether you would enjoy reading about your life in a book written about you by someone else? Are others seeing in you what you see in yourself? Are you showing your true self to the world? Is what you intend to come out coming out? Are you performing your magic and is the world receiving your magic?

A PhB is a magical person because of the display of his or her own personal and natural talents. He is in touch with his gifts and it shows. There is no one like him—or you—among our six-billion family members.

In my Professional Human Being workshops, I often present the certificate of a PhB degree to a deserving member of the host organization. I don't do the judging; the members of the organization do. The criteria for the certificate are based on the Seven Lessons presented in this book, one of which, as I talked about in this Lesson, is Performing Your Magic. The organization solicits feedback on possible recipients and then chooses the award winner.

MEET LLOYD ROGERS, PhB CERTIFICATE RECIPIENT

From among several candidates, Chief Rogers was chosen to receive this recognition. The event was the 2007 Hawaii Fire Chiefs Association Annual conference, held at the Turtle Bay Resort on the island of Oahu in Hawaii. I was hired by Manny Neves, Assistant Chief of the Honolulu Fire Department, to give the keynote address at the conference. Prior to the event, attendees were asked to nominate candidates for the PhB certificate and to describe why they chose that person.

At the time that he received this certificate, Chief Rogers had been a fireman in Honolulu for 31 years and was two months away from retiring. He had helped the city reduce costs associated with fire calls and emergency responses during his tenure. He had initiated special programs that saved the state of Hawaii more than $70,000 annually. His service to the community extended to the elderly by initiating special smoke-alarm programs. He also served as the administrator of the Hawaii State Fire Council. Chief Rogers was named Manager of the Year in 2007. What really stood out for me about how others characterized Chief Rogers, PhB, were the words *service* and *community*. Here is how he was described by his colleagues:

- Chief Rogers' greatest strengths are his compassion for mankind, the ability to empathize with his acquaintances, and a good-natured, lighthearted attitude toward life.
- When given a task at a moment's notice, he accepts it with that mischievous smile, a gentle "okay," and then delves into the task wholeheartedly, giving it his all and doing it well.
- I have seen him with tons of work: fire-prevention work, fire council responsibilities, fireworks and building code issues, legislative testimony, setting up tents for parking lots, attending numerous meetings, just to name a few. He always approaches everything with an attitude of service. "What can I do? How can I help?" He handles it all with that same impish smile and lively eyes.

- He is loyal, dependable, trustworthy, and one you can count on to listen to you with a kind ear, even if he's pressed for time.
- He has not shown favoritism for special friends. He deals with everyone in a considerate and respectful manner.
- His quiet demeanor, gentle smile, easygoing attitude, and malleable personality belie a man of strength and character. He is an outstanding employee, boss, and friend.
- One of Chief Rogers' strongest character points is his ability to stay calm under pressure. (He should consider becoming a professional poker player when he retires because you will never know by his facial expressions and body language what kind of adversity he is battling at that time.) I have found myself trying to pattern my reactions to stress and adversity after his model. He is a fine example of being cool under pressure and keeping his composure under duress, and this is just one of the many characteristics that I will miss when he retires.

As you can tell, Chief Rogers is a man who is showing his true self to the world. He is a happy, simple, caring, hardworking person, and well liked as a leader and human being. He is an ordinary man doing extraordinary things. He is performing his magic. He loves his work, serves his coworkers and the community, handles adversity well, envisions a safe, better community, has very high standards, and lives them. What fascinated me was the comment, "I found myself trying to pattern my reactions to stress and adversity after his model."

Chief Rogers is someone we would all like to be like.

Epilogue: Recently I spoke to my friend, Assistant Fire Chief Manny Neves who informed me that Chief Rogers is back on a contract basis to help the department. If you love what you do for a living it's hard to stay away.

10

Lesson 2: From Here I Am

to

There You Are

From what we get, we can make a living;
what we give, however, makes a life.

— ARTHUR ASHE
tennis legend

I belong to the National Speakers Association. At an annual conference of the organization back in the early 1990s, I met the man widely considered the guru of public speaking, the late Bill Gove. I immediately built a rapport with him because we had a lot in common: we were both former baseball players, and had become professional speakers. Bill's magic was the same as mine: we educated, entertained, and inspired through our speaking craft. We were also both the same impressive size—short!

At our meeting, I asked Bill what he regarded as the most significant thing he had learned in his then 37-year career as a public speaker. He told me that, at the time he first hit the stage, there were very few people speaking for a living. He was confident to an extreme and felt that he was doing his audiences a favor; after all, he could stand up there and speak and they couldn't. He was cocky. But, as the years passed, he realized it was really about the audience and their needs. It wasn't about him. It was all about service. He said that his focus transformed from "here I am" to "there you are."

Bill's realization helped me establish the cardinal direction of my speaking career toward serving others *while* I serve myself. This is a philosophy that I share with my audiences. You give to others and you serve yourself in the process, the essence of which is captured in PhB Law 4: *I cannot help another without helping myself.*

Although I didn't spend much time with him, Bill had a profound influence on my perspective, not only in relation to speaking, but also to life itself. He was a kindhearted and intelligent man and quickly became one of my mentors. Of course, I took his legendary course called *Everything You Need to Know About Speaking*, which is still available and I recommend to anybody interested in becoming a better public speaker. You can get more information about the course at www.govesiebold.com

Bill, in many ways, demonstrated the qualities of a Professional Human Being.

SERVE OTHERS AND SERVE YOURSELF

I walked into the Austin Shoe Hospital on West Highway 290 in Austin, Texas, about five miles outside of town, to a booming and exuberant, "Hello! Welcome!" I had gone in to get my shoes repaired but felt like I was entering someone's home. You should have seen the smile I received. It was infectious! The guy had energy.

He stretched out his hand, "Hi! I'm Emilio. How can I help you?"

Emilio assisted me with my shoe problem in a way that saved me money and got the job done, the whole time exuding the excitement one would find in Disneyland. We became friends in a few minutes. I stayed for a while and had the chance to observe him with other customers. He radiated the same infectious smile and high energy. If people came in down in the dumps they would leave with a grin. When I complimented him on the excellent service he provided me and the other customers, he replied that, since he had been serving customers for over 40 years, he should be good at it.

Emilio told me he had worked 30 years for H-E-B, a large grocery chain in Texas and northern Mexico, before retiring. He stayed at home for a short time and then he felt he had to serve somebody. He considers himself a *serve person* and says he has been one since age 13, when he began selling the small-town, highly successful newspaper *Grit* in Taylor, Texas.

I asked Emilio what he did at H-E-B. He started by saying he had been a meat cutter, but quickly corrected himself saying his real title was a Bovine Dissection Technician. I told him about my old friend, the Leather Technician, and we both laughed.

What I discovered is a new term: We have a salesperson, a marketing person, an accounting person, an IT person, and now we have a serve person. What is a serve person, and why should we become one? Here's why.

After spending a warm, wintry Christmas season with my parents in Canton, Ohio, a few years ago, I boarded the plane for my trip back home to Austin and sat in my first-class seat. As I was speaking on my cell phone, I noticed a U.S. Army sergeant coming down the aisle. He looked like a professional soldier and walked ramrod straight; he was proud, strong, handsome, and impeccable. I turned my head to watch as he made his way to the back of the plane and sat down in one of the last rows.

The thought occurred to me, *Who am I to sit here in first class when this individual who has put his life on the line has to go all the way in the back.* I ended my phone conversation, got up, and walked to the back of the plane.

"Would you mind switching seats with me?"

He looked at me, "Where is your seat?"

"In first class."

He was taken aback. A little confused. Then happily surprised. "Why do you want to switch seats with me?" he asked.

"To honor you and all our armed forces around the world who are serving us and our country."

The sergeant seemed slightly embarrassed. "But I've never sat in first class before," he answered.

"Well, it's about time. You deserve to sit up there."

I noticed that he got teary-eyed. I think I did as well. He shyly agreed and we switched seats. I knew he was very happy inside that somebody, a complete stranger, had gone out of his way to thank him for service. As for me, I felt great inside. This was Christmas to me. Several passengers noticed what had happened and stopped to tell me what a great gesture that was. One lady was actually in tears. The flight attendant told me that this was one of the nicest things she had ever witnessed on a flight.

When we landed, the flight attendant gave me a bottle of wine as a token of her appreciation. At baggage claim, some of the other passengers came over to thank me, including a Vietnam veteran. I looked over and saw the sergeant waiting for his duffle bag to appear on the conveyor belt. I was curious to find out whether he enjoyed the experience in first class. I walked up to him and asked, "How did you like it?"

He answered me with a big, satisfied grin. Then he carefully opened his hat that he held securely in his hands. His hat was full of miniature bottles of liquor! We burst into laughter, and so did many people around us. He thanked me again and told me how much he enjoyed getting to fly first class and how well the flight attendants treated him.

I wished him a nice visit with his family. He was headed home to visit with them, and then he had to return to Iraq.

I received many thanks for my simple gesture, but nothing could surpass the happiness that grew inside me. The random act of kindness—was it for the sergeant or was it for myself? The experience was a personal validation—that giving and helping is a gift to oneself.

Be on the lookout for opportunities to give gifts to yourself by giving to others.

It is well known that people who exercise vigorously describe feeling exhilarated or high during their workouts and then later they experience a sense of calmness and resistance to stress. But few people connect what they do at work to such a potential for getting *high*. Scientific research tells us that the same emotional and physical highs can also be produced through much less exertion—helping and serving others. People have told me that when they serve and help others, they feel fantastic, physically and emotionally. By serving others, they actually serve themselves. PhB Law 4 says it perfectly: *I cannot help another without helping myself.*

Mind/Body Connection

In 1988, Allan Luks, director of the Institute for the Advancement of Health in New York, coined two terms: *helper's high* and *helper's calm.* The first term describes the euphoria, increased energy, and general feel-good sensation during the act of serving. *Helper's calm* refers to the calmness felt immediately after the act. These experiences promote health by reducing stress via the release of endorphins, which are the body's pain-killing, mood-altering hormones. These experiences are the opposite of the stress response.

HELPER'S HIGH AT ANY AGE

Alaska fire chief, Pete Brown, was a guest on an *Oprah* show honoring individuals who have inspired others. Pete had developed a program for high-school girls to learn how to become members of the all-girl fire-fighting and emergency medical team, Dragon Slayers. These young women were trained to save lives. They worked for the fire department for 10 to 15 hours a week while maintaining their grades and staying drug and alcohol free.

The Dragon Slayers have saved people who have fallen through ice into freezing water, helped mothers in delivering babies, rescued people caught in fires, and treated gunshot victims. One of the girls talked about how she felt working at the fire department: "After you've helped someone, no matter what you've done, you get this unexplainably good feeling after which you feel so good and calm."

When I heard this, I recall thinking, "Wow, she just described the *helper's high.*" She described perfectly what scientists have been finding at the Institute for the Advancement of Health in New York and at Arizona State University, where they have been studying helper's high.

Mind/Body Connection

Psychologist Robert Cialdini of Arizona State University found that frequent *givers* experience the *helper's-high* euphoria. He found that these good feelings lower the output of stress hormones, which improves cardiovascular health and strengthens the immune system.

Emory University brain scientists have discovered that cooperating with or serving others activates an area in the brain rich in dopamine—the chemical that produces pleasurable sensations.

It is so easy to get stuck in a rigid routine and forget the reason why we work. Lift your head up every now and then and connect with the bigger purpose: and that is always service. You can enjoy these incredible helper's-high feelings every day at work when you connect *what you do at work* with *helping people*. This is what Leroy Grant thought every time he shined someone's shoes. Whatever you are doing at work, you can and should think, "I'm solving somebody's problem." In fact, we are all professional problem-solvers. We actually *get paid* to solve somebody's problem.

I would like you to start thinking in terms of what you're doing on the job and how you might shift into *helper's high* and experience *helper's calm*—the exact opposite of the stress response. What can you do to grab that feeling on a daily basis?

Mind/Body Connection

University of Michigan psychologist, Stephanie Brown, found that, when we give a lot and help others or do good to others, we release chemicals in the brain and the body that increase life expectancy. She monitored

423 couples for five years. All of the men were at least 65 years of age. She found that the frequent helpers among them had a 50 percent reduced risk of dying during the monitoring period.

DO YOU WORK FOR MONEY OR DOES MONEY WORK FOR YOU?

I want to tell you about two extraordinary people—both Professional Human Beings—to help you understand what the act of giving and helping does for happiness and health.

Paul Navone is an 80-year-old resident of Millville, New Jersey. With only an eighth-grade education he began working at age 16 in local glass factories, often putting in 60-hour weeks, and never in a half-century did he earn beyond $11 an hour. He never experienced a windfall and never won a lottery. But Paul was a thrifty man and invested wisely in the stock market and rental properties. And get this: Paul became a local hero at age 78. How? He donated two million dollars to two local schools. What an amazing feat! He lived frugally but experienced great joy in the act of giving. His philosophy: "What I invested in is enriching people's lives."

Cut from the same cloth was Matel Dawson, Jr., of Highland Park, Michigan. He passed away a few years ago at age 81. He had worked as a forklift operator at a Ford plant. Like Paul, Matel had only an eighth-grade education, yet he gave more than a million dollars to universities for scholarships. How is that possible?

Matel never took vacations. He often worked 12-hour shifts and lived frugally. He never made more than $26 an hour and drove a 1995 red Escort. But he routinely invested his money and eventually become a philanthropist. In the last decade of his life, he gave $680,000 to Wayne State University and $300,000 to Louisiana State University. He also contributed almost $250,000 to the United Negro College Fund.

His supervisor at Ford was asked if he knew about the philanthropy. He actually didn't know until he heard about it on the radio. Matel Dawson was a very humble person. The only thing the supervisor could say about him was that he was always the one who collected money for the sick workers. So here is a truly giving man after whom we can model ourselves.

President Clinton invited him to the White House. Matel's first response was to ask whether or not the President would make up for his lost wages—the answer was no but he went anyway. In a magazine interview in 1998, he was quoted as saying, "I need money to make me happy—it makes me happy to give money away. It gives me a good feeling." In a subsequent interview, in a magazine called *Black Issues in Higher Education,* he said, "I just want to help people, to leave a legacy and be remembered."

These men are certainly remembered. They are Professional Human Beings we were lucky to have on the planet. They both have lived out our PhB Law 4: *I cannot possibly help another without helping myself.*

How can you apply this law to your life? Helping another doesn't mean just giving money. It can also mean giving your time, a little kindness, and your expertise.

Set aside some time and seek out some volunteer activities in your community. The feeling of making a difference in the lives of others is so totally rewarding; you'll get to meet people, develop skills and hidden talents, and broaden your perspective. Some companies allow employees to volunteer several hours per week and they pay for it as well. That's exciting. For the company, the payoff is immense in terms of employee morale, energy, and productivity levels, not to mention the impact on individual health. It is a cost savings for the company.

Mind/Body Connection

There's a telltale piece of research from the University of Michigan that I like to refer to in my presentations. It involves a study of 2,700 people over a 10-year period. At the end, the researchers found that, more than any other activity, doing volunteer work increased life expectancy. Now that's about as powerful a payoff you could ask for! Giving begets a longer life.

Just recently I presented at a conference in Houston for Quality Service Contractors. This organization provides contractors with a means of finding solutions to the many issues service and repair contractors face. During the conference, I met a business owner from Dallas by the name of Sonny Friedman.

Sonny and his wife Carolyn run the very successful Atlas Plumbing Company. On their website (atlasplumbing.com) you can see the elements of the business clearly displayed as well as Sonny's most prized affiliation, Challenge Air for Kids and Friends. This latter is where Sonny's heart is. He sits on the board and volunteers his time (challengeair.com).

The Challenge Air for Kids and Friends takes participants who are physically challenged or have a life-threatening illness on a 30-minute flight in a four-seat, single-engine, general aviation aircraft. All pilots are volunteers and give the children and young adults (ages 7-25) the flight of a lifetime.

Sonny's friend, the late Rick Amber, founded Challenge Air. Rick believed "every disabled person should see the world—out of their wheelchairs and crutches—from the sky." This belief came from Rick's life experiences. As a fighter pilot and training officer in the U.S. Navy from 1967 to 1971, he lost the use of his legs when his jet crashed during a landing attempt. So he used his sky savvy to perform his magic. "You just have to see the faces of these young people when they return from this flight. They talk about it for the rest of their lives."

As Sonny said this, I watched his face. I could see clearly what Sonny's participation did for him. He glowed. His face radiated an indescribable happiness. He was excited about the joy he gave to children. He was unaware of the obvious joy he received in return, but I could see the years peeling away.

Sonny demonstrated what the research describes: Doing volunteer work increases life expectancy; and helping others during your working hours has the same effect even if you get paid for the service. It is a measure of whether or not you perform your magic. Want to live longer? Give more! Help more!

ARE YOU PROFIT OR OVERHEAD?

I have had a long, rewarding relationship with The Kroger Company, one of the biggest grocery chains in the United States, with more than 300,000 employees.

When I trained in the stores, I would ask the employees, "Who do you work for?"

They would say, "My boss."

I would say, "No, that's not who you really work for."

Then they would try, "The store manager?"

"No, you don't work for the store manager either."

"Kroger?"

The answer is the person who comes through the front door. I would say, "Through that door comes a shopper. Imagine that the shopper has a little tag on her chest and it says $5,000."—That's what most shoppers spend in a year for food—"So she's spending $5,000 a year." I would continue, "So you could stick a label on her forehead that says 'profit.' There's your profit, walking through the door."

Then I point to the group in front of me and ask, "What label would you stick on your forehead?" Usually a few people in the audience have gotten the message, and somebody comes up with the right answer: "Overhead."

That's it. "You're *overhead*," I say. "*She's* profit. Now, watch her as she walks around the store and shops. She has a very large cart of groceries. When she comes through the checkout line and pays for her food, some of that money goes into your Friday paycheck."

Now, I ask the question again, "Who do you work for?" The answers are generally quite different from before. They get it: They work for the customer. She pays you. She allows you to afford your car payments, your mortgage, your food, everything you own.

In my case—and in Bill Gove's case—our audience is our customer. Keeping my focus on the customer makes the customer happy and makes me happy, too. By not keeping the customer primary, the customer will suffer. Eventually I will suffer.

So you need to shift the way you look at work. You need to develop a customer-centered focus. Ask yourself these questions daily to stay serve-conscious: 1) Was my experience with the customer positive? 2) How can I make it better? 3) Did I ask my customer what I can improve upon to better serve her?

You are there to help the process and in the process you help yourself. You're not there in a manager-centered focus nor are you simply in a company-centered focus nor a profit-centered focus. Of course, you must make a profit. But you'll make it if the customer is at the center of everything you do.

Nonprofessional human beings are *me-centered*, not service-oriented. They do only what they are supposed to do—nothing more and usually less. They have an "I don't care" attitude that completely turns off customers. They don't like their jobs and it shows loudly and clearly. They are there just to get by. They'll do just enough so they don't get fired. That often manifests as employees who are paid for eight hours but who actually work four or five.

The new social contract is that *we are all self-employed*. It requires us to be professional problem-solvers and givers. Given the opportunity competitors will gladly serve the customer we should be delighting and are not.

Mind/Body Connection

Research shows that our health is at risk when we perform in ways that produce anxiety, boredom, or frustration. Anxiety suppresses the immune system, inhibiting, for instance, the function of the natural killer cells that fight infection. Boredom suppresses our ability to be creative. It taxes the heart and overall mental health. When we're bored we feel a

> general lack of satisfaction in whatever we're doing.
>
> According to a research study carried out by the University College, London, people who complain of boredom are more likely to die young. Findings on heart disease show sufficient evidence to say there is a link with boredom. Boredom can also lead you to deep depression and frustration. Boredom shuts down the creative part of the brain.

To generate healing in ourselves, we should be focusing on our customer, on whoever is being served. At home, as wife or husband, you are serving the family; at work, you are serving the employees and customers. If we take the right approach and have the right perspective—we actually lower our stress hormones, improve our cardiovascular health, and strengthen our immune system. We can significantly help our own health by helping others!

KROGER SERVICE

My favorite example of a self-employed, service-oriented attitude involves a seventeen-year-old bag boy at a Kroger supermarket in Dallas. As the checker diligently rang up the purchases of a shopper, he asked the routine question if she had found all she needed.

"No, I actually haven't," the woman answered. "I couldn't find the Albertsons mayonnaise."

This store was a Kroger supermarket, of course. The Albertsons supermarket was across the street.

When the bag boy heard this, he quickly thought, *Well, we want to keep her shopping here. We don't really want her to go to Albertsons.* He told the woman, "Please wait a minute and I'll get the Albertsons mayonnaise for you."

He ran out the door, jumped in his car, drove across the street to Albertsons, bought three jars of mayonnaise with his own money, and hurried back to his store. He gave the woman a jar of the mayonnaise with a smile, and said, "This jar is on us. We want you to be happy here. We'll keep the others in the back and you can purchase them when you like. Just ask for the Albertsons mayonnaise and we'll go in the back and get it for you."

I'm sure when the woman realized that Albertsons was across the street and, as an extraordinary act of customer service, this spirited young man was kind enough to go and get it for her and not even charge her, she was converted into a Kroger loyalist.

The young man's action was reported to his manager and he was very proud when he was named *Employee of the Month* because of his quick, innovative thinking. After making his customer feel like Queen for a Day, I'm sure the bag boy experienced that feeling of *helper's high*. Who wouldn't?

When you understand whom you are working for, it becomes much easier to experience the *helper's high* and *helper's calm*. Because you can experience it. Everybody can. And you can experience it all the time when you make a routine out of giving and treating people royally. You can give millions if you have it. Or you can give a smile or an extra courtesy. It can be very, very simple. And I'll tell you this: *the person who does the giving goes away with more joy than the person who does the receiving.*

One such Kroger employee I learned about was James Levy, a store manager in Dallas and a real PhB. One day he noticed a longtime customer crying while she was shopping. She was an elderly widow. He pulled her aside and asked her why she was crying. She told him that her property-owners association had initiated action to force her into a retirees' home because she was no longer able to take care of her home and lawn.

James felt compassion and assured her that he'd do whatever he could to help. He offered to take her home after she was finished shopping that day, so he could see her residence and determine how he could help.

After he returned to the store, James had a meeting with his employees about her. They decided that once a week they would do volunteer work at this customer's home and they notified her association accordingly. So every Saturday, different employees went over to cut her lawn, clean her house, and even paint it. It wasn't long before the house was sparkling. After some time, and perhaps embarrassed, the association informed her that it would be happy to take over the work. But here's the kicker: The Kroger volunteers were enjoying it too much. They weren't interested in giving it up.

What a great example of how to infuse the *helper's high* throughout the workplace by providing an extraordinary service to a customer and the community. I'll never forget the words of my friend Bob Zincke, former Kroger Executive Vice President of merchandising strategy: "What you are most happy about in the end are the things you did to help others."

Here's another Kroger example. John Woodall used to be a Kroger store manager in the Houston area before he was promoted and moved to Dallas. One Sunday, while in Houston, his house and belongings were badly damaged by floodwaters. He called around to some of the other store managers and asked if they could come and help move some of his furniture onto a truck to prevent further damage. Arthur Oden, the district manager at the time, heard about John's plight and came over on his own. He worked almost an entire day and gave an active hand to the very same managers who reported to him at Kroger's.

I asked John about this experience at a workshop and he said, with a straight face, "This is not good for me." He was joking, of course. "Well, the problem is, I'll never be able to say no to Arthur again for making such a deposit in my account."

Later, when I met up with Arthur Oden, he told me he got great delight out of serving somebody who reported to him.

Stop and think about the implication. Imagine the ripple effect and goodwill created over that part of the Kroger operation. If a manager serves an employee, does energy rise or fall? Arthur's action certainly energized the team.

Another time I heard that Arthur had taken his store managers on a recreation day and, during the bus ride, he personally served them food and drinks. Here is an example of what management can do for their employees to model who works for whom; the manager works for the employees. The dividend is *helper's high* for managers and an environment where people enjoy working.

WILL THE REAL MICHAEL JORDAN PLEASE STAND UP?

PhB individuals come in all shapes and from all strata of society, from barbers and glass factory workers all the way up to billionaires and superstars. I once heard a story about the great basketball player Michael Jordan, which made him a real PhB in my eyes.

After a Chicago Bulls game, Michael stayed behind for a long interview in the locker room. After the interview, a reporter observed him come out of the arena and was greeted by two young boys. They had waited for an hour with a camera in hand. They were hoping to have their picture taken with the basketball superstar but, as the first boy tried to take the picture, his camera jammed. The reporter watched Michael Jordan then spend the next 15 minutes patiently trying to get the camera to work. He succeeded, and then posed with each boy for a photo. With a big smile, he waved goodbye to his young fans and climbed into his limo.

When I think of this story, I think of the two Michael Jordans: one is an extraordinary athlete in the greatest professional basketball league on the planet—somebody who could amazingly average 30 points a game over a 15-year career; and the other is a Professional Human Being, a caring, giving person who takes time to be there for others. Michael's single act of compassion and generosity with those kids told me who he really is. He's a people person. He made an emotional connection with these kids that they will never forget. There's a saying: "People don't really care how much you've accomplished, they don't care how much you know, until they know how much you care." Michael's actions tell us how much he cares.

Another superstar is actor Denzel Washington. One time he visited Brooke Army Medical Center in San Antonio, a facility specializing in burn treatment for soldiers. On the base are buildings called Fisher Houses, hotels where the soldiers' families can stay for little or no charge. These residences are almost always filled.

During his visit Denzel was given a tour of one of the Fisher Houses and was told about the shortage of rooms. His reaction? He asked how much it would cost to build one of these buildings. A few months later they received a sizable donation from him. Denzel Washington is one of my favorite actors, so I wanted you to know what kind of a human being he is.

These examples bring to life those wonderful words of Mother Teresa: "In this life we cannot do great things. We can only do small things with great love."

HELPING SOMEBODY WHO IS DOWN CAN BRING YOU UP WHEN YOU ARE DOWN

Let me introduce my friend Jesse. I met Jesse while we were both attending the University of Santa Monica. A few years before, Jesse had finally succeeded in his long struggle with addiction and was working with Action Family Counseling Center. He did outpatient counseling for teenagers and adults who had substance abuse challenges.

One morning Jesse and a colleague were walking to work when they saw a man sleeping outside near the Center next to a mountain bike. Familiar with the appearance of someone on drugs, Jesse looked down empathetically at the man knowing that he could help him but only if the man were willing. The two walked around the man and continued on their way, entering the building and carrying on with their day as usual.

About half an hour later, Jesse heard the door open and he smiled as the same man ambled into the Center. His name was Joe and he was dirty and scruffy. He told Jesse and the office staff how miserable his life was and that he wanted to get off drugs. He had heard that the Center provided help for people in his situation. Jesse responded by sitting Joe down, ordering a pizza, and spending some time counseling him. Jesse told his own story to Joe explaining how he had changed his life for the better; Jesse tried to build up Joe's self-esteem and told Joe that he was worth getting clean. He then gave Joe a phone card and some money and told him to call his family. As Joe left, Jesse hoped his words had made an impact on Joe's life.

About four months later, Jesse was headed to work and on this particular day he was feeling depressed even though it was his two-year anniversary of being clean. Shortly after starting his day, a man walked into the office. Jesse didn't recognize him. The man was clean-shaven and well dressed. After a minute or two of talking, Jesse realized that this was the very same Joe.

The story Joe told was that, after he was treated so well at the Center, he was powerfully motivated to get clean. Joe described the impact that Jesse's actions and words had on him—it was just the inspiration he had needed. Jesse was deeply touched. The two men spent some time talking about the breakthrough Joe had had.

After Joe left, Jesse sat down at his desk and wept. It was a joyful weeping. His depression disappeared. He felt great about himself.

He was having a helper's high.

Jesse felt that this was the best gift to him on his anniversary. It was the most powerful cure for his depression. He realized that, by reaching out to somebody else, he had been an inspiration. Sometimes we don't get validation or even feedback for acts of service. But, in this case, Jesse received direct feedback that gave him renewed motivation and purpose in life—and the reminder that life was about helping others.

BUMP A NOSE, CHIQUITA

Here is a beautiful story from *Open Hands: Lessons on Giving and Receiving*, a book written by one of my friends, Jana Mullins. The story combines the first two lessons on becoming a PhB—*Perform Your Magic* and *From Here I Am to There You Are*. The story is called "Bump a Nose, Chiquita."

My name is Connie Mendez, I was born in Houston, Texas in the year 1953. I came from a very poor family, and, to top it off, there were nine children. But that was okay because I always heard people saying that God gave us all a gift when he gave us life, so I'm here for a reason. I am second to oldest and was severely abused physically and mentally by both parents. At the age of nine I was super skinny because there were days I only ate one meal and on others nothing at all. I had a real bad allergy so my nose was always running.

I have a big sister who is two years older than I am. She had only two dresses to wear and we both had to share them. She had this one green dress that I had to wear—it was too big and it kept falling down from one side of my shoulders. I had a pair of red shoes that a neighbor gave me that were one size too small for my feet so they tore from the front. I had no socks so I used my father's socks. The socks stuck out of the front of the shoes, making it look like the shoe had a tongue.

So I went to school looking like a clown. As I walked into the classroom, all the kids turned around to look at me and they all laughed at me. Then my teacher said, "Leave her alone, she's mentally retarded." Her words hurt me so much that I just wanted to die that day. I was thinking nobody loved me, not even God. I asked God, "Where is my gift? Did you forget me?"

At the age of eleven, I felt all alone in the world. I tried to commit suicide. No one knew why I did it, and nobody asked me why. Life went on. I needed to be loved, but I goofed again. The first man who said, 'I love you' to me, I married. He didn't like to work and he beat me and my children. I had three kids and ended up raising them by myself. My husband left me when my children grew up and I was alone again.

Then one morning I woke up feeling very depressed. I asked God, "Why am I here? Where is my gift? Did you forget me?" Then I had a flashback to my childhood years. I was crying and feeling very sad. Then I said to myself, "You can't do anything right, can you?" I said, "I just want to die. I can't take it anymore. But before I do, I'm going to take a walk one last time around the park." As I was walking around the park with my head down and crying, I heard some voices and people laughing. I lifted up my head and saw some people walking into a small building and they looked very happy. Why were they so happy? I followed them into the building. There I saw a group of ladies laughing and having a good time, sorting out boxes of clothing. This one lady, who had a big smile, came up to me and said, "Hi, I'm Linda, what's your name?"

I said, "Connie."

Then she told me to come and join them. "I really need all the help I can get. I need to sort out some clothing. I work for the Center for Faith and Health. We help out people in need with jobs, food and clothing. Will you please stay? We need you."

"Sure," I said. The words "we need you" made me so happy. My heart was beating fast with excitement.

When we finished, I said goodbye and Linda said, "I'll see you tomorrow, be sure to come back." I walked out of there feeling like a new person. The words "we need you" stayed in my mind. Thank God, thank you my God, I thought. All I want to do is live because Linda needs me tomorrow.

I kept coming back. Our group also helped seniors. Whenever I gave a senior a cup of coffee, I was told, "Thank you, we need you, we are sure glad you are here." I would get big hugs.

What they didn't know was that their hugs and love kept me from committing suicide. The funny thing was that the situation was really the other way around. I needed them. I stopped thinking about suicide.

Never in my life had I ever received an award for anything, but in 2002 I received an award for volunteering for the Center for Faith and Health. The group actually raised funds for me to go to clown school and I graduated as a clown. My clown name is Chiquita. And now I know it's true. God does love me and he did not forget me. He did give me a gift. He gives us all a gift. Now I understand why all the kids laughed at me in school. God gave me the gift of making people laugh. I'm not weird; I'm gifted. Thank you, God, and to all the people who volunteer. Thank you for my gift.

Once you move from *Here I Am* to *There You Are* and realize how powerful giving and serving are, you also realize that you couldn't possibly help another without helping yourself!

Thought Provokers

- *I slept and I dreamt that life was all joy. I woke, and saw that life was but service. I served and discovered that service was joy.*
  – Rabindranath Tagore, author of India's national anthem

- *Life is not worth living without service.*
  – Roy Mootoo, retired district commissioner, Trinidad and Tobago Scout Association

- *Service is the rent we pay for living in this world of ours.*
  – Nathan Tanner, teacher, business leader, Canadian politician

- *Anytime a customer comes into contact with any aspect of a business, however remote, is an opportunity to form an impression.*
  – Jan Carlzon, former president of Scandinavian Airlines

- Always do more than you are paid for. *It's not the hours you put in your work that counts; it's the work you put in the hours.*
  – Sam Ewing, American baseball player

Action Ideas

- Focus on others by listening well. One way to keep yourself engaged is by repeating back to the speaker what you've heard in your own words.

- Watch the movie *Dead Poets Society*. Robin Williams portrays an English teacher who inspires his students to become extraordinary. Let this inspire you to inspire others.

- Read the classic book on service, *Moments of Truth* by Jan Carlzon. Carlzon turned three European corporations around, including Scandinavian Airlines, by revolutionizing the service concept.

- Serve someone in an extraordinary manner—and *enjoy* it!

- Read the book *The Only Thing That Matters: Bringing the Power of the Customer into the Center of Your Business* by Karl Albrecht. It is about doing the right things exceedingly well, as revealed by your customer.

Spotlight
THE CUBAN-AMERICAN DREAM

Back in high school, Margie was the life of every party. Wherever she was, there was laughter. I remember her as intelligent, warm-hearted, vibrant, and with an infectious, positive nature. This disposition was key in overcoming her biggest challenge: Margie was a refugee from Cuba.

In 1962, Margie along with her older sister and younger brother were sent by her parents from Cuba to the U.S., in what was called Operation Peter Pan. Over 14,000 children of parents who opposed the revolutionary government were air lifted from Cuba between 1960 and 1962. The Department of State, the CIA, and the Roman Catholic Diocese of Miami collaborated to assist in the transporting of the children and then placing them with friends, relatives, and in group homes in 35 states.

Within 24 hours of landing in Miami the three children found themselves in my hometown of Canton, Ohio, with an aunt and uncle, who had emigrated from Spain. Unfortunately, their uncle had a heart attack and subsequently lost his job, which ended the living arrangement. The Catholic Charities then placed Margie and her siblings in the home of Patrick and Mary White. The Whites were an incredibly generous family. They already had six children, three girls and three boys, and yet opened their hearts up to three more.

While staying at the Whites, another tragedy struck: Margie's father passed away in Cuba. When Margie's mother finally made it out of Cuba and met the children, she had to tell them that there was no money. However, her mother already had it figured out: she advised her children that their only hope would be through education. "You will need to be an A student throughout high school and get a scholarship to college." This was not news to Margie. There were already high expectations for her; all of her relatives had advanced degrees—including the women, which in Cuba was rare.

After another year of living with the Whites, the three children were finally able to move into a little apartment in a tough side of town, not far from where I lived in an equally tough side of town. Margie never let her surroundings get the best of her. She was a member of the Student Council, the National Honor Society, and the Girls' Athletic Association just to name a few. She was also one of the best leaders at Central Catholic High School. All three siblings earned full college scholarships. Margie attended Marian College in Indianapolis, Indiana, and then came back to my own alma mater, The University of Akron, where she earned a master's degree in Higher Education.

I lost touch with Margie after high school. Fast-forward 35 years to 2002. Our class reunion was being planned and many of us had sent information to be disseminated to all our classmates in preparation for the festivities. In May, I received an e-mail from Margie Diaz Kintz with the subject line of "Are we Neighbors?" It turned out that Margie lived five minutes from my home in Austin, Texas! We had been living near each other for four years. It was fantastic to be reunited with Margie. As I got to know her again, I was fascinated by how Margie's past had influenced her future, and how she has found her magic and let it tumble out into service.

Margie's first job was as a grant writer for Stark Technical College. This launched her career into the fundraising arena. Then, in 1977 she became a fundraiser for St. Edward's University in Austin, Texas. Margie later became the Director of Development at Trinity University in San Antonio, Texas.

Behind every successful man is a very surprised woman! (I'm speaking from experience. Ask my wife.) Behind every successful woman, however, is a great man. Especially in Margie's case! Margie's husband, Tom Kintz, another Cantonian, was a very successful manager with Intel, the world's largest semiconductor-chip maker.

When Tom's job transferred to Oregon, Margie left her job and headed there with him. She had no idea what she was about to do until talking with an Intel recruiter who told her about a job opening to run the company's community giving program. "You are making this up!" she screamed disbelievingly. This needle-in-a-haystack job was made for Margie. She couldn't contain herself.

She was hired as the manager of corporate contributions. When she took over the program, Intel was giving away about one million dollars annually. Margie created a foundation and took the program worldwide; by the time she retired, Intel was giving away $150 million annually to the global community! No small feat!

Margie's legacy lives on in the growth of Intel's giving program, which, not surprisingly, was recently praised by President Obama; he credited Intel's STEM education programs for helping prepare youth for high-tech jobs.

Margie had started that ball rolling. How did she achieve this? She has always been a people-person: That's her magic! "Fundraising is a connection with people, and I was really good at fundraising. It is fundraising *sales*. I could have been a salesperson for the corporation but I really didn't want to sell technology."

Her connection with people continues to drive her. "Fundraising is telling the story of the organization. This is what I do now as a volunteer, as a service. Once you raise money from an individual, organization, a corporation, or a foundation, you circle back and reconnect with them to let them know that this is what you've done with their money.

"And I know how to give money away. It is not just a passion, I have the knowledge of how to do this. I know what boards are supposed to do because when I was working I would manage boards. I had to manage boards at universities. I also created advisory boards at Intel. I had to make sure boards were working effectively and that they had what they needed. I have always had to manage volunteers."

What Margie used to do for a living has now become her life's passion and she continues to "pay it forward" with her own charities. "Ninety-five percent of Tom's and my personal giving targets education. I have a passion for education because I know what difference it makes in someone's life." They have created a scholarship in honor of Margie's deceased brother Julio, and an endowed scholarship at St. Edward's University targeted to women and minorities going into science and math.

Margie now serves on three boards: the Christel House International, ACCESO, and KRLU, Austin's public television.

Christel House's vision is to help underprivileged children break the cycle of poverty, realize their hopes and dreams, and become self-sufficient, contributing members of society.

ACCESO provides humanitarian outreach to the people of Cuba who are struggling to obtain basics such as medicine, medical supplies, and reading materials. Their annual missions also help build relationships between Americans and Cubans. Working with ACCESO has given Margie the chance to fulfill her dream of returning to her homeland of Cuba. Margie continues to serve by using her time and energy working towards ending the embargo and lifting the travel ban. "I see that as the only way to see change in Cuba in my lifetime."

I admire Margie's serving nature. She attributes her "pay it forward" philosophy to the influence of Patrick and Mary White and the extraordinary love and generosity they showed to her. "Watching them and how they lived their lives was inspiring. They opened up their home to us. They moved out of their large bedroom and moved five girls into it. The other good-sized bedroom was used as the boys' dormitory with bunk beds for four. Pat and Mary moved into the tiny baby room. We had absolutely nothing to offer, but the way that they treated us was absolutely no different than the way they treated their own children. Each child had chores to perform. Every Monday morning, Mrs. White would dole out milk money to each one of us. It was total equality as love was given to each one of us. They totally transformed me." Mr. and Mrs. White were obviously PhBs.

Margie is an example of someone who uses her magic in service. Both Margie and Tom are two highly successful, self-sufficient individuals who retired from Intel at age 50. They haven't retired from serving though.

When I grow up, I want to make global contributions like Margie.

11

Lesson 3: Stop Going Out of Your Mind

We don't get a choice about what hand we are dealt in life.
The only choice we have is our attitude about the cards we hold
and the finesse with which we play our hand.

— SYLVIA BOORSTEIN
author and meditation teacher

W e were standing in line at the airport in Naples, Florida, waiting to
catch our flight to Miami. My wife Sais and I had been to Marco
Island to relax and attend a family reunion to celebrate my parents'
fiftieth wedding anniversary. Vacationing on Marco Island in Florida was
fantastic!

Getting to my next destination wasn't going to be as pleasant. I was
headed to Denver to give a workshop at eight the next morning at the Western
Management Development Center. And Sais was headed home to Austin.

We had arrived early for the flight and were sitting in the lounge
relaxed and happy to be early. At just about the time we should be boarding,
things changed dramatically. Instead of the regular boarding message, we
heard an announcement that our flight to Miami had been cancelled because
of "a mechanical problem."

My first thought popped out of the sympathetic nervous system. I
was annoyed and angry. I thought, *Hey, I was here first!* As if that mattered to
anybody. The second thought that followed was, *I'll bet they probably didn't have
enough people to put on that plane, so they cancelled the flight.* And the third thought:

I'm a Platinum member! I've flown almost three million miles on American Airlines. They can't do this to me! Meanwhile, everyone was lining up to get a new flight.

For the next five minutes, I went *out of my mind.* How could they do this to me? I even got here early! My mind was seething. I was angry. Temporarily insane!

Sais noticed my reaction and remarked, "You're making a big deal about this. I'm sure it'll all work out." And then, to make matters worse, she continued, "Why don't you do some of those things you talk about in your class?"

Such words, of course, could easily have fueled further agitation. What did she know? She was going home. She didn't have to present the next morning in Denver! However, her words stopped me in my tracks.

After a few seconds, I regrouped and burst out laughing. She was right. My perspective changed. I stopped my suddenly spinning, victimized mind. Up until that moment I hadn't taken my own advice. I was out of my mind—temporarily insane. Now the gears started turning again. I stayed calm, alternate arrangements were made, and I got to Denver that night and was ready for my class the next morning.

The title of the class my wife had referred to is *Stop Going Out of Your Mind Over Change: Become a Quick-Change Artist.* But right at that moment I was *out of my mind.* I did not make a quick change to the new reality, and I was what I call *a prisoner of the moment.*

Professional Human Beings understand this: You create your situations and challenges in life, and you can get yourself out of them—change is an opportunity for advancement. The opposite is thinking it is everybody else's fault. This is a victim mentality. If you think this way, you are stuck. You are a victim of a mentality that says, "I didn't create this, so I can't uncreate it and create something else. I'm helpless."

Life constantly brings change, and your reactions can either make you the architect or the victim. We all encounter this many times every day.

MOMENT MANAGEMENT

What do I mean by "going out of my mind"? Well, my initial reaction to the flight cancellation activated the fight-or-flight response in me. Blood shunted away from the prefrontal cortex, the CEO in the brain, where we think, make decisions, and plan properly. The blood was rerouted to my arms and legs preparing me to fight or to flee the scene, or, in this particular case, get upset over my cancelled flight. I've covered this reflex earlier. It's something that can erupt in an instant and spew negativity multiple times day in and day out.

How do I normally handle situations that can produce a stress response? Ideally I use the model I introduced back in Chapter Five: *Moment Management*. Well, for sure, I'm not perfect, but I try to use this model as often as I can. It helps me make positive, effective choices instead of damaging ones. I'm aware that I can't enjoy the present unless I'm here.

Here's how we apply the model to the situation of my flight cancellation.

The Elements of Moment Management

1. **THE SITUATION**: The actual external event or circumstance you're experiencing. In this case my being told that the flight was cancelled.

2. **YOUR INTERPRETATION**: Your internal evaluation of the event; how you explain the event to yourself. In my case, I told myself I was the victim and they did this to me to make my life miserable.

3. **YOUR RESPONSE**: How you choose to react, whether in a fit of anger or with calmness or with joy.

Now, there is a fourth dimension to Moment Management: the physiological consequence of your choice. The body follows the mind. Your response is based on the explanation you attribute to the experience or event presenting itself; in my situation blood flowed and my body began to feel enraged.

As far as I am concerned, if you can't manage the moment, you can't manage the bigger changes that life inevitably serves up. We have to manage each moment, moment by moment.

When the moment gives you an event that you do not expect, can you create enough mind space between what occurs and how you interpret it? Can you slow down your thinking at the moment in order to respond properly to the situation? Intentionally *see* the situation in a way that is to your advantage?

Response is a choice! It is not by chance. Initially, it is not automatic or involuntary to interpret the situations in a way that is beneficial to you. But, with practice and intent, you *can* see them that way automatically and then your response will follow your positive outlook.

Your interpretation of any event can make you, as it did with me at the airport, a *prisoner of the moment*. It activated the sympathetic nervous system in the direction of un-wellness. It put me temporarily out of my mind. At that moment in the airport, I wasn't rational. The passengers were lining up to re-book their flight and I was still seated thinking irrelevant, disease-producing, and irrational thoughts.

Laughter created by my wife's remark, "Why don't you do something you teach in your class?" brought me back in my mind, back to sanity. Blood started to flow back to the brain. Laughter is one of the easiest ways to recover from any stress. It steered me back to becoming a *sovereign over the moment* and activated the healthy parasympathetic nervous system.

Remembering my Platinum status with American Airlines, I called the Platinum Desk. "Hello, I'm stuck in Naples and I need to get to Denver." I explained what happened and asked what I should do.

The agent asked, "How far is the drive from Naples to Miami?"

I found out from someone in the line that it was about two hours.

"Okay. We have a flight from Miami to Denver leaving in four hours. If you rent a car right now, you can get to Miami and make that flight. We will make the reservation."

I now had a reservation and a plan. At that moment I remembered the man with the thousand-dollar suit. Have you heard this story? A flight had been cancelled and all the passengers were angry. A well-dressed gentleman—looking as though he were a man of importance, wearing a thousand-dollar suit—approached the agent and asked, "Do you know who I am?"

She looked at him and said, "Sir, excuse me for one second, okay?" She pulled the mike over and announced, "Ladies and gentlemen, can I have your attention, please? There's a gentleman here who doesn't know who he is."

Everyone laughed hysterically. Except the man with the thousand-dollar suit. He just walked away, angry and red-faced with embarrassment. A few minutes earlier that was me, I must confess! I had been in a similar mental location: temporary insanity!

As I walked over to get the rental car, I heard an announcement over the loudspeaker, that American Airlines would have vans waiting out front. They were going to take us all to Miami to get our connections. Perfect. The stress had now completely disappeared. I was back in control and I was happy. It seems we are happy to the extent that we feel in control of our lives. We are *always* in control of our interpretation and therefore our response.

SOVEREIGNTY AND RESPONSIBILITY IN THE MOMENT

What is the main reason we tend to go temporarily insane? The answer I have come up with is this: I am not happy when something occurs that wasn't what I expected, what I planned for, or what I wanted to take place. In other words, unexpected change. This for me is any experience that is not on my list of preferred expectations for the day, week, month, year, or life—or moment!

My response at the airport shows how very easy it is not to take responsibility for how we see whatever appears before us. The question is, "Is the situation in our control or not?" The answer is that it is placed before us. It is *what is*. I believe that from early childhood we learn that if we don't like *what is* we throw a tantrum. As babies and young children, we likely threw our share of fits and quickly learned, if we throw a fit, things might go our way. We would get what we wanted. Most of us have carried this over to adulthood thinking: Get upset, get angry, raise my voice, and I may get what I want. The mind clings to *what I want the situation to be* instead of *what is*.

Is the tantrum-reward assumption invalid? Absolutely. All of this is really a lesson about responsibility. Remember: Responsibility is your response-ability, your ability to respond appropriately to the situation, taking full responsibility for action in the moment. Most of us have a tendency to identify ourselves as victims of our circumstances rather than as architects.

Thinking about this more philosophically, if something is delivered to my doorstep, if something ends up in front of me, then the laws of nature are pretty clear why it did so. We are handed something we have co-created. It wouldn't show up unless we were part of it. This is sometimes very difficult to understand.

Let's go back to the three-stage moment: situation, interpretation, and response. In life, we find we cannot possibly be responsible for the external, but we are responsible for the internal. That is, how I interpret and how I respond are in my control. An African proverb is: "When there is no enemy within, the enemies outside cannot hurt you." It's all about our internal framing of the situation. It is about our own perspective of the situation. It is not about the situation itself, however uncomfortable that situation may be.

Martin Seligman, psychologist and former president of the American Psychological Association, coined the term "learned helplessness." It applies to people who portray themselves as victims, blaming the external for whatever is in front of them for which they will not take responsibility nor respond appropriately. The mind/body connection in this situation is fairly interesting. This victim mentality creates a feeling of being out of control; whenever we feel out of control or helpless, our stress level goes up and switches on the sympathetic nervous system. You may have noticed that when people are going through extraordinary change, they may fall ill and have a dark, gloomy state of mind.

Mind/Body Connection

Learned helplessness or victim mentality creates a feeling of being out of control and increases stress levels markedly. Prolonged feelings of helplessness make the body secrete excessive levels of the hormone cortisol, which interferes with the immune system's ability to fight off infections and some forms of cancer. It can also deplete the brain's supply of dopamine, a chemical that helps fight depression.

From *Learned Optimism: How to Change Your Mind and Your Life* by Martin E.P. Seligman, Ph.D.

When we face a challenge, an unexpected change, and find we are not in control of changing the external event or situation, we need to make a mental adjustment. The famous American economist, John Galbraith, put it extremely well by saying, "Faced with the choice between changing one's mind and proving that there is no need to do so, almost everyone gets busy with the proof."

However, the laws of physics, philosophy, and business tell us: "What we're reaping we have to have sown. Every action has an equal and opposite reaction. What goes around comes around."

So the change in my mindset—or the change in perspective, or the change in interpretation, or the change in evaluation—is a change in thinking. In short, the challenge we have with change, moment to moment, is a thinking problem.

To be sure, it's not what comes to us; it is how we come to it. The situation or circumstance does not make the person. It reveals us to ourselves. It is that conversation we talked about in the earlier chapters that we are carrying on with ourselves. How are we explaining the world to ourselves? When we apply the Moment Management model, it is clear that we have to change our minds, which means change our thinking.

This change of thinking or perspective has to take place within 1/10th of a second after the occurrence of what is happening to us, what we are experiencing. We have to expand that 1/10th of a second to 5 seconds, then to 10 seconds, and in that 5 or 10 seconds, we need to begin to talk to ourselves in a different way. Talking to ourselves in a different way amounts to changing the way we relate to ourselves as we go through an event or situation. Ron and Mary Hulnick, President and Chief Academic Officer of the University of Santa Monica, could not have said it more clearly: "The issue is *not* the issue. How you *relate to yourself* while you go through the issue *is* the issue."

MOMENT MANAGERS

Check out the list below of what I call Moment Managers. I apply these questions—pretty automatically now—in situations that crop up in my life. I may use one or several at a time to get me back *in* my mind or prevent me from spinning out in the first place. Professional Human Beings can go temporarily insane, like anybody else, but they know how to restore equilibrium quite quickly.

When presented with an unwelcome situation that is not on your preferred list of expectations for the day, how do you react? Will you be sovereign over the moment or its prisoner?

Remember these questions as you manage your reaction:

1. Am I in control of this situation?
    a. Am I sovereign over this moment or am I its prisoner—which do I choose to be? I am a prisoner when I blame someone for the situation that I find myself in, and I am sovereign when I recognize my role in it.
    b. Can I interpret this as a test? Is this God, Nature, or the universe testing me?

   c. What are my unmet expectations? What was it I wanted that did not happen? What must I let go of?

2. Can I change the situation?
   a. What can I do to influence the situation?
   b. What is the new reality? Once I realize this is what I did not expect to happen, I must embrace it because I can't change it.
   c. Do I understand the longer I take, the longer I stay out of my mind, the more stress I accumulate, the more miserable I make my life, the more prone to illness I become, and the faster I age?

3. Do I have an effective solution?
   a. How fast can I realign myself with the new reality?
   b. What do I need to think and do to accomplish swift alignment?
   c. How can I make this experience serve me?

One book that I often recommend to people in my workshops is *Leadership and Self-Deception: Getting out of the Box* by The Arbinger Institute. This book is about self-responsibility in the light of business. It is an engaging story that follows an executive through his daily life at home and at work. Through him, we see the subtle psychological processes that keep us trapped in the box of self-deception. The book shows us a way out of the box by posing the following questions:

- What role do I play in the obstacles that confront me?
- Can I take responsibility for my part of the situation?
- Can I see that I am part of the problem?
- Can I see that the challenge is not the problem itself, but rather how I relate to the problem?
- How do I treat myself, and others, as I am going through the problem?

Recently, for example, I helped some employees confronted with an unwelcome situation. This client company had spent $2.5 million on a new software program. Not only did team members grumble about the change but they actually resisted it for up to a year. With this resistance in mind, I asked the team at one session, "Will the organization purchase another software program?"

The obvious answer was, "No. This one cost too much."

Then I asked, "Since the software isn't going away, wouldn't it be better to realign with the new reality now? Learn how to use it now?"

I received reluctant nods in return. They begrudgingly had to let go of their unmet expectation. They had to let go of their comfort zone because the new reality was that the new software system was here to stay.

In my own case, I learned back in my university job that phone calls were not interruptions of my work but were part of my work. I shifted my mindset and was able to serve those students calling me just as I served those coming into my office. My new response served me and better served all of my customers.

However you feel about your control over the external situation, remember that you are always *in control of your reaction.*

I have always been fascinated by research on older people, individuals who have survived the ups and downs and challenges of life. I once read a survey of healthy centenarians (people over a hundred years of age) about what they believed helped them live long and healthy lives. Surprisingly, the most common answer was not a special diet, regular exercise, nor avoidance of alcohol or tobacco; it was the ability to let go of situations they were not in control of—and the flexibility that comes from that letting go. That flexibility and embracing the uncertainty slows down biological aging. This is a clear demonstration of PhB Law 5: *Body follows mind;* the mind released its resistance, and the body followed with health.

Mind/Body Connection

Optimists catch fewer infectious diseases than pessimists. Optimists have better health habits than pessimists. Our immune system may work better when we are optimistic. A study conducted during the 1930s on the lives

---

> of Notre Dame nuns showed that the optimism expressed in the nuns' diaries correlated with their longevity.

Conversely, resisting change, holding on to our ideas of how things should be when that reality isn't manifesting, causes stress, strain, aging, and a disease-producing physiology.

Microbiologists tell us that almost 100 percent of our atoms are replaced within a year's time. The stomach lining renews every five days. You sport a new suit of skin every four weeks. Your liver is reconstituted every six weeks and your skeleton every three months. Even your DNA has a new generation of atoms every two months. In other words, you get a new version of yourself every four months! We have a constantly changing physiology.

Certainly, the mind needs to learn a lesson from the body. The body is completely comfortable with change while in many cases the mind will resist it. The challenge is to get the mind to change routinely and smoothly as well. That's the big problem and disciplining your mind to be flexible is the answer.

My proposition is that having the creativity and optimism to come up with innovative ideas makes us able to make any situation serve us. An opportunity arises almost daily in the workplace. Management is doing its best to meet the requirements of the most challenging economy since the Depression. Roles, processes, approaches, systems, products, and missions are all shifting beneath our feet. We have a responsibility to ourselves and our associates at work to make the healthiest choices in the face of change. Choices affect everyone in our environment!

I would like you to recall what we have discussed concerning manual muscle testing in Part I of this book. Using this technology or imagining the use of this technology, you might readily see what kind of thinking and self-talk are *enabling and empowering* and what kind are *disabling and disempowering*.

What kind of choices do you make in the face of change in the workplace?

StOP Thinking	PhB Thinking
I am angry and upset over this recent change. I will resist it! I may even sabotage it!	I will realign to the change we are facing. I will do my best to adjust.
I think management makes changes just for the sake of change!	I believe that management creates change which is directed toward a goal which represents a more desirable outcome than we have now.
When difficulties occur from changes, I see it as proof that these changes are bad.	I realize that problems are a natural side effect of change.
I think that supervisors and managers enjoy withholding information from us.	Managers don't always have the right answers as the process unfolds because change is a discovery process.
Management keeps changing its direction. It seems lost!	I understand that management needs to be creative and improvise as they go. Course corrections are smart.
I assume that managers and supervisors don't really care about their direct reports.	I agree that being a supervisor or a manager is not easy. They must make unpopular decisions and not everyone will be pleased.
I can't make a difference anyway from my position.	I will make a difference one way or another. Why not make it a positive difference?

I didn't create this plan anyway, so let the managers and supervisors complete it.	I realize that a plan has been put in place and now it's everyone's job to make it work. If I get a paycheck it is my plan too.
I believe that management doesn't know what it's doing.	I agree that there's no such thing as a mistake-free project, especially a change project. If I am tolerant of management's mistakes, they will be tolerant of mine.
I feel that change is not necessary. It will go away in time.	I understand that change is here to stay. I believe that change can help us create a better future.

This chart was adapted and formulated from a presentation by Price Pritchett, the renowned organizational change expert. (Pritchettnet.com.) His main premise is congruent with the proposition of this book; that "the organization can never be what the people are not."

ARGUING AND ITS EFFECTS

ABC's *20/20* program once aired a segment called the "Bickering Couples," which dramatically demonstrated the effect of our emotions and actions on our bodies—the mind/body connection. The segment featured an experiment conducted by psychiatrist Redford Williams, M.D., director of the Behavioral Medicine Research Center at Duke University, and known as the guru of anger management.

He hooked up a number of couples in order to measure blood pressure and cortisol levels as they *discussed* touchy issues. As tempers and decibels rose, so too did the blood pressure. It skyrocketed and the cortisol levels rose significantly. Such behavior is clearly unhealthy and can shorten life span—or stop it abruptly, as in strokes and heart attacks. Like a polygraph, this experiment was a clear demonstration of how quickly a psychological mood could affect the physiological state.

The experiment reminded me of earlier research showing that the way we approach communication, especially when we argue with hostility, can do real bodily harm—the immune system weakens while blood pressure and stress hormones rise. Emotional conflict creates a toxic environment within our bodies that can promote arterial disease and, in general, make it difficult to combat illness.

In part two of the experiment aired on *20/20*, the couples trained in communication and conflict-resolution techniques taught by Dr. Williams and his wife, Virginia Williams, Ph.D., president of Williams LifeSkills, Inc. The two are coauthors of seminal works, *Anger Kills* and *LifeSkills,* that describe the potent effects emotions can exert on the body.

The Williams' approach, in many cases, is to create a space between the stimulus—the stressor—that causes the upset and the interpretation one chooses to make. As I mentioned earlier, you are in control of your interpretation and response to any event. So in that context, this would mean learning to talk to ourselves differently.

The Williams devised the following four questions (found on their website: williamslifeskills.com) to create the gap between the experience of the stressor and the response to it:

1. Is this matter important to me?
2. Is what I am feeling and/or thinking appropriate to the facts of the situation?
3. Is this situation modifiable in a positive way?
4. When I balance the needs of others and myself, is taking action worth it?

If all your answers are "yes," then you should have a conversation on the topic. If you get one "no," then it isn't worth bringing it up; drop it! According to the Williams, using the questions not only changes our interpretation and perspective about the subject at hand, but also slows down the process. Anything we can do to slow down the process is helpful. I call it the process of moving from *thoughtless reaction* to *thoughtful responding.* The couples learned to think before reacting. They also learned a second skill—to listen before reacting. Listening has many aspects:

- Don't interrupt.
- Ask questions.
- Repeat what you heard in your own words to that person.
- Don't move off the topic until the speaker feels your under-standing is complete.
- And don't argue about the solution to the situation—just repeat what you heard.

In the second part of the experiment, the couples were hooked up again to the same measuring devices used previously while they talked about their hot issues. But this time, they were instructed to use the four questions above as well as to listen fully before reacting. Now, with the use of the new techniques, both blood pressure and cortisol levels actually dropped during the session. The takeaway was that a change in approach, a change in their skill of handling the moment, resulted in positive changes in the body.

CHOOSE YOUR RESPONSE: A MIND/BODY FRAMEWORK

There are traditionally four approaches to communication with others. In the face of change, or at worst, a crisis, people often tend to repeatedly fall back on a particular style. Think about the success or failure in getting your desired outcome by using one particular approach or another. Here are the styles and a description of the way people act when they use that approach in dealing with others.

1. **Passive**. You avoid conflict, don't make eye contact, rarely express feelings or your own opinions, sometimes lack confidence, may get embarrassed easily, but never complain. You usually are compliant and may be submissive at times.
2. **Passive-aggressive.** You avoid conflict and rarely speak up but complain about the situation to the wrong person at the wrong time.

You use silence, guilt trips, sarcasm, and gossip. You play the victim or the martyr. You suppress outward expressions of aggression but channel your anger into passive non-cooperation and obstructing the actions of others.

3. **Aggressive.** You are prone to fly off the handle, are usually opinionated, loud, tactless, and sometimes finish other people's sentences. This type of communication style is argumentative, rebellious, and sometimes resistant. You appear overly confident, but have low self-esteem.

4. **Assertive**. You express your opinions and feelings openly and honestly without denying the rights and needs of others. You are usually firm without being dominating. Communication is calm without an emotional edge or charge on it. It is direct but non-confrontational. It is using tact with diplomacy. Assertion is telling someone "where to go" in such a way they actually look forward to taking the trip!! This style can be described as calm-assertiveness.

These approaches are pretty simple to understand, but what is not appreciated is the physiological outcome of each style. Think also about your style in terms of the mind/body connection, as represented by the chart on the next page.

Evidently, the first three approaches to communication are less healthy for us physiologically than the fourth category. In the fourth category we express ourselves openly and honestly, without denying the rights of others or our own needs and rights. It is the ability to say "no" when appropriate. It is the most balanced response and does not contribute to the activation of the stress response in others—most of the time. I am saying most of the time because nothing works all of the time and, in some cases, it may be appropriate to use one of the three other approaches.

Unhealthy	Unhealthy	Unhealthy	Healthy
Passive	Passive-Aggressive	Aggressive	Assertive
Compliant/submissive. You are actually aggressive toward yourself for not speaking up, for not defending yourself and/or for not standing up for your rights and needs. You turn on yourself psychologically and physiologically.	Wrong person, wrong time. You flee from direct confrontation but are chronically emotionally agitated.	Argumentative, combative, rebellious, resistant, and emotionally charged.	Firmness without domination or emotional charge. Direct but non-confronta-tional.
Flight response. Your body responds as if you are running away from something. You activate the sympathetic part of the autonomic nervous system.	Fight _and_ flight response. You activate more of the sympathetic part of the autonomic nervous system.	Fight response. You activate most of the sympathetic part of the autonomic nervous system.	This is the healthy response.

Not only are the first three approaches unhealthy, but in the end, they may not get you what you want. For instance, if one of your coworkers is doing something you don't like, one of your choices could be to complain to someone who is not directly involved in the situation. The important question is this: Would this really solve your problem with the other person? In most cases, the answer is no! This is the passive-aggressive choice.

A passive approach might be to say nothing to anyone, including the person who is causing your upset. Does this solve your problem? Again, in most cases, this would not solve your problem.

You could get very aggressive with the person and bring a lot of emotion to the table, convey a lot of negative charge, even raise your voice demonstrating anger and hostility toward the person. This normally is not a successful way to communicate either. What occurs when someone is aggressive toward another is that he doesn't listen to the content of the speaker's message! The listener is overwhelmed by the emotional outburst and uses this as an excuse to rationalize away your content. The listener doesn't respond to aggressiveness.

Assertiveness means you are firm, clear, and honest with the person who is causing you distress. You are not confrontational, but direct, and address the behavior, not the person. This is the assertive choice. Of all the responses, assertiveness seems to be the most healthy response; but for most of us, in most cases, it can be difficult to pull off. Assertiveness can require extraordinary patience and equanimity.

In summary, when we are faced with a situation we are feeling upset about, we have four choices, and in that moment before we respond, we make a decision about which style to use. So the question is this: Which communication approach serves me best in the situation? My vote in most cases is to be assertive.

COMMUNICATION APPROACHES—HAWAIIAN STYLE

Many of my clients are located in the beautiful state of Hawaii. When I first went there as a consultant, I realized that a large percentage of the people have Asian ancestry. Consequently, the culture has a strong Asian influence. Having worked in Japan, Hong Kong, India, Indonesia, and Singapore, I had some familiarity with Asian cultural values. There are a few key phrases used to describe personal interaction in some quarters of the Asian culture: *no shame, save face, fit in,* and *don't stand out.*

In light of these strong attitudes, as you can imagine, it's very difficult to communicate directly and even more difficult to give and receive feedback. It is also extremely difficult to be assertive. Because of these inhibitors, assertive behavior is sometimes seen as aggressive. I was wondering how my understanding of the Asian culture would relate to Hawaii. And I pondered how the previous four traditional communication approaches would be used there in challenging situations.

An experience in a Honolulu movie theater gave me a good test case. I had gone to a movie with some participants from one of my leadership classes. We all sat in one section of the theater.

On either side of me sat a woman of Japanese descent. Several other people occupied rows in front of and behind me. Within the first few minutes of the movie, a lady a few seats away from us answered her cell phone and began talking in a fairly loud voice. She was totally ignoring the earlier, on-screen reminder to turn off cell phones.

She continued talking well over a minute. She was saying things like, "No, I'm not going to go to that restaurant," and "Well, we decided to come to this movie, not go to that other one." Everyone in our area could hear her clearly. It was disturbing and rude. The two women seated next to me started to look in her direction and give her what they call in Hawaii "the stink eye"—a very harsh stare that you wouldn't want coming in your direction. They said nothing but they were visibly boiling inside. They just held in their emotions and kept looking in the offender's direction.

Now, in which category would you place their response?

Passive, of course. I wanted to say, *You know, ladies, I don't think the "stink eye" works in the dark.* The lady on the phone continued talking. I was curious to see which approach would be used.

Another minute of this passed and then a man about three rows up began throwing popcorn at the woman. The popcorn buzzed right by her head and a couple of pieces hit her. She responded by turning to the side and making herself into a thinner target. But she continued to talk.

In which category would you put the man tossing the popcorn grenades?

Yes, that's right: he was aggressive. Unfortunately, he wasn't getting the result he wanted either.

I continued observing and she continued to talk. I saw most of the people in my area of the theater turning to the person right next to them and talking to that person about the cell phone lady. They were passive-aggressive to the problem at hand.

After about three minutes of this I stood up and wormed my way past a few seats and, leaning over, said to the woman, "Ma'am, would you please turn off your phone now? You're disturbing everybody."

She immediately shut off her phone right in the middle of a sentence and sat there looking at the screen as if she never had the phone on.

When I got back to my seat, the two ladies who sat next to me were so embarrassed they both looked down and away from me. It was as if they were saying, "Excuse me," to the rest of the theater, "we're not with this *Haole* boy." (Whites are referred to as *Haole* in Hawaii.) They were embarrassed to be with me.

The rest of the movie went on without event. On the way out of the theater I asked the ladies how they enjoyed the movie.

They responded, "Great, really enjoyed the movie!"

I then asked, "What did you think about the woman with the phone?"

The ladies said, "Oh my gosh, we don't do that here! That's just not right!"

"What did I do?" I asked.

"Well, you were aggressive with her!"

"Well, I would call it something else," I replied.

"What would you call it?" one woman asked.

"I was being assertive! I wasn't aggressive. I didn't raise my voice. I didn't show any anger. I didn't have any emotional charge around it, so I call that assertive."

One of the women said, "No, no, no, no! To us that was upsetting because you were aggressive with her."

I asked her, "How did you expect her to know that she was disturbing us and we wanted her to turn the phone off? You were being disturbed, right?"

"Yes," they said, "but you didn't have to be like that!"

"May I show you what being aggressive would have been like?"

"Sure."

"I would have said something like, 'Ma'am, you turn that phone off right now, or I'll shove it down your throat!' Now that's aggressive."

One of the ladies looked at me and said, "That's not aggressive...that's evil!"

I laughed good-naturedly but inside I thought it was hilarious. I had just learned a fifth communication approach—evil! Add that to passive, passive-aggressive, aggressive, and assertive.

What I really learned—and I've since found this to be true with most teams I coach in Hawaii—is that people prefer to save face, to not shame anyone, and to continue to use what they call "talking stink" about people. In no sense is this approach exclusively Hawaiian. On the mainland we call it "gossiping," talking to the wrong person at the wrong time and not resolving problems in the process. The contrast seems greater, though, in the Aloha spirit of a loving and caring culture.

It's very easy to not respond and keep our thoughts to ourselves, even if negative. It's very easy to talk about other people behind their backs and not to them. It's very easy to get angry, lose our temper, and become hostile toward another. What is not easy is to maintain an assertive approach, avoid the fight-or-flight response, and stay calm. Healthy responses lead to a healthy individual. Healthy individuals contribute to a healthy organization.

When choosing your approach, consider these two questions: What's the healthiest response for me? What will get me what I want?

Remaining calm and assertive in the face of difficulty also allows us to be more creative, as we'll see in the next chapter. Once we divert our blood away *from* the brain and *to* other parts of the body—legs and arms—by activating the stress response, we sacrifice our creativity and become less capable of making good decisions and thinking clearly.

This lesson has been about asking yourself the following question: "Do I go out of my mind often?" If you do, you'll find this is one of the reasons for your lack of success in the workplace. In addition, it definitely affects your personal life, whether your friends and family will tell you or not.

ASSERTIVENESS-ASSESSMENT QUESTIONNAIRE

Where do you fall on the passive/assertive/aggressive scale? To find out, take this brief questionnaire, developed by my friend and colleague, Warren Blank, Ph.D. Warren developed this to help team members know how and why they relate to each other as they do. They were able to see that the reason they didn't get along was that they had different communication approaches. This survey measures how passive, assertive, and aggressive you are. I have modified it slightly by adding the passive-aggressive category. How true are the following statements as descriptions of your behavior? Write down the number that represents your answer. Please respond to every statement.

Never True	Sometimes True	Often True	Always True
1	2	3	4

_____ 1. I respond with more modesty than I really feel when my work is complimented.

_____ 2. If people are rude, I will be rude right back.

_____ 3. Other people find me interesting.

_____ 4. I tell others how someone's negative behavior made me feel but not the main offender.

_____ 5. I find it difficult to speak up in a group of strangers.

_____ 6. I don't mind using sarcasm if it helps me make a point.

_____ 7. I ask for a raise when I feel I really deserve it.

_____ 8.   I have something to say but only after the fact.

_____ 9.   If others interrupt me when I am talking, I suffer in silence.

_____10.   If people criticize my work, I find a way to make them back down.

_____11.   I can express pride in my accomplishments without being boastful.

_____12.   I fuel the rumor mill.

_____13.   People take advantage of me.

_____14.   I tell people what they want to hear if it helps me get what I want.

_____15.   I find it easy to ask for help.

_____16.   I tell people how I feel but it's not the right person or the right time.

_____17.   I lend things to others even when I don't really want to.

_____18.   I win arguments by dominating the discussion.

_____19.   I can express my true feelings to someone I really care for.

_____20.   I don't speak up during times of conflict but later complain to colleagues who weren't directly involved.

_____21.   When I feel angry with others, I bottle it up rather than express it.

_____22.   When I criticize someone else's work, they get mad.

_____23.   I feel confident in my ability to stand up for my rights.

_____24.   I gripe about things but don't voice my opinion at the appropriate time or place.

When you're finished answering the questions, score them as follows:

1.   Sum up your answers to items 1, 5, 9, 13, 17, 21.
     Enter your score: _____ (Passive)

2.   Sum up your answers to items 4, 8, 12, 16, 20, 24.
     Enter your score: _____ (Passive Aggressive)

3.   Sum up your answers to items 2, 6, 10, 14, 18, 22.
     Enter your score: _____ (Aggressive)

163

4. Sum up your answers to items 3, 7, 11, 15, 19, 23
   Enter your score: _____ (Assertive)

Your scores will reflect what you lean toward most of the time. The goal is to be assertive in your communication. Reread questions 3, 7, 11, 15, 19, and 23, the questions that address assertiveness. Now be aware of these situations in your life. Your challenge is to increase your choice of assertive communication. Similarly, look at the questions in the other categories and take action steps to move you towards your desired goal.

Thought Provokers

- *Courage is what it takes to stand up and speak; courage is also what it takes to sit down and listen.*
  – Sir Winston Churchill, British prime minister

- When you smile, your facial muscles activate endorphins in your brain! These are feel-good molecules.

- *If you don't like something, change it. If you can't change it, change your attitude. Don't complain.*
  – Maya Angelou, American author and poet

- Like the law of gravity, the law of cause and effect, action and reaction—*as you sow so shall you reap*—is a natural law. Understanding this law helps you understand that everything happens by law, not by chance.

- What you cannot change is *what is*. Accepting *what is* removes your suffering. See *what is* as friend not enemy. Accept *what is* as if you had chosen it. Complaining is non-acceptance of *what is*.

Action Ideas

- Watch the movie *Get Shorty*. John Travolta's character, Chili Palmer, inspires assertiveness.

- Stop being so surprised when obstacles arise. Get used to them. And change your interpretation of them from roadblocks to stepping-stones.

- Read *Zero Limits: The Secret Hawaiian System for Wealth, Health, Peace, and More* by Joe Vitale and Ihaleakala Hew Len, Ph.D. This book introduces the profound Hawaiian practice of ho'oponopono, which in the native Hawaiian language means "making things right."

You will learn how to "[wipe] your mind's slate clean and [start] over without preconceived notions, so you can live in a world of daily wonder. Imagine if anything and everything were possible. In fact, everything *is* possible when you look at the world free of mental constraints. This book is a key that opens your life to a new universe of possibility and accomplishment—a universe with *Zero Limits*!"

- Let go of always having to be in control of what happens to you.

- Catch yourself blaming and find your part in it. Refuse to blame anyone for anything. It's not good for your physiology and it's a sign you don't want to take responsibility. We are at least partially responsible for every outcome in our lives. Blame focuses on what cannot be undone or changed. Blame looks backward. Accepting responsibility looks forward!

Spotlight
THERE'S NO PLACE LIKE USM

Neal Donald Walsch, author of *Conversations with God,* says about the University of Santa Monica, "There is no place quite like USM; if you haven't heard about it you need to." And I agree. Lesson Three is an examination of accountability and responsibility, and USM is the best place to gain these powerful tools and qualities. In a two-year course of study you will come away armed with the most practical skills and strategies to amazingly transform the rest of your life.

Do you go out of your mind often? Do you find yourself being triggered often? The curriculum at USM is uniquely designed for you to learn the skills of healing unresolved issues. And what is an unresolved issue? Anything that disturbs your peace. Imagine a technology that results in more peaceful people—people who are learning how to embrace the reality that, first and foremost, we are spiritual beings having a human experience.

USM squarely tackles three fundamental questions so many of us are asking:

- Who am I?

- Why am I here on earth or, what is my purpose in being alive?

- How can I make a more meaningful contribution in my world?

I'm sure Neale would agree, that USM is the best in the world at what it offers, a Master's degree in Spiritual Psychology.

At USM you'll have the opportunity to experientially explore the largely unexplored territory of spiritual reality. And more important, you'll learn how to be in this world while also learning how to see through soul-centered eyes—eyes that perceive through the lens of spiritual reality—and how to operate effectively from within that reality.

I'll give you an example. In a soul-centered reality, it is clear that peace can never be found through people fighting for peace no matter how well intentioned they may claim to be. The only logical way peace can ever truly occur is as a result of large numbers of people daring to transform within so that they experience greater levels of inner peace. And how does one find inner peace? By learning the principles and practices of healing unresolved issues.

Check out the transformational new book, *Loyalty To Your Soul: The Heart of Spiritual Psychology* by the President and Chief Academic Officer of USM, H. Ronald Hulnick, Ph.D. and Mary R. Hulnick, Ph.D. They are also the designers and senior faculty of USM's Spiritual Psychology Program. For more information visit universityofsantamonica.edu

12

Lesson 4: See Yourself on Broadway

Don't label growth as trouble and painful
and standing still as safe.

— NEALE DONALD WALSCH
author of *Conversations with God* series

A s a young boy, I dreamed of the day when I would go to New York to see a show on Broadway. I got my wish with Doug Henning's musical, *Merlin*. The show was being produced by a major studio, Columbia Pictures, and directed by the very successful Ivan Reitman. It was the first of its kind to incorporate magic into the plot of a Broadway musical. The chance to be involved in the production process was way beyond what I had dreamed of.

This show fulfilled the dream of someone else as well.

Long before the show opened, Doug's wife Debby had a dream. Her desire was to work with her husband. She and Doug were newly married and she dreaded being away from him. She knew the best way to spend time with him was to get a role in the play. But, even while she was strongly motivated to be a part of *Merlin*, she realized it was a long shot.

Debby had done some summer stock and community theater but never anything professional. If she wanted to achieve her desire, she would have to appear before the most intimidating and critical play-going audiences in the world. Before auditioning and casting for the production began, Debby started asking about how she could possibly get a role in the play. She also expressed doubt and trepidation at the same time. Some time before the auditioning began, Doug and Debby made a trip to Europe to see their

167

spiritual mentor, Maharishi Mahesh Yogi. During a conversation with Maharishi, Debby talked of her desire to be in the musical. But even as she expressed her desire, she declared her doubts: "Broadway is so big! I don't know if I can do that!"

Maharishi chuckled. "Broadway? Big?"

And he began spinning the tabletop globe he always kept next to him. He stopped at that little spot on the globe called Manhattan. Somewhere on that tiny island was a street called Broadway. Maharishi pointed to it, asking, "Broadway? Big?"

He paused a moment then pronounced, "You have to think big. Thinking small will not get you what you want. You have to stretch your imagination so that it's big enough to see you there. Anything is possible, and anything means ANYTHING, even Broadway. You've got to *see yourself on Broadway.*"

THINK BIG

Armed with this inspiration and perspective, Debby returned to New York. She was on a mission! She convinced herself that the theater was just one small location at one small spot on the earth. She wrapped her mind around the idea that she could do it and started preparing for her dream. She immersed herself in getting ready for the audition. She took lessons in voice, dance, and mime.

She was set on auditioning for a major role in the play—that of the magical unicorn—a close friend of Merlin, who would be played by Doug. On the day that Debby auditioned, Doug and I sat in the audience watching one professional actress after another perform for the producers and director. Finally, Debby's turn came. She sang "Memories," from the musical *Cats*, which was playing on Broadway at the time. She was amazing! Doug and I looked at each other. We both had tears running down our faces. Her reading, performed with full confidence, stage presence, heart, and beauty, left Doug and me speechless. Doug could not have been more proud.

Remarkably, Debby, the longshot, got a role in the play—not the role of the unicorn, since the director and writers changed the role of the unicorn to one for a ballerina—but she gladly took another role. She got the role not because she was Doug's wife, but on her own merits as a talented performer. She had competed against professional actresses from all over the world and got a part. It was a huge personal victory for her and an inspiration to all of us.

It goes without saying: She was a great success in the show. In fact, it was the beginning of her stage career with Doug. After *Merlin*, she routinely appeared as his onstage assistant for television shows, tours, and stage shows.

Debby turned her thinking upside down. She stretched her imagination. She thought big enough to wrap her mind around the idea of getting the part. She could see herself there.

You've certainly heard the phrase: "I can see myself doing that." Or the flip side: "I can't see myself doing that." Debby's story verifies the truth of both sayings. If you can see yourself doing something, you will; if you can't see yourself doing something, you won't. Henry Ford put it this way, "If you think you can do a thing or you think you cannot do a thing, you are right."

Mind/Body Connection

The chronic feeling that it is impossible to improve a situation or to feel better about yourself reduces the efficiency of your immune system and the ability to stave off disease.

ENVISION THE FUTURE

One of my all-time favorite books is *The War of Art: Break Through the Blocks and Win Your Inner Creative Battles* by Steven Pressfield. This book addresses the internal obstacles to success and helps to unlock the inner barriers to creativity. See if these questions describe you: Do you dream about writing the Great American Novel? Do you regret not finishing your paintings, poems, or screenplays? Want to start a business or charity? Wish you could start dieting or exercising today? Hope to run a marathon someday?

The seeing is done by our inner eye of imagination. Your imaging power lies within your own mind. It is as if you have the ability to draw plans in your mind and then, just like an architect, expand on those plans until you actually create them. The thinking/vision must be clear, and on that basis you can create what you see.

So there's great power in envisioning: There is power in our thinking big!

The brain is set up so that, when you rehearse mentally, the same neurons fire in your brain as if you were doing the exact thing physically, and yet you are sitting with your eyes closed. Athletes know this process very well. If you picture yourself performing an action in great detail the same neurons fire in your brain. So, if you see it perfectly, you are rehearsing it perfectly. This is why *mental rehearsal* is used as a tool to achieve goals. It's a powerful use of imagination!

Sages have pronounced, "What you put your attention on grows," and if you want to increase the reality of something in your life, continue to think about it. If you want to be creative and a better problem solver, then you must find out what can put you into that state to prepare you for activity.

As a humorous sidebar, when I was growing up, I used to listen on the radio to personality development guru, Earl Nightingale. He would speak about what he called "The World's Greatest Secret." It was "You become what you think about most of the time." Not surprisingly, at that time, I wondered, "If that's the case, how come I'm not a woman?"

At work, we sometimes get creative insights by getting up and away from our desks, taking a stroll, or doing some deep breathing. Meditation is another method through which we can experience the deep rest that releases creativity and imagination. Others close their eyes and get more in touch with the thinking process. For some, the creative spark comes while in the shower or during exercise. For others, it's at night, while they are in the dream state.

I have known people, who, during sleep, wake up and write ideas down. Ideas and insights often come when the mind is calm and relaxed. The challenge is to find out when you get most of your creative insights. Another challenge is to capture those insights before they slip away. I have made a tiny pad and miniature pen my constant companions.

Creativity expert, Chic Thompson, in his book, *What a Great Idea!* refers to the ideas presented by Joe McMoneagle, a consultant at the Stanford Research Institute who uses a technique called "Envision the Future."

McMoneagle asserts that there is a direct link between how we see the future and how it will in fact *be*. "Envisioning the future is a natural ability—all men and women have at least some capacity to do it." He compares this ability to playing an instrument, which some can master as a virtuoso and others can barely make squeak. "The degree of success is determined by the openness that you want to apply to the process."

In envisioning the future, McMoneagle believes that "we do in fact create our realities [through our intentions, Thompson clarifies] and the only limitations on what the future might be occurs in our own minds—*the birthplace of limitations*." Thompson says, "If so, and even if not literally so, it behooves the person envisioning the future to project a positive one and not to block the view with unnecessary assumptions." Looking ahead, or in this case *imagining ahead*, is a great method for achieving success.

After attending Thompson's seminars in creativity, new-product-development managers at Apple told him that his envision-the-future approach to idea-making had worked like a dream.

They recounted that, afterwards in their own planning meetings, they used the envision-the-future approach; they envisioned "what the industry would be like, what consumers would be demanding, what the competition would be doing." This envisioning cleared the path for them to see their role in the industry's future. They were then able to work backwards step by step to accomplish their goals.

Chic Thompson summarized, "By reframing their problem or goal, the Apple execs gained a perspective unlike any they would normally have had."

Clearly, this is a technique for business as well as for our personal lives.

171

THE JUKEBOX LESSON

During the 1980s, Doug Henning's production company was hired by Worlds of Wonder, the creator of the talking bear Teddy Ruxpin as well as Lazer Tag. The folks at WoW wanted Doug to introduce their new toy line in a magical way at the New York Toy Fair. The illusions were built, all the planning complete, and rehearsals had taken place. Then the whole team went to New York City. Upon our arrival, Doug announced, "Tomorrow morning we'll rehearse one last time." The actual show was the following day.

The crew collectively let out a big sigh. Nobody really wanted to rehearse again. Everyone wanted a day on the town to have fun—it was New York City after all. Doug, being the consummate professional, insisted, "You can never rehearse enough. We've got to rehearse on the actual venue's stage." He decided that the rehearsal would take place in the morning and then everyone could take the afternoon and evening off. Doug was the star of the show. So the rehearsal took place.

The first couple of illusions went smoothly. No hitches. The third illusion was built around the model of a large jukebox. Doug was going to produce several toys out of a jukebox that, when open, appeared to be empty. After the previous illusion, Doug segued into the jukebox illusion; then he gave the signal to the stage manager to wheel the jukebox onto the stage. As the stagehand did so, we all let out a gasp. The jukebox was too big to get through the doorway!

THE IMPORTANCE OF REHEARSAL

Worlds of Wonder was paying us as professionals. And professionals rehearse. Can you imagine if, during the actual performance, a similar glitch had occurred? In front of all the executives from Worlds of Wonder, their buyers, and the audience? It would have been a disaster! Lesson learned: You cannot perform any better than you've rehearsed.

I once read that Nancy Kerrigan, Olympic medalist in figure skating, went through a time when she had trouble with her performance. She never practiced perfectly; she would always leave out some part whenever she practiced her sequence, maybe a spin or a move. She never managed to skate through an entire program. After she began working with a new sports psychologist consultant, who helped her work through her issues of holding back, Kerrigan no longer let herself skip anything in practice and her performance improved dramatically.

As I mentioned before, we think 1,200 words a minute, a total of over a million a day. Most of these words are in our minds at a subconscious level. We consciously use 2,000 of the neurons in the brain, but we use about 4 billion subconsciously. This implies that most of our thinking, or rehearsing, is incessantly taking place at the subconscious level, without any conscious direction.

Everyone has experienced this. I drive to an important meeting and upon arriving, realize that during the drive my brain was mostly rehearsing the event ahead instead of the road ahead. How fast did I go? Did I stop at red lights?

There was little recollection of the drive. I was lost in the traffic of my mind and the car was on automatic pilot. I'm not sure that such activity is particularly good when you drive, but mental rehearsal in general is a darn good idea.

It serves us all to grab the reins and make conscious use of the constant chatter in our thinking process. I'm sure you've done this on different occasions. When I have a meeting coming up, I'll try to rehearse scenarios in my mind along these lines: "When he says this, I'll say that. Then he may get upset, so I will respond in such and such a way, et cetera, et cetera." That's rehearsal. If you rehearse it, you're more likely to have a situation unfold just as you have rehearsed it. You create a blueprint in your mind as to how that meeting should proceed.

Scientifically speaking, when you rehearse mentally like that, you still fire the same neurons in the brain as if you were actually doing the activity. This mental exercise of rehearsal strengthens connections in the brain circuitry and allows for a clear picture or an image of what we want to create; therefore, a more exact duplication becomes possible.

As I said earlier, athletes, especially elite athletes, know this technique perhaps better than any other segment of society. This is what my psychologist friend, Dr. John Anderson, tells me. He has helped many top athletes improve their performances through mental rehearsal. Their routines have been played out in their minds more than they have been played out on the actual playing field. John once told me of a boxer who was perspiring profusely during a mental-rehearsal session and actually ended up on the floor exhausted after the session.

Many baseball players visualize successful performances. Batters often mentally rehearse every pitcher they will face, reviewing how a particular pitcher threw to them in the past. And pitchers do the same with opposing batters.

Some of you may also remember the story of Colonel George Hall, an American fighter pilot, shot down in Vietnam in 1965. The flier spent seven years as a POW in a North Vietnamese prison, much of the time in solitary confinement. He kept his sanity by pacing the floor of his tiny cell and visualizing that he was playing a round of golf every day.

Before the war, Hall had been a 4-handicap golfer—meaning he shot about 76 on a 72 par golf course. During his imprisonment, he replayed every golf course he had ever seen over and over again using his visualizing capability. He used his sense of sight, sound, smell, touch, and taste in as vivid imaginary detail as he could conjure. One week after his release from prison, and back in the United States, the colonel played a round in the New Orleans Open golf tournament. He hadn't played in seven years. He shot a 76, four over par!

Quite an amazing example of how mental activity actually was enough to maintain a high level of skill without ever having to pick up a club. I heard this story in 1990 and it remains a convincing reminder of how powerful the mind actually is.

SIMONA ENVISIONED THE FUTURE

I first met Simona Baciu in 2004 at the Cluj Chamber of Commerce in Romania, where I was presenting on how to become a Professional Human Being. After my presentation, several people came up to talk with me. Simona was one of them. She introduced herself to me, and after telling me how inspired she was by my workshop, handed me some square stickers with the words "Be Happy." Then she began excitedly telling me about what inspires her—the kindergarten she had been working on for the past ten years. It was called the Happy Kids Kindergarten.

Simona's aim was to change education in her country, which had been living under a Communist regime for more than 50 years.

Her story began in 1989 after the Romanian Revolution. Simona, then a high-school technology teacher, also desired to bring happiness to children. At the time, there were no soft toys in Romania so she created a teddy-bear company, with the intention of using the money to open a kindergarten.

One year later, with her profit of 100 DEM (about $70 U.S.), she opened Happy Kids Kindergarten. She chose this name because she believed when children feel loved and secure, they are happy, they learn more, and they become productive members of society. Initially, the kindergarten was housed in one of the two bedrooms in the Baciu's apartment and became part of the family's everyday life. Simona ran the school herself; she had 12 students. As more families heard about this happy place, more students enrolled in the kindergarten. Simona hired additional staff and moved Happy Kids into a rented apartment. It was often a struggle but she kept on with the goal of creating a legitimate school with a happy learning environment.

Simona and her husband, Dr. Dan Baciu, pushed through more doors by establishing Happy Kids Foundation. Through this foundation, they were able to receive financial support from individual sponsors and institutions abroad. By 1998, they had accumulated enough money to start construction on their own building to house Happy Kids—the very first kindergarten built in Romania after the Revolution.

Their hard work continued to pay off in the next years, when they accomplished in 2000 their vision of building the Happy Kids primary school, and four years later the secondary schools.

This is when I met Simona at the Cluj Chamber of Commerce.

"Jim, I would be honored if you would come visit my school. The children have never met an American. Please come say 'hello' and say some words to them in English."

I went the next day. It was great. The kids, about 100 of them, were happy and well behaved. But the "school building" was small, just a few rooms.

While I was there, Simona declared that she had accomplished her dream of offering Romanian children the *best* school. However, she had told me before that her aim was to change the education system in Romania and, looking around, I thought she would have to push further than these modest accommodations. She must expand her vision even more. First of all, she needed a larger building: "You're dreaming too small," I told her. "Dream big!"

Simona's eyes grew large. She later explained to me that she had thought of this place already as huge. However, at the same time, she had been thinking about whether to go further or stop here. She told me that my words followed her for many days.

Fast-forward to 2010 at another of my Cluj workshops. I received an e-mail from Simona, asking me to come see her new school. So, the day after my presentation, I followed her and her son to her school. When we arrived, I saw a beautiful, expansive, five-story building. We got out of the car and I asked her, "How many rooms in this building are yours?"

She turned to me and exclaimed, "Jim, this *is* my new school!"

My jaw dropped. "Wait a minute. The *whole building*?"

She smiled, "Yes. The whole building."

I was dumbstruck by what she had been able to accomplish. The school building was modern and very impressive. She translated what the banner outside the school proclaimed: "International School of Cluj, School of the Year in Romania." I stood amazed.

She looked at me, "Do you remember telling me to dream big and daring me to do more? That's what I did!"

She showed me around the building. The classrooms were colorfully painted and well equipped with computers and modern technology. The staff of 42 included Simona and her daughter. There were about 300 students enrolled, both Romanians and students from international families. Some of the Romanian students came from disadvantaged backgrounds or were orphans, benefiting from scholarships. I was entranced by all the bright, happy faces.

I congratulated Simona on her major accomplishments—that of the building and of the award!

Simona thinks I inspired her, but as always in the end she's the one who inspires me! She's running the *school of the year* in Romania and changing education in her country. What an inspiration!

BREAK LOOSE—LOBSTER STYLE

Many people like to stay safe and secure in the confines of their assumed limitations, even though, like a lobster's shell, it can pinch and hurt and stop the growth process. Others, like Simona, are more valiant. They push against the shells of life, even if it hurts to break loose and even if they can't always quite see clearly beyond the shell.

A lobster's shell is inflexible and rigid. The lobster grows but the shell does not. Therefore, the only way for a lobster to develop is to break out of its shell. After shedding its outgrown shell the lobster waits vulnerably, unprotected, for its new, larger shell to grow. The lobster cannot attain its full growth potential without taking risks.

Do you see where I'm going with this? Are *you* prepared to shed your old, uncomfortable shell? Are you prepared to lie vulnerably waiting for your new shell to grow?

It can actually hurt to take a chance, break out, and grow. The lobster is programmed to do it. Nature has predestined this crustacean. We are not programmed that way. Human beings are given the power of choice, so we must voluntarily take a risk and even become vulnerable for a while, until we "grow another shell" and the process starts all over again. Does this sound like a process we repeat many times throughout our lives? Each time we have to choose to go beyond our boundaries, our limitations. Breaking out and taking risks are really part of life. If we didn't take the risk of saying or doing something wrong, creativity would not exist.

I agree with the Peter Drucker, who wrote, "To try to eliminate risk in business enterprise is futile … Even the attempt to minimize them … can only result in the greatest risk of all: rigidity."

THE THREE Rs: RELAX, REHEARSE, RISK

Risk-taking is the beginning of real personal growth. I had been a student financial-aid advisor at the University of Akron for just a few months when Bob Larson, my boss and mentor, asked me to speak at college nights at local high schools. Though I was just a 22-year-old rookie and a few weeks into my job, he saw some potential in me to speak in front of mature adults. I, however, did not yet see this potential and, though it boosted my ego, I was very nervous.

I now had to go out to speak to adults—to parents! I had to prepare a presentation on financial aid and admissions. So, before providing my guidance, I went over to the admissions office to get some guidance myself. I spoke with my boss and several staff members. I became thoroughly educated about financial aid and the admissions process.

The first college night was held at a high-school gym. I opened the door, saw what seemed like five-hundred people in the bleachers—it might have been one-hundred—waiting for me. I spooked, shut the door, and hightailed it back to my car. I was shaking in my boots. I thought to myself, *These are adults, and I'm a kid. What are they going to learn from me?*

I had to pull myself together. I psyched myself up by thinking of the first varsity football game I played in. Lined up on the field with my teammates, I was tense and felt weak. The referee blew his whistle, the football was kicked, and then my butterflies flew away. Somewhat fortified by this memory, I became more relaxed; I headed back, walked through the gym door as confidently as I could act, and kicked off my speaking. My knees were still shaking and I was perspiring as if I had been playing that football game, but I kept going.

After my twenty-minute spiel, it was time to take questions. I quickly realized that I—the kid—knew more than these adults did about this one subject: financial aid. I became more comfortable and confident standing in front of them.

My comfort and confidence built with each and every stint. I became less stressed, and soon I began enjoying those Wednesday college nights. I didn't know it at the time, but this was the launch of my public-speaking career. Mr. Larson had noticed that I had the potential to be a good speaker, and this led me to see my own potential as well.

Those first presentations I gave were my breaking out of my small lobster shell. I continued to grow as I was asked to speak to larger audiences. Little did I know then that one day I would be invited to give a keynote speech. Giving my first keynote address, like the lobster, I was required to break through my next career shell.

I had to really step up as a speaker. And I was apprehensive.

Early on, I started to prepare for my speaking appearances by utilizing three techniques: relaxing, rehearsing, and risk-taking. I continued to use this same approach many years later when I prepared myself for that first keynote address.

The setting was an international conference in Heidelberg, Germany. I remember getting myself in a relaxed mood and letting the ideas flow for the content of my presentation, and then rehearsing, rehearsing, and rehearsing. I envisioned how I would interact with the audience and how the audience would react to me. Perhaps learning from Doug Henning's jukebox experience, I even went into the meeting hall before the session; I envisioned entering the room, standing in the front, walking up the aisle toward the back of the hall a few times, how I would get my subjects for the muscle test, and how the subjects would access the stage. I warmed up the room with my thoughts long before the session ever opened. Which I still do today!

My presentation was a great success, if I may say so myself! That one talk earned me repeat invitations back to Germany, and it advanced my career to the next level of success. Since that time, I've done scores of keynotes.

Even though you may have some jitters throughout, I find that it is important to find a way to relax yourself so the creative juices flow, and then rehearse thoroughly before you take the risk. Rehearsal prepares you for the boldness necessary to take the risk. Practice yields confidence. Not engaging in mental rehearsal is the equivalent, in athletic terms, of not having a pre-game warm-up. You must warm up your mind like a baseball pitcher warms up his arm, or like a musician warms up with an instrument before a performance. Mental acuity is not sharp without physical and mental exercise. You have to exercise the mind, and you also must exercise the body.

Personally, I have found that both mental and physical exercise give me a sense of self-esteem, strength, and a boldness to do things I may not feel capable of doing. I'll be talking more about physical conditioning later on, because this too is part of overall excellence and mustering the stamina and energy to becoming a PhB.

Mind/Body Connection

We think of risks in terms of having a negative effect on health. Perhaps we can't make a blanket statement.

- A survey of British psychologists during the height of World War II, when the German Luftwaffe was bombing England, concluded that people with mental disturbances actually showed remarkable improvement as a result of involvement in dangerous tasks of firefighting and rescue.

- Experts believed that the heart-attack rate during the war would increase because of physiological stress. A study in France showed

---

that the rate actually decreased.

- Studies have linked cases of spontaneous remission from cancer to instances where patients started activities totally foreign to their temperament that involved physical risk such as skydiving, scuba diving, and mountaineering. An active immune system is essential in rejecting cancer and infections and it can be stimulated in this way, (say researchers) by risky, exhilarating behavior.

I once read a pretty startling statistic: more than 75 percent of the population have a fear of public speaking. It is the leading fear. Number six on the list was dying. Doesn't it seem strange that more people would rather be dead than speak in public? They would rather be lying in the coffin than delivering the eulogy!

If you have a fear of speaking, join Toastmasters! There is sure to be a local chapter in your area. This may be the single-most important recommend-dation I give you in this book. I have donated my time, and given talks, on many occasions for this great organization that has chapters all over the world. I've recommended Toastmasters to many clients. Some organizations I've worked with have even established their own Toastmasters clubs, such as the Babbling Brook Club at the Honolulu Board of Water Supply.

Toastmasters is one of the best leadership programs in the world. It allows you to practice three main elements in this PhB lesson: relax, rehearse, and risk——the three Rs. People in business and in many other fields need to be creative enough to craft their own speeches, be bold enough to stand up and speak, and need to be open enough to take the risk of receiving feedback. These are essential skills for a leader, and Toastmasters is a superb organization for honing them. You can't beat the value—membership is about a hundred dollars a year.

"It is a liability not to be a good public speaker," said Warren Buffett, who took the Dale Carnegie Public Speaking Course in 1951 and credits his launch into the business world after having improved his skills as a speaker.

PhBs are possibility thinkers. They influence their success, happiness, and even their health profoundly by rehearsing mentally. They prepare to take risks through rehearsal and then complete the task by following through. All three elements—relaxing, rehearsing, and risking—contribute to successful careers and longevity.

Mind/Body Connection

To make full use of your mental potential, you must first take into account your physiologic responses. A constant stress mode causes interference with much of the operation of the higher brain (cerebral cortex) where the impulses of creativity originate. Blood is routed away to the skeletal muscles and extremities, inhibiting verbal and problem-solving activity as well as creativity. A calm-state physiology enhances blood flow to the higher brain and generates brain-wave synchrony that translates into more creative thinking.

DOUG TAKES A RISK

In 1975, Doug Henning's magic career was about to take off. The NBC television network needed higher ratings. Doug needed a television show. He had done tours, Broadway, and off-Broadway shows, but hadn't yet broken through into television. Now, he and his team were given the opportunity to present a proposal to NBC. Doug offered some pretty amazing illusions to them, such as walking through a wall, levitating a woman, and transforming himself into a shark.

After his pitch, one NBC executive said, "All of those illusions sound good but to me I think any magician could do them! Can you tell me something you can do that no other magician can do?"

Doug was stunned and momentarily silent. He looked out the window, paused, and then looked the executive right in the eye and stated, "I'll do Houdini's Water-Torture Escape. No one has done that since Houdini's death."

Doug was, of course, referring to Harry Houdini, perhaps the greatest magician and "escapologist" of all time, who passed away in 1926.

The NBC exec asked, "How does that work? What do you do?"

"Well, they handcuff me," Doug began. "They hang me by my ankles upside down in stocks and put me in a tank with 200 gallons of water. From this, I have to escape within a few minutes."

The NBC guy asked, "Is that life threatening?"

"What do you think? Of course!" Doug exclaimed.

The NBC execs liked the real danger element. "Okay, if you do all the other illusions plus this one, we've got a deal."

After the meeting, everyone walked out and got on the elevator. As soon as the door closed, one of Doug's team members spoke up. "I didn't know you knew how to do Houdini's water-torture escape."

"I don't." Doug stated.

Everyone was shocked.

"But we have six months to figure it out," he added.

Talk about a risk. This was the biggest risk of his career. Even though it was an illusion, Doug still had to learn how to hold his breath hanging upside down under water for at least two minutes. It's no easy feat, I can assure you. To make a long story short, the TV special was a grand success, and Doug pulled off the illusion superbly. It certainly created a big ripple of wonderment and surprise in the audience. They saw him hanging upside down in the tank full of water. A screen dropped over the tank. About two minutes later Doug had miraculously escaped, standing outside the tank in a hooded costume, axe in hand, ready to smash the tank of water in which he was last seen immersed. Doug's big risk launched a television career and a widely watched special every year after that for the next seven years.

BODY FOLLOWS MIND

Body follows mind is the essence of this lesson. To experience this on a physical level, here is an exercise that I use in my Professional Human Being workshops. People often have an "aha" experience.

Have a friend read the following aloud as you perform the actions. Don't start this exercise unless you have someone else read it to you. Resist the temptation to read it and wait for the experience.

Body-Follows-Mind Exercise

Stand a few feet in front of a wall, facing the wall. Stand with your feet flat on the floor and about shoulder-width apart. Make sure your feet are planted like roots growing into the floor. Raise your right arm and point with your index finger to the wall in front of you. Next, with your arm acting as a compass, slowly turn your body clockwise so your arm begins to move to your right. Twist your body as far as it will go, without moving your feet. Your finger will now be pointing to the opposite wall. When you can go no further, mark that spot mentally on the wall.

Now return to the starting position, put your arm down and rest. Close your eyes. With your mind's eye, I want you to see the spot on the wall that you were capable of going to. Now visualize a spot one-foot beyond that spot you were capable of reaching on your first try. Now open your eyes, raise your right arm, point your index finger to the wall in front of you as you did before and slowly turn to your right again without moving your feet. Keep them firmly planted as before. Go to your new spot.

What people usually experience is that they go a good foot or more past their original spot. I call this the chiropractic move because the body is not always ready to turn that far.

The lesson: The body follows the mind. If you can see it, you can achieve it. If you can't see it, you probably won't achieve it. So, when you say, "I can't see myself doing it," all the cells of your body are eavesdropping on that language and restrict themselves to exactly what you tell them. Body follows mind.

The two-time, Olympic pole-vault gold-medalist, Bob Richards, really knew what he was talking about when he said, "Ingenuity, plus courage, plus work, equals miracles."

That's what this lesson is all about: ingenuity, which is calm-inspired creativity, the courage to take risks, and hard work through practice. The result: You can soar higher than anybody, like Bob Richards did.

Rehearsing is the hard part. You noticed from this last exercise that when you mentally rehearse, the body follows the mind. There is a relationship between the mind and body that is played out time and time again. In each lesson, we've seen that all states of mind reproduce themselves in the physical.

Finally, I've learned from life that in order to be idea-prone and idea-filled I have to be a learner. I read or listen to, on average, a book a week. I know that learning affects the brain as well as the body. Not only does it provide us with resources to solve problems and to plan and make decisions, but it also has an influence on our whole system.

Mind/Body Connection

A January 1993, *USA Today* article titled: "Brain Power: A case of 'use it or lose it,'" by Marilyn Elias, suggests that the brain is changed by education and a stimulating adult life. It's like a mental muscle that flexes better with workouts. This physical change promotes an even greater capacity to learn, while those who lead mentally inactive lives, show signs of ever decreasing ability, scientists say. It's definitely a case of *use it or lose it!* "You have to stay mentally active to keep that anatomical edge you get from a college education," says Bob Jacobs of the UCLA School of Medicine who measured the length of dendrites in the brains of 20 deceased adults. Dendrites are root-like parts of neurons that bring information to brain cells and promote sophisticated processing. The longer the dendrites, the more information the brain is believed capable of receiving and understanding. Dendrite lengths varied up to 40 percent. Longest: college-educated people who were mentally active all their lives at home and at work. Shortest: high-school dropouts, who were mentally unchallenged on and off the job. In between: college-educated who led mentally inactive lives and less-educated who pursued more challenges. Overall, the dendrites shrank with age, but a vigorous mental life minimized the decrease.

In summary, I believe that we act on what we think about. Our tools of creation are thoughts, words, and actions. All of our states of mind reproduce themselves in the physical, first by creating molecules that can either be disease- or health-producing.

Thought Provokers

- *Life begins at the end of your comfort zone.*
  – Neale Donald Walsch, author of *Conversations with God*

- *Opportunity dances with those already on the dance floor.*
  – H. Jackson Brown, Jr., author of *Life's Little Instruction Book.*

- The more you think about something, the more you attract it into your life.

- *Progress always involves risk; you can't steal second base and keep your foot on first.*
  – Frederick Wilcox, English football player

- *A man carries his success or failure with him: it is not dependent on outside conditions.*
  – Ralph Waldo Trine, author of *In Tune With the Infinite*

Action Ideas

- Read three good, recommended books on any topic. You will know more about that topic than most of the population; you'll become part of the creative minority. The less you know about any given topic, the more fearful you are of taking the risk of stepping into your discomfort zone.

- Memorize poems, jokes, or quotes. The exercise of remembering them does your brain good. Researchers have found that memory loss is reversible. A group of older study participants significantly increased their recall after training and practice. You can also play word games. We can warm up our brains just as if we were a pitcher warming up his arm or a musician warming up before a gig.

- Eat foods containing choline, which boosts the brain's energy and memory functions. Such foods are soy, egg yolks, or a choline supplement.

- Watch the movie *Stand and Deliver,* starring Edward James Olmos. It is the true story of *the power of expectation.* Very inspiring. This film is a must-see for all teachers, coaches, parents, and managers.

- Read *Building Your Field of Dreams* by Mary Manin Morrissey. In it she suggests you ask yourself five questions to determine if your dream—your goal—is big enough: Does this dream enliven me? Does this dream align with my core values? Do I need help from a higher source to make this dream come true? Will this dream require me to grow into more of my true self? Will this dream ultimately bless others?

Spotlight
PETRUTZ CONQUERS HIS FEARS

Meet my Romanian friend, Petrutz Pacuraru. Petru is based in Bucharest and is my agent for Eastern Europe. I've known Petru for ten years now. I was one of the best men in his wedding, in which I was honored with the title of Godfather. Petru is a powerfully built, large-framed athlete, who is deathly afraid of heights and public speaking. When he first introduced me at programs, he was so nervous I could barely hear this bear of a man; his head was lowered as he read from his notes, rarely looking up at the audience.

Petru has taken several steps to face his fear of public speaking. He earned an advanced degree in project management, where he was required to do a lot of speaking in front of groups; and he took part in Aspen Institute leadership programs, where he had to give many formal presentations. The change I've witnessed in Petru is remarkable. Now, when he introduces me, he looks out into the audience and speaks freely without notes. Just recently, his text to me read: "Wish me luck. I am going on a television program to talk about leadership and our workshops in Romania."

In addition, he faced his fear of heights, a fear that began in childhood. Petru couldn't even stand near a window at elevations higher than the first floor. Some time ago, I asked him when he was going to come visit me in the United States. He, of course, doesn't fly. He sent a message that read, "I will fix the problem." One month later I received an e-mail from him with a video of two single-engine planes in flight. One plane was video taping the other plane—which was being flown by Petru! What an accomplishment.

However, this wasn't without struggle; Petru told me later that it was a horrible experience. "In the beginning, it was the worst ten minutes of my life. I had the huge fear of death and felt the imminence of being crushed!"

My courageous friend discovered that it is amazing to face your fear and prove to yourself that you can beat your fearful side. "It is like a drug, and I have done it with most of the things that had a fearful impact on me. I have won this battle."

Congratulations to my godson, Petrutz. He is so proud of his enormous feat and deserves to be.

13

Lesson 5: Stand Up for What You Value Most

I so desire to conduct the affairs of this administration that, if at the end,
when I come to lay down the reins of power, I have lost every other friend on earth,
I shall have at least one friend left, and that friend shall be down inside of me.

— ABRAHAM LINCOLN
16th U.S. President

We were at the Ed Sullivan Theater in New York City and Doug Henning was in the middle of performing. His six months of planning and 16 hours of taping before a live audience would be condensed into a one-hour TV special, the last of his series of eight for NBC.

After six intense hours of the first day of filming, Doug was completely exhausted. He needed rest, and he decided he wanted to take a break to meditate. I cautioned him that his decision could be a problem because so many people worked with us on the production, and I reminded him that every moment of the day was costing him money.

"I need to do it, Jim," he said. "I'm no good like this. You know how much better I'll perform with a couple hours of meditation and rest. If I do it, I know the remainder of the filming will be super and I want to be at my best for my audience."

As a meditator myself, I understood perfectly what he meant, and I went immediately to the producer who oversaw production costs. He became quite stressed at the prospect of shutting down the operation and idling over a hundred workers. A couple of finance guys came over and ran

189

some numbers and came up with $25,000. I was shocked! It would personally cost Doug that much for his break!

I hated having to take that bad news to Doug.

His eyes grew wide when I told him the figure. He paused for just a few moments to weigh the costs. He took a breath and agreed that he would be happy to pay that amount. The cost on himself would be greater without the rest.

To Doug, nothing was worth missing his meditation because he felt that it was the basis of his success. The finance guy was totally astounded.

A little while later, the producer came running up and excitedly knocked on the dressing room door. "I have to tell you—something miraculous just happened! When we told everyone you needed to rest and meditate and it would take about two hours, and you had agreed to pay them for the break out of your own pocket, they had a meeting and decided to take a two-hour break also. Without pay! Can you believe it? They said they don't know what this TM thing is, but since Doug is that committed to it, they will take a break without pay. They think that if the meditation and rest are so important for you that you are willing to pay them for it, they are willing to support you."

When Doug valued something, he did not compromise. And people respected him for it.

It's been more than twenty years since then and I'll never forget Doug's decision. I learned how important it is to stand for what you value—and Doug highly valued his performance and his meditation time. He valued keeping his mind/body battery charged.

Don't compromise your values, even if it costs you money.

WHAT DO YOU VALUE?

Those elements of life we value most become our values. What we cherish determines what we think is right or wrong, and what we do or don't do. Values serve as standards for personal behavior and examples for those whom we lead. They represent our personal bottom line. Deciding what we stand for and not compromising these values enables us to become the person we want to be. This means holding oneself accountable. Therefore, it doesn't matter who knows your values; what matters is that *you* know them and you refuse to compromise them. And when you do, it creates unstoppable self-esteem and character. It forms your solid core. Decide what your core is and stick with it.

There is a scene in the movie *City Slickers* that depicts the essence of this lesson perfectly. In it, Mitch (played by Billy Crystal) and his friend Ed (played by Bruno Kirby) are having a conversation in the middle of a cattle drive. A woman—the only woman in the cattle drive—rides by on a horse and Ed makes a sexual remark that triggers a conversation on sex.

Ed poses the question to Mitch, "What if you could have sex with someone very attractive and your wife never found out?"

Mitch pauses. "It's a big trap."

Ed continues, "Look, let's say a spaceship lands and the most beautiful woman in the universe gets out and all she wants is to have sex with you, and the second it's over, she will fly away for eternity; no one will ever know. Are you telling me you wouldn't do it?"

Mitch answers—and here's the big point: "No, it wouldn't make it all right if my wife or anyone else didn't know. *I would know it and I wouldn't like myself.*"

Remember your PhB Law 2: *The most important relationship is the one you have with yourself.*

"Actualizing the self," as Abraham Maslow puts it, is a process which infuses self-esteem with indestructibility. And self-esteem, the unconditional acceptance in liking or loving oneself, is fundamental to good health. In short, compromising our values compromises our love of self. Low self-esteem can cause psychological and immune-system depression, as well as diseased arteries. Thus, by compromising what you believe in, you make yourself sick. It's self-sabotage and creates disease in our own bodies. Moreover, psychologists say if you do not like yourself you cannot like anyone.

Mitch's answer is a mind/body winner.

If you say you value your family most but always work on weekends, it is not just your family that suffers. In compromising your values you are also undermining yourself. If you say you value honesty over everything, yet you lie about practicing what you value—you won't like yourself.

Identifying your values and not compromising them brings unstoppable self-esteem. This is a solid foundation—the core criterion—for good mental and physical health. What you will glean from this lesson is that when you compromise what you believe in you will not like yourself. You will begin to turn against yourself and the immune system will begin to sputter, making you vulnerable to things you are much better off without.

> **Mind/Body Connection**
>
> The chronic feeling that it is impossible to improve a situation or to feel better about yourself reduces the efficiency of your immune system and the ability to stave off disease.

STAND UP FOR VALUES

There are a lot of companies built on the idea of socially responsible investing, where both the company and the greater good benefit.

Patricia Aburdene, author and speaker on predictions of how values and consciousness transform business, indicates in her book, *Megatrends 2010*, a trend toward socially responsible investments. The following corporate story exemplifies a socially responsible company.

Former chairperson of Johnson & Johnson, Robert Wood Johnson, in 1943 penned the credo which the company still uses to guide them. The credo emphasizes the responsibilities the company feels towards various groups: healthcare workers, and patients, their employees, the community, and the stockholders. But do they live their credo?

The Harvard Business School used an entire case study to demonstrate how J&J translated this credo into action. They didn't compromise what they valued most. Their credo was the blueprint for their response to the tragedy that occurred in 1982.

Seven people died in the Chicago area after taking J&J's Extra Strength Tylenol. The product had been tampered with and was found to be laced with cyanide poison. J&J took swift action by immediately removing all Tylenol capsules from stores throughout the entire U.S.—the first-ever recall—at a loss of over $100 million. The company absorbed the entire cost. This was done even though the deaths had occurred only in the Chicago area. Furthermore, J&J launched a 2,500-person team to alert the public.

Soon afterwards, the company came out with Tylenol Gelcaps, the first inherently tamper-proof capsule, and recaptured the 92 percent of capsule-segment sales lost to product tampering. Implementing their credo was critical in saving Tylenol. And by remaining true to their values J&J may have also ensured the future of the entire company.

J&J's reaction had been guided by the company's credo. The Washington Post wrote, "J&J has succeeded in portraying itself to the public as a company willing to do what's right, regardless of cost." But the reality is that what at first seemed a costly defense of its values turned out in the end to be a wise investment in the future of the company. Altruism can be the healthiest form of self-interest.

WHAT'S YOUR CREDO?

Doug Henning put his money where his mouth was by making meditation his highest priority. Mitch, from City Slickers, made his own integrity his highest value. And the J&J credo set the company's compass. What do you value? What is most important to you? What do you stand for? Do you have a credo?

A credo can be your guiding force. To help you get closer to clarifying and building your credo, consider and select the values of greatest importance to you from the Values Chart below. Then prioritize them. You'll begin to see your primary focus.

Adventure	Fame	Loyalty	Security
Appreciation	Family time	People	Service
Challenge	Fun/Humor	Personal development	Solitude
Charity	Friendliness	Physical appearance	Spirituality
Cleanliness	Integrity	Independence	Productivity
Competition/ Winning	Power/ Influence	Structure/ Orderliness	Purpose
Creativity	Inner harmony	Honesty	Travel
Education	Respect	Recognition	Wealth
Enlightenment	Simplicity	Health	Wisdom
Faith/Religion	Love	Satisfying job	World peace

SAMUEL STONE'S CREDO

You might not know your credo and you might not know others' credos, but you can figure them out from what they do.

Since I'm from Canton, two of my friends, Margie Diaz Kintz (a fellow Cantonian you met before) and Brad Fregger, recently sent me articles about a legendary Cantonian. Normally, what I hear about my hometown relates to the Pro Football Hall of Fame, which is located there. However, the article my friends sent me was about the celebration of a local man named B. Virdot.

The celebration brought 400 residents together to talk about a Mr. "B Virdot," who 75 years ago wrote an ad in the Canton Repository, Canton's newspaper, during the holidays offering help for families in need. This was right smack in the middle of the Depression and families were definitely in need. Mr. B. Virdot offered modest cash gifts if the family would do one thing: write a letter describing the challenges they were having and how they would spend the gift of money. He promised not to divulge the letter-writers' names. Hundreds of residents of Canton received checks of $5 and $10 that Christmas.

How was this legend uncovered? Journalist Ted Gup received an old suitcase from his 80-year-old mother. The suitcase had belonged to Ted's grandfather, Samuel J. Stone. When Ted opened the suitcase, which had been stored for some time, he found that it contained hundreds of letters and cancelled checks. It turns out that B. Virdot was really Samuel J. Stone. Mr. Stone had opened a special account under the name of B. Virdot. He had sent the gifts out from that account, maintaining his anonymity so that no family would feel shame in asking for help. Samuel Stone was Jewish and came from Romania, where he had struggled with poverty and persecution. After coming to the U.S., he opened a chain of clothing stores and became a successful businessman.

Time to go back to the celebration. The 400 people who attended were relatives of those who had received the checks along with the only remaining direct recipient, 90-year-old Helen Palm. Not surprisingly, everyone spoke glowingly of Samuel Stone and his generosity. And the hope that he generated in the community at a time in 1933 when it seemed that there was little hope. Mr. Stone created such warmth, gratitude, happiness, and hope without anyone even knowing who had created it.

You can read many heartwarming stories about Samuel Stone in Ted Gup's book, *A Secret Gift*. The book includes interviews with over 500 family members of the many recipients of generous gifts from "B. Virdot."

Coincidentally, I have a friend back home in Canton, who is the modern-day version of Mr. B. Virdot. My friend—who I will also call Mr. B.—has been an anonymous donor to many people, foundations, and causes for many years and remains unknown to many of the recipients. He spreads great progress and fulfillment in the community like Mr. Stone.

Though wealthy, he continued to work for many years; I once asked him why and his response was, "I make money so that I can give it away!" And give it away he did! When he sold his company, Mr. B. unlike many owners, gave every employee a generous bonus. Even I got a generous check and I was not a full-time employee, but I had served as a consultant to his company for many years.

I am honored to hear about Mr. Stone and to count Mr. B as one of my dear friends.

I have gained many lessons about values from these two gentlemen but I will share the most important lesson: our relationship with ourselves is indeed the most important one we have. Only the men themselves knew of their actions. They felt good about themselves and their contributions without anyone else's knowledge. No one had to know.

Mr. Stone's generosity was an outstanding value that he lived. We may never know the exact reasons why he did what he did, but we can deduce which values he held dear. Look back at the Values Chart above and decide for yourself which values guided his actions.

THE ALL-ENCOMPASSING VALUE: THE ALOHA SPIRIT

Have you been to Hawaii? It is heaven on earth! Not just visually but also in its essence. Aloha is its essence. Aloha is what makes the destination of Hawaii unique.

In the Aloha state, Aloha spirit is almost a state law. Law may sound harsh; strong guideline would be closer to the truth. Native Hawaiians will tell you that "Aloha" means "love, respect, hello, goodbye, affection, kindness, mercy, spirit, sending and receiving positive energy, and living in harmony"—so many positive values!

"Aloha" reminds me of the Indian greeting, "Namaste," which means "I honor the *God* that is *within you.*" Similarly, "Aloha" is made up of "alo" (meaning "in the presence of") and "ha" (meaning "divine breath"). This Hawaiian greeting reminds us that we are *in the presence* of the *Divine*. Do you see why Hawaii is *heaven* on *earth?*

Once, after I presented my Professional Human Being workshop, a gentleman of Native Hawaiian descent came up to me and handed me a card. I was so impressed with it that I'd like to share it with you. One side described the Aloha spirit at work and the other, the absence of that spirit. It shows a clear sequence of thinking being the basis of action, action being the basis of habit, habit the basis of values, values the basis of character, and finally, character the basis of destiny.

Notice what a clearly laid-out demonstration of how a lack of value-based action could cause unhappiness in one's life and, in this case, unhappiness in Hawaii's workplace! This gentleman chose to take on the mission of reminding people of the consequences of living or not living Aloha.

ALOHA
The Aloha Spirit at Work

Seed Planted	Fruits of Seed	Harvest
Forgiveness	Unity	Joy
Patience	Order	Security
Respect	Admiration	Friendship
Honesty	Trust	Confidence
Responsibility	Maturity	Self-Control
Commitment	Perseverance	Strength
Discipline	Character	Success

As I read the card, I am reminded of Mahatma Gandhi's teaching:

Keep your thoughts positive because your thoughts become your words.
Keep your words positive because your words become your behaviors.
Keep your behaviors positive because your behaviors become your habits.
Keep your habits positive because your habits become your values.
Keep your values positive because your values become your destiny.

Becoming a Professional Human Being

On the back of the card was a description of the destiny that could be created by the absence of value-based action.

MISERY		
Where is Aloha?		
Seed Planted	*Fruits of Seed*	*Harvest*
Unforgiving	Disunity	Bitterness
Impatience	Disorder	Confusion
Dishonor	Rejection	Anger
Disrespect	Enemies	Loneliness
Lies/Deceit	Distrust	Suspicion
Irresponsible	Immaturity	Recklessness
Uncommitted	Insecurity	Weak

I am reminded to live with the Aloha spirit outside of the state of Hawaii. Spreading Aloha in our environment is spreading value-based living, or what Patricia Aburdene describes as "social responsibility."

This is a clear description of how values not only influence our lives but ultimately create our lives.

HOW VALUES ARE LIVED IN HAWAII

My work takes me all over the world and I feel privileged to work with so many different peoples and cultures.

During a workshop at the Pacific Leadership Academy in Honolulu one Friday afternoon, I was unconsciously rubbing the side of my jaw.

Someone asked, "Jim, do you have a problem with your jaw?"

I apologized and said, "Yes, I do. Tomorrow I'm going to get a root canal!" Another participant wanted to know why I didn't take a pain medication, and I admitted, "I would not be able to speak to you coherently. I'm very sensitive to any medication and usually get drowsy, especially from painkillers, so I'm going to have to endure this for the rest of the day."

198

My tooth had started hurting the previous day. I called my dentist, Dr. Richard Hlista, back in Austin, whom I'd seen earlier about the tooth. Dr. Hlista confirmed that I was going to need that root canal sooner than we thought.

"Where are you?" he asked me.

"Honolulu," I said.

He was silent for a while, then continued, "Okay. I've got a buddy near there in Aiea. He's a root-canal specialist. We served in the military together as dentists and became good friends. I'll give him a call."

What luck that Dr. Hlista had a dentist friend in Aiea, the only city in the United States spelled with all vowels—it is a very small town close to Honolulu. Dr. Hlista called back and gave me his friend's name—Dr. Glen Biven, who was still working full time at the age of 72. I called Dr. Biven and set up an appointment. He worked around my schedule and agreed to see me on his day off, Saturday. That's where the Aloha began! Dr. Biven was a very nice man, a great dentist, and he did a fantastic job. He gave me another good dose of Aloha with his kind smile, his calming approach, and his military stories during his time with Dr. Hlista.

That night, Saturday night, I was spending a quiet evening in my hotel room, lying in bed, watching a movie, recovering from the root canal. I was nearly pain free but now kind of stoned from the painkiller. Suddenly I heard a knock on my door. It was unexpected because I had the "Do Not Disturb" sign hung outside. I wondered who was knocking on my door at this time on a Saturday night. Through the peephole I saw room service standing there with a cart of food. I opened the door.

"Sir, I have your meal!"

I was confused. "My meal? But I didn't order one. In fact, I can't chew a thing because I just got a root canal."

The waiter insisted, "Well, you ordered this meal."

"I'm sorry, I did not order this meal."

He asked to use the room phone. When he got off he said, "Oh, it's a gift."

A gift?

He took the lid off and I was greeted by the aroma of spices. My mouth began to water. I looked at the soft tofu and tender vegetables in the soup and thought, *Wow, what a treat! I can actually eat this!*

The waiter said it was an anonymous gift.

My immediate thought was that it was from someone in my Friday class since only they knew about my tooth. I ran through the list of attendees in my head and immediately knew it was Jan Kemp, whom I'd known for a long time. I called her cell phone and left a message, "Did you by any chance just order my dinner?" She returned my call on Monday. Yes, she was my benefactor. Both Dr. Biven and Jan Kemp demonstrated the Aloha spirit.

What can we learn from Jan Kemp? She showed me that you don't need a big, demonstrative, festive approach to make a difference in people's lives. It's living values and treating people with value-based action that creates Aloha. It's the little things that make a big difference—as little as miso soup.

DO YOUR ASSOCIATES LOVE YOU AT WORK?

Let me tell you about Jan Kemp and her family. Jan was the Deputy Director for the State of Hawaii's Department of Human Resources Development when I met her, and now she is the Chief Human Resources Officer at Honolulu Board of Water Supply. Her husband Garry is a successful and well-liked manager in the Attorney General's office. They are both very proud of their daughter Kanani. Jan is truly one of the most extraordinary women I've met.

People often ask me who the best leaders are in Hawaii, since I have coached many of them, and I always include Jan in the top five. She is a lawyer, highly intelligent, completely competent, an extremely caring manager, and one of the most humble people I've met. Once, while consulting with the Department of Human Resources Development, I administered a feedback survey allowing Jan's direct reports to anonymously evaluate her as a manager and Jan's results were fantastic. Jan's associates love her.

This reminds me of the movie, *A Knight's Tale*. In it a peasant squire, William, played by Heath Ledger, masquerades as a knight so he could joust with other knights as it was illegal for peasants to joust. He was an excellent jouster and won several tournaments. He once competed against a knight to whom he dealt a crippling blow, but agreed to a draw rather than finish him off and dishonor him. No one knew that this man, whom he could have defeated, was really the Prince of Wales in disguise. Fast-forward to the end of the movie. Found out to be a mere peasant, William was imprisoned in stocks and was being ridiculed by a mob. Out from the mob appears the Prince of Wales. He silences the crowd and says to William, "Your men love you! If I knew nothing else about you, that would be enough. Let me repay the kindness you once showed me." He then draws his sword and knights William, proclaiming him Sir William.

William dramatizes the truth of true-life stories that show us how competent and caring leaders like Jan through her selfless service and devotion to others creates love and loyalty in the hearts of those she serves. If I knew nothing else about Jan Kemp except how much her people love and appreciate her as a person and a manager that would be enough for me to award her a PhB.

HOW VALUES ARE LIVED IN INDIA

I mentioned the use of the Hindu greeting, "*Namaste*." This represents one of the cultural values that exist in India, just as Aloha exists in Hawaii. *Namaste*, as I explained before, means honoring that which is God within you. This greeting reminds Indians of one of their ultimate values as participants in one of the world's oldest cultures: honor others as divine beings. Indians put their hands together as if in a prayer position in honor of the person they are greeting. How does this respect and honor translate into action in everyday Indian life?

I've experienced these values personally. For 40 years, I have worked with my friend Guptaji, who's from Haridwar, India. His real name is Ghanshyam Das Gupta but I call him Guptaji as a sign of respect. I consider him one of my best friends along with his wife Prem, his son Vipul, and daughter Nidhi. As early as the late 1970s, I would fly to India for business or meditation courses, and he and his wife would unfailingly make an incredible five- to six-hour trip from their home in Haridwar to the airport in Delhi to meet and greet me. At first they traveled by, believe it or not, scooter, and later they came by car.

Each time, they would meet me in the wee hours of the morning and Prem would be carrying a stainless-steel canister in hand with a freshly cooked meal inside. They would accompany me to the hotel, talk to me while I ate, and in some cases turn right around and head back to Haridwar. Talk about a tradition of respect and honor—I couldn't ask for better friendship!

On one occasion while preparing to travel to India on business, I decided that I would not let the Guptas know when I was coming because I didn't want to put them out yet again; I would instead call them after my arrival. I was heading for Delhi to work on a project with my employer, who was at that time Doug Henning. I didn't even tell Doug my exact arrival time.

I arrived in Delhi at 3:30 a.m., extremely exhausted and stumbled half-asleep through the airport. I approached the arrivals hall and headed to the baggage carousel. I suddenly heard someone calling out, "Jimmy!" I looked up and there they were! The Guptas! Prem donned in her sari and carrying her stainless-steel food canister and Guptaji with an incredulous look on his face. I blurted out, "How in the world did you find out I was coming and what flight I was on?"

Guptaji exclaimed, "I was irritated and angry until just this moment when we saw you!" He went on to describe the previous night: "Prem woke me from a deep sleep and announced, 'Jimmy's coming.' How do you know that? 'I just know,' she said. I told her to go back to sleep. He would have called us; he's not coming! She insisted, 'No, I'm going to cook.' So she cooked and the rest, as they say, is history. I didn't really believe her. But I should because she does this a lot. She will warn me not to do business with this or that person or something's wrong. If I don't listen, there is always a problem, just as she predicts. It's about time I started listening, Jimmy! She has great intuition. Obviously! You are here!"

This is a taste of the magic of India!

Six months later on another trip to India, I visited the Guptas' home. To accommodate me, they moved out of their main bedroom and into a small room, giving me their room. I protested, "No, no, no, this is not good! I can't do that!"

They responded, "You must. It would be an insult not to stay in our room."

There I was in their room and they were crammed into the small room. Talk about feeling awkward. The next morning, I expressed that I felt uncomfortable and that I would feel better if they moved back into their room.

They explained, "In India, we treat our guests, our parents, and our teachers like God. If you don't let us do that, we would not be following our Hindu tradition. We would not be happy."

The Guptas are great examples of respect, love, friendship, honor, and cultural integrity. They have taught me how to live according to these values. Their hospitality towards me continued even after they moved to the United States. They now own two restaurants in a small town in Iowa, and do you think they ever allow me to pay for my meals when I'm in town? No such luck! They treat me as a family member.

I think we in the United States could learn these value lessons when it comes to our guests, our elders, and our teachers. The essence of Namaste has flowed into how the Guptas raised their children, who continue to carry on strong values. I like this Indian proverb: "The world is my family." And my Indian friends demonstrate how to create that reality. The Guptas and I are lifetime friends.

IT IS OUR DUTY

In the late 1990s, I was working in Jeddah, Saudi Arabia, an ancient coastal city on the Red Sea, known as the gateway to Mecca. I had been hired by the Presidency of Civil Aviation/Airways Engineering to conduct a five-day leadership course for branch managers who ran the airports. Every evening, I combined my daily walk with exploring the sights and sounds of this ancient place. On the fourth evening I went too far. The sun was setting and I suddenly realized I was lost!

I began looking for a taxi but none was around. I was deliberating what to do when a car stopped. The Saudi driver rolled down his window and asked in English if I was lost.

I hesitantly admitted, "Yes, I am."

"Where are you going?"

"The Sheraton Jeddah."

"Please get in," he instructed; "I'll take you."

I hesitated. I was in a foreign country, I was completely lost, and I didn't know who this was. We had also been told to be very cautious about interacting with strangers. I summoned all my intuition to feel whether or not to get in the car. The man seemed friendly. I got in the car and we sped off.

I used this chance to ask the man about himself and the place. I also told him how grateful I was for the ride.

He answered simply, "You appeared lost."

I had to laugh. I asked whether or not the hotel was on the way to where he was going.

He responded, "No, not really, but I'll take you anyway."

I was taken aback, "It is so nice of you to do this!"

He looked me directly in the eye, "It's my duty! Allah has put you in my path so I must help. It is my duty!"

I was impressed by his dedication to his faith. "Thank you. I hope I can repay this good deed someday for someone else," I replied. That is your duty," he instructed. Then he told me a famous quote from Imam Ali: "If you see a man, he is either your brother in religion or he is your brother in humanity."

This man put his values into practice.

ANCIENT CITIES TIMELESS VALUES

I became acutely aware of the complexity of the Israeli/Palestinian conflict while working in Jerusalem for an engaging two months. Let me say that the land which makes up Israel and the Palestinian Territories is not only considered sacred by three great religions but it is also one of the most beautiful pieces of real estate I have visited globally.

There are four quarters in what is called old or East Jerusalem; the Moslem, Jewish, Christian, and Armenian quarters. I stayed in a Palestinian-owned hotel in the Muslim quarter almost the entire two months. I, of course, made several Muslim friends there. However, I also was there working with an Israeli organization and had many Jewish friends. I lectured on behalf of the Israeli-based organization to Christian Palestinians.

I also befriended an Armenian family living in the Armenian quarter of Jerusalem and was pleased to have several meals at their home. I also became acquainted with a Coptic priest from Ethiopia. In my conversations with all of my new friends concerning the conflict, I found that each perspective was ironically both contradictory and simultaneously made perfect, logical sense. I felt completely confused and dismayed. It was heartbreaking observing firsthand the fear and suffering there.

Amidst the chaos, confusion and tension, though, I found PhBs there just as I have in every corner of the world. They gave me tremendous hope for the region.

Allow me to introduce Ismail Khatib. He and his family lived in Jenin, one of the more than 50 Palestinian refugee camps spread through several bordering countries. His family lived in the camp with about 12,000 Palestinians outside the city of Jenin. He had a 13-year-old son named Ahmed. One afternoon Ahmed asked to go buy a tie for the celebration of an Islamic holiday that was planned in school for the following day. Ahmed's father gave him permission to go. After shopping Ahmed ran into his friends who were playing with realistic-looking, plastic guns. He decided to play with them.

Jenin is located on the border of Israel where Israeli patrols are the norm. The kids were playing with the toy guns and a patrol of Israeli soldiers came upon them. From a distance, the soldiers saw what appeared to be a gun. Ahmed was shot. It was a horrible mistake. He was rushed to Rambam Hospital in Haifa, Israel where he died twenty-four hours later. His father

Ismail, in the face of incomprehensible grief and anger, decided that he had to do something other than strike back in revenge and continue the hate.

He decided that he could do something in the direction of peace. The killing had to stop. He decided to donate his son's organs to Israeli children as a peace offering. He spoke to his family and his Imam about his intent. He even went to the Brigade of Martyrs, a supposed terrorist organization in Jenin, and all agreed it would be a good gesture towards peace.

Ahmed's father and mother donated their son's organs and saved 5 Israeli children from the age of 7 through 14 and an Israeli woman 58 years of age.

Ismail and his wife met with the parents of the children whose lives were saved by transplant operations using Ahmed's organs. As you might imagine it was an extremely emotional meeting. Men, women, doctors, nurses, and visitors at the Schneider Children's Medical Center sobbed. They met the parents of 12-year-old Samah, an Israeli Druze girl who received Ahmed's heart; Fairouz Gaboua, whose 5-year-old son Mohammad received one of Ahmed's kidneys; Tovah Levinson of Jerusalem, the mother of 3-year-old Menouha who received Ahmed's second kidney.

This amazing family gave Samah a new life. Yousa, Samah's mother said, "It is difficult to express in words what's in my heart." Tovah Levinson said, "We are really grateful to you for saving our daughter's life. God will pay you back for this good deed." Ahmed's parents responded by saying, "We hope her wounds will heal soon. We hope that she will work to promote peace once she grows up." Ahmed's father addressed the Israeli public through a letter that called on both Israeli and Palestinians "to instill a new culture in your children's minds."

There could be no greater sacrifice for anyone! This man is one of my heroes. I am not sure I would have been able to do what he did. He is truly a Professional Human Being. The word "Islam" means peace and they demonstrated that fully. I see the real face of Islam in the face of Ismail and his wife. Ismail said, "I want to create a bridge of peace to Israel." Ismail is right! Unless the values of peace, acceptance and tolerance are taught to the children of Palestinians and Israelis alike, how will the hate end?

I also want to honor two Israeli doctors I met. They represent the real face of Judaism. They risk their lives while volunteering their time. They are members of an organization called Physicians for Human Rights-Israel. These two doctors, as well as other doctors, nurses, and pharmacists risk their lives every week. They enter the Palestinian refugee camps, dangerous for Israelis, to serve the poor who have little or no medical assistance.

Since the 80s the organization has included the Mobile Clinic project, consisting of both Israeli and Palestinian health professionals. This project's mission is as follows: "Through consistent collaborative work, the mobile clinic aims to serve as a gesture of trust and solidarity with Palestinian patients and medical professionals and help to foster greater recognition for human rights values among the Israeli medical community while sensitizing the Israeli public to the need for Israeli policy change vis-à-vis the occupied Palestinian territory." When they enter the occupied territories the reality is that they do risk their lives. Their service though is their bridge of peace. There is no question in my mind that these brave Israeli and Palestinian health care professionals are also, along with the Khatibs, perfect examples of what it means to be a PhB.

What they teach us is that the enemy is not the Israelis or the Palestinians; the obstacle to peace is continuing the conflict by instilling hate in the next generation towards the other. Actually, the people who started this conflict died long ago. For peace to dawn the idea of peace must supplant what occurred centuries ago. New values must be modeled for the generations to come. The children must be taught a new way of coexisting. Today this is beginning to occur in some families and schools, but not all. Ismail and these Israeli and Palestinian health care volunteers are bold pioneers of that change.

To me the way to create change seems clear—it must take root in the hearts and minds of the people. These two examples are extraordinary displays of forgiveness and compassion. But perhaps it all begins with simple humility. When both sides are certain they are absolutely right and the other side is completely wrong, what room is there for change?

HUMILITY: THE DOMAIN OF KINGS

On the border of Israel is the Hashemite Kingdom of Jordan. It was also the home of a remarkable man, the former Jordanian king, King Hussein I. He passed away a few years ago but remains a PhB for me to this day. His son, the current king, has big shoes to fill.

During his reign King Hussein was known as the father of modern Jordan. He created an oasis of peace and moderation in the Middle East. During his 47-year reign he upgraded the standard of living for his people and put them on the path towards democratic government. He was known as a great mediator of peace in the Middle East. He recognized Israel as a State in 1994, Jordan becoming only the second Arab state to do so. During his long reign, what made an indelible mark on me was one, simple, personal act of humility, not any of his grand, political achievements.

On the Jordanian-Israeli border a tragedy occurred. A rogue Jordanian soldier shot and killed seven 11-year-old Israeli girls and injured many others. They were on a school outing with 40 other students on a scenic outlook on the border. Ironically the place where this occurred is called "the Island of Peace," a park which was established as a tourist promotion area in the Israeli-Jordanian treaty. The king was so distraught that he went to Israel to visit the grieving families. In a courageous act he knelt before them and asked for forgiveness. One of the women said, "I looked in his eyes, he was authentic, he was honest and he was hurt, which helped me."

At the time of King Hussein's death Prime Minister Netanyahu had this to say about him and this one act of humility. "On the personal level there was no one more gracious, considerate and kind; no one more hospitable and generous; no one more capable of understanding and empathy. The people of Israel will never forget his visit to the bereaved families of Beit Shemesh. Coming to ask forgiveness for a heinous act of terror, he knelt before parents mourning their slain young daughters, tears in his eyes, words of comfort and condolence on his lips. It was an act of greatness of a great man, a man who knew war and grew to hate it, a man who tasted violence and vowed to banish it. He was an apostle of good will, a visionary with a healthy grasp of the real, a dreamer with a thorough understanding of the possible, a man of infinite courage who craved peace with all his soul."

Humility was the domain of this king. I am astounded by the influence this one man has had on his people, the Israelis, the Middle East, and me. The values of forgiveness, compassion, and humility have the potential to end ancient conflicts but only if each individual makes a decision to own them. We have the king, the Khatibs, and Physicians for Human Rights-Israel to teach us.

Mind/Body Connection

Loving oneself is fundamental to good health. If we compromise what we consider to be our values, we end up not liking ourselves. Our immune system is weakened when we act counter to our deeper values and conscience. Childre and Cryer, *From Chaos to Coherence.*

The risk of low self-esteem is depression of the immune system and vulnerability to arterial disease. You can read more about this in Harriet Braiker's book, *Lethal Lovers and Poisonous People: How to Protect Your Health from Relationships That Make You Sick.*

MEN WHO LIVE THEIR VALUES

Everyone knows the name Nelson Mandela, the anti-apartheid activist who would not compromise his values and spent 27 years in prison for his beliefs. He became the first democratically elected president of South Africa. Mandela is an example of someone who stands up for what he values. Surely he ranks among the most inspiring freedom fighters of modern times and to this day, in his 90s, he continues to travel the world to inspire justice and equality.

Mr. Mandela received many honors, including the Nobel Peace Prize in 1993. His life is an inspiration, one of non-compromise for what he values most: freedom for his people. He truly fits my description of a PhB. As president, he was literally the primary beneficiary of his work of trying to bring freedom to South African people. He personified PhB Law 1: *I am the main and first beneficiary of everything I think, do, and say.*

By living his values, Nelson Mandela was able to inspire one of my best buddies in college, Larry Jenkins, not to mention the many others he has inspired. Larry Jenkins, my buddy from the University of Akron, held Nelson Mandela in such high regard that he legally changed his name to L. Mandela Jenkins. The name Mandela is on his license plates. He has also asked his son to give the name to his next grandson so that the Mandela spirit lives on. It is powerful to see how a man can inspire another man from another continent, across the ocean, and from another time.

At college, Larry and I lived in the same dormitory and played intramural basketball together. I wasn't quite in his league though. He later joined the varsity basketball team and was one of the school's all-time leading scorers. When his basketball jersey number was retired, he called me up to come and be with him during that honor. My buddy, L. Mandela, is a hardworking man of principle and by the way, L. Mandela Jenkins was an All-American basketball player.

Jeff, an acquaintance of mine, had a long, thriving, enjoyable career at IBM and left to start his own woodworking company. As he left IBM, someone asked him, "What are you going to build?" His response: "I'm going to build a good life!" Today he is a happy, successful business owner enjoying a good life.

"Make decisions based on your values and you will value your decisions."

— JEFF MITZEL
Owner, GreenAward Custom Woodworking, Austin, Texas

Thought Provokers

- *Do your best each and every game and each and every day. On the field and off.*
  – Dominic Bagnola, my dad

- *The world is full of people that have stopped listening to themselves or have listened only to their neighbors to learn what they ought to do, how they ought to behave, and what the values are they should be living for.*
  – Joseph Campbell, American mythologist

- *Values provide perspective in the best of times and the worst.*
  – Charles Garfield, author of the Peak Performance trilogy

- *Until you value yourself, you won't value your time. Until you value your time, you will not do anything with it.*
  – M. Scott Peck, author of *The Road Less Traveled*

- As software drives hardware, our thoughts drive our habits.

Action Ideas

- Read and incorporate *The Four Agreements* by Miguel Ruiz. In his book, don Miguel Ruiz helps uncover those self-limiting beliefs that rob you of happiness and create unnecessary suffering. Based on ancient Toltec wisdom, *The Four Agreements* offers four rules to live by that can make your life richer.
  - Be impeccable with your word.
  - Don't take anything personally.
  - Don't make assumptions.
  - Always do your best.

- Watch the movie *Rob Roy*, starring Liam Neeson. It is a story of integrity, honor, and values. Values are a gift to yourself.

- Forgive yourself for all mistakes. Forgive someone who did something "to you." It's the best thing for your physiology and your mind's capacity. You will no longer have to carry it in your mind or body.

- Be resourceful. Figure out what to do, how to do it, what more you need to learn to do, and do it—before being asked or told.

- Read *The Culture Code: An Ingenious Way to Understand Why People Around the World Live and Buy as They Do* by Clotaire Rapaille. This is an amazing book, which cracks the code on why we do the things we do and helps us to better understand others as well as ourselves.

Spotlight
DOMINIC BAGNOLA, MY DAD

My dad, Dominic Bagnola, is a kind and gentle guy. I've never, ever heard my father use a curse word. He is also a fantastic athlete and at age 84 was still playing Silver League Baseball. He was an all-round, natural athlete, a confident, talented, and very competitive player. His greatest loves (besides my mom) are baseball and softball. Off the field, he is bashful and soft-spoken. On the field is where he comes alive.

Dad began playing ball at age thirteen and he has been playing nonstop for 72 years. He was talented enough to play professional baseball but the Second World War drew him out of high school before graduation at age eighteen. He was drafted into the Army and went to the Philippines and Japan in the Asia-Pacific Theater for twelve months.

While in Asia, after the Japanese surrendered, Dad played on the Armed Forces Baseball team for Army. The Army had bulldozed areas to make fields and had put lights up. When he received his discharge from the military, he was asked by an Army colonel to play third base in the Military World Series which was going to be held in Tokyo. He declined; he decided he wanted to go back to the home he missed in Canton.

Dad was a competent defensive player and a superior hitter on offense, attaining a batting average in the mid- to high-.300 range during his entire career. He has been playing in the Akron Silver League since he retired from Diebold Safe and Lock Company at age 65. In 1984, he was inducted into the Amateur Sports Hall of Fame in Canton, Ohio, for softball; by then he already had 40 league championships under his belt. Dad played in five Silver League World Series and was a member of the winning World Series team in 2000.

The highlight of Dad's baseball career came on April 6, 2002. On this unusually cold and windy spring day in Canton, we drove my dad to a brand-new baseball field behind St. Thomas Aquinas High School. My dad had no idea what was up. A group of fans, friends, and family awaited us. We led my dad onto the field and directed him to look towards the fence. We watched as several men lifted the sign up. It read, "Dominic A. Bagnola Field." I heard my dad gasp. He glanced at me as tears came to his eyes. He looked around at all the familiar faces and was moved that so many people had come out for him on such a cold day. (It was actually snowing heavily and everyone had been called and discouraged from attending.) More than sixty years of playing gracefully, competently, and humbly was recognized and honored.

I had the honor of giving a speech about my dad. It was cold so my speech was short! I began by asking the crowd if they remembered the Hall of Fame football player who was nicknamed "Sweetness" because of his sweet and graceful moves on the football field and the qualities of grace and dignity off the field, which he never lost.

Many yelled out, "Walter Payton!"

I yelled back, "That is correct!" I consider my father the "Sweetness" of the softball diamond. He is graceful and dignified on the field and humble and unassuming off the field. Two beliefs lead his life. The first and foremost is, *If you are going to do anything, do it right, whatever it is.* Something my brother Dean reminds me of almost every time we talk. And second, *Keep exercising and playing and you won't rust out.* My dad has lived this: He has done what is right, played, and hasn't rusted out! Congratulations, Dad, from all of us!

Later that night, Dad's teammates, friends, family, fans, and well-wishers showed up at St. Thomas High School for the banquet to honor my dad. Dad asked me to speak on his behalf. To prepare for this I asked my dad what his guiding principles were. My father is not a man who would sit and write in self-reflection, but this was an occasion for him to articulate his beliefs. As Dad talked about his success philosophy and described what was important to him, my brothers, my sister, and I were taken back to moments in our childhood where we saw our dad live out these beliefs.

Dad's Constitution:

Dominic Bagnola's Principles For Athletic and Life Success

★ There is no need to talk big; just play big.

★ Don't become depressed with yourself when you don't perform well.

★ Don't become too impressed with yourself when you do perform well.

★ There is no problem with playing your hardest and best and losing. There will always be another game and another challenge.

★ It is always good to play to win, but never forget to honor your opponent.

★ Always do your best. Never give up.

★ Practice is as important as the game itself. Be prepared to play. Practice is rehearsal.

★ Remember to make your teammates look good. Make a lot of fanfare over their successes and don't make any over your own.

★ Athletes don't have to smoke, drink, use drugs, take performance enhancers, or use profanity to fit in or achieve anything.

★ Remember to transfer all of the above to everyday life. Sports are a rehearsal for wholesome living.

You really must stand for something or you will fall for anything! You have a set of values that have framed your life thus far and have brought you to this point in your life. What are those values? Frame your own constitution.

14

Lesson 6: If You Don't Know Where You're Going, Speeding Up Won't Help

How can I go forward when I don't know which way I'm facing?

— JOHN LENNON
from the song "How"

Doug Henning's signature was his ability to create wonder and entertain people. It took Doug some time to realize that all the passion he felt and all the fun he was having meant that this was his calling. "What is entertainment?" was the question Doug posed to Maharishi Mahesh Yogi as they sat together in India, discussing life's great questions.

The wise sage responded that entertainment allowed people to enter into the Self, to go beyond their busy, mundane, thinking mind. He said that you transcend when a comedian makes you laugh, and you transcend at the height of a magical illusion when wonder is created. Doug realized that his real magic was that he transformed people, allowing them to experience their inner selves, and putting them on the path of self-discovery.

When Doug would make someone levitate, he'd produce a waterfall spouting from the stage and lay the person horizontally on the waterfall. Then he'd raise her body up, and the water would rise with her. The minds of the viewers in the audience would go into high gear trying to figure out the angles. They would search for clues to the illusion. Surely something was behind the waterfall holding her up?

Next, Doug would stop the water, leaving the person floating in midair.

The intellect went to work again. There must be ropes holding her up!

Then Doug would take a hoop, light it on fire, and pass the hoop completely around the floating body. Right at that moment, when the hoop went completely around the body, there was nowhere else for the intellect to go. That's the moment when the viewer transcended and felt wonder.

With each illusion, people transcended. If you looked at the audience, as I often did, many people were smiling, in awe, except of course for those hardcore skeptics who refused to be entertained and were still busy trying to figure out the illusion.

Doug would sometimes say at the beginning of the performance, "These are illusions without the use of trick photography. Just enjoy." His mission was to create a sense of wonder in the viewer.

I used to wait in the lobby before some of the performances and watch people streaming in tired from their long week. Then I'd watch them leave the show, and they'd be beaming, their faces glowing. They left having had the experience of entertainment, of wonder, of transcendence, of *anything is possible,* and of awe. Creating that joy and wonder was Doug's signature. He spent his whole life focused on that goal.

WHY DO GOALS AND DESTINATIONS MATTER?

A British friend of mine, Dexter, once related an experience to me that will answer this question. He said, "When I'm spending time at my vacation home in County Clare, Ireland, I often set that address as 'home' on the GPS (Global Positioning System). Not only does this make it simpler to navigate back to the house, it also provides a sense of closure and subconsciously reinforces a 'sense of home' in an unfamiliar area.

"Once, back home in England, I took some relatives to their hotel about an hour away. I clicked *Go Home* on my GPS and started on the route. About a mile down the road, I glanced down at the GPS and knew something was wrong; it was estimating the time to home as several hours. I realized then that the GPS was directing me not to my home in England but to my vacation home in Ireland—via ferry across the Irish Sea! Fortunately for me, I lost less than 5 minutes in this detour."

Setting the wrong destination or having no destination at all can be costly. On the GPS, once you set a destination, the satellite system will give you feedback when you go off course. It, or I should say *she* (the voice on my GPS), says, "Recalculating!" However, without a destination she can't tell you whether or not you're going on the right course.

In our lives, we set goals and then we either recognize when we are off course or the unseen forces of Nature say *recalculate* so we can course-correct. Without a goal then, how could we get an indication to recalculate or course-correct? We couldn't even leave our driveway without a destination!

I often lecture to AIESEC (Association Internationale des Étudiants en Sciences Économiques et Commerciales), a large international student-driven organization. The students frequently ask me, "What if I don't know what I want to do? I don't know what courses to take." My advice always is to pick the best goal you can right now and start moving in that direction. It may not be the ultimate goal for you. No worries. You will find something more suitable along the way by having a short-term goal. If you are not moving, you can't find something better. Goals and destinations are important. They set direction, a basis for feedback or *recalculation*, and perform the task of the boat's rudder.

Years ago during a visit to one of the offices of Canon, Inc., I learned the importance of setting up a planned strategy and destination in the business setting. Businesses have what is called "strategic intent." This means they make a statement of intention for their business. They may use it for one or two years. At the Canon office, I saw the company's strategic intent posted on the walls. It was a mission that pervaded the corporate climate. When they started a meeting, they would put this strategic intent at the top of the flip chart: "Beat Xerox." This was their guiding purpose at that time.

I've played sports and I've been around business for a lot of years. I understand what is behind that focus. But I believe that businesses, as well as the people who work for them, have to have something greater to steer them.

217

Of course, if you don't know what your purpose is, no one can tell you. You have to figure it out yourself. I know mine because long ago I figured out what my magic is, how I can use it in the service of others to make a difference in their lives and mine, and how I can make a living from it.

Everyone comes with a purpose. Everyone comes with a mission. It is in our DNA. When you figure it out, and then fulfill it, you feel good about yourself. It makes you healthy. You work toward your destination with commitment, zest, and positivity.

Mind/Body Connection

Norman Cousins wrote: "Hope, purpose, and determination are not merely mental states. They have electrochemical connections that play a large part in the workings of the immune system and indeed, in the entire economy of the total human organism. In short, I learned that it is not unscientific to talk about a biology of hope—or of any of the positive emotions."

Just as a rudder on a ship, we can direct our energies toward success by establishing our current objectives (which may change over time and circumstances), visions, and personal values as our daily operational guide. Keeping this larger goal in mind promotes inspiration and self-motivation, which in turn brings psychological happiness and a sense of well-being. This feeling produces the molecules of health.

Mind/Body Connection

Cynicism occurs when mission and a sense of purpose are missing. This triggers anxiety, loss of self-esteem, and depression.

Having a strategy is the compass that guides you through life. Personally, I want to inspire people to turn within and become Professional Human Beings who are awakened to the reality of their own greatness.

Imagine how many ships in ancient times were lost at sea without a compass. We need an inner compass as well, something to serve as a guide to carry us for the long haul that includes inevitable rough seas.

YOUR INNER COMPASS GUIDES YOU

Shannon Lucid had that inner guidance. She knew at a very young age what she wanted to be. In grade school in the mid-1950s, she had written an essay about wanting to become a rocket scientist. Her teacher told her that there was no such position nor would there ever be such a position and, if there were such a thing, a woman would not be given that kind of a job anyway. Shannon was undeterred.

Fast-forward to 1996. I was watching a television program where an astronaut was being honored. It was Shannon Lucid, the first woman to receive the Congressional Space Medal of Honor. Only ten others have received this honor. She had flown in space five times, and held the record for the longest stay in space by a woman. One of her missions was a prolonged visit aboard the Russian research space station *Mir*.

When I tuned in, Shannon was thanking her eighth-grade teacher. Her teacher's opinion had only made her more determined. And prove her teacher wrong, she did. She earned a Ph.D. in biochemistry and was selected in 1978 to NASA's astronaut corps. Imagine Shannon's thought process and how powerful her focus was.

What do you focus on? What do you want to create? How would you like to serve? What type of mission have you decided to be on, here on Earth or maybe—à la Shannon—out in space? What would you like to accomplish? How do you want to be remembered?

LEE IACOCCA'S COMPASS

While working with Doug Henning I had many wonderful adventures. One involved a TV commercial Doug did for Chrysler, in connection with the company's introduction of its first minivan, the Dodge Caravan. The car acquired the nickname of the *Magic Wagon* because Doug introduced the van in a magical way. The real magic for me, however, was getting to know the history behind the magician of Chrysler—Lee Iacocca, its then CEO.

Iacocca tells the story about how he loved cars from the beginning and was sure about his future in the car business. When he was 19 and attending Lehigh University, he told his fraternity brothers that, by the time he was 35, he would become the vice president of Ford Motor Company. They asked him if he thought he would ever be its president. Probably not, he said, because a Ford family member would always run the company.

At 35, Iacocca indeed became a very successful VP at Ford. By 40, he became president of the Ford Division, and later became president of Ford Motor Company. He was right, though, about a Ford always running the company. In 1978, despite having posted a $2 billion profit, Henry Ford II and Lee Iacocca decided that Iacocca should "resign." The two didn't see eye-to-eye.

Iacocca mapped out his career with the Ford Company down to the detail of even not running the Ford Company in the end. Iacocca said that leaving Ford was the worst and the best thing that ever happened to him. Worst, because he had to leave. Best, because it gave him the chance to move over to Chrysler, and raise it from the ashes of near bankruptcy to a robust company. He introduced a line of compact cars as an answer to the oil crisis of the 1970s.

He later went on to write bestselling books and start other businesses, including the development of the E Bike, an electric bicycle that you charge by plugging into any wall socket. The profits have gone to diabetes research. He has also been actively involved in fundraising to

---

refurbish the Statue of Liberty and to feed impoverished children around the world.

One of his books praises the innovation, energy, courage, and creativity of Americans—personal qualities that certainly characterized his life, inside and outside of business.

In 2007, he launched a website intended to encourage open dialogue about the challenges of our time, such as soaring health-care costs and why the U.S. lags so far behind in developing alternative energy sources and hybrid vehicles. The site also features Iacocca's book, *Where Have All the Leaders Gone?,* and allows users to rate presidential candidates by the qualities Iacocca feels every true leader should possess: common sense, communication, creativity, conviction, competence, courage, character, charisma, curiosity.

On his website, he makes this insightful comment: "What have I learned from philanthropy? That it's no different from business. To be successful you have to be focused, to have a plan and stick to it, with the help of a great team."

Lee Iacocca manned a strong rudder to guide his ship through life. He has left a powerful signature.

I shared this story about Lee Iacocca with my mother and wondered aloud, "Why didn't I do something like that?"

She laughed and went down into the basement and returned with a small box. After reminding me that my favorite subject in grade school was geography, she proceeded to pull out some maps which I had meticulously drawn when I was in fourth grade. Maps of many, many countries. As we reminisced on these old drawings, I realized that I did know where I was going. I had drawn the blueprint and then began to build unknowingly. I have now visited over 80 countries.

MAHEALANI CYPHER'S COMPASS

Mahealani Cypher (Denise DeCosta) is one of the guardians of the Native Hawaiian culture and lands. Mahealani's compass is more of a divining rod—leading her towards protecting the water!

Although of mixed ancestry, she has Native Hawaiian blood—which is a rarity. The number of Native Hawaiians is estimated at 200,000. And the number of Pure Hawaiians is about 8,000. When you meet Mahealani, you will know right away that she is a passionate Hawaiian and proud of it. She is the current president of the 26-member Oahu Council of the Association of Hawaiian Civic Clubs.

My introduction to Mahealani was when I saw her on television when she was the spokesperson for the Board of Water Supply in Honolulu. She occupied that position for many years until she transitioned into the powerful position of city clerk for the city of Honolulu. Now retired from full-time work, she performs her real, personal mission: preserving Hawaiian culture, traditional Hawaiian values, and the land itself. It isn't as though she just recently started this mission; she has been doing this her entire life.

A single mother who raised her own children as well as her grandchildren, while performing as a powerful manager and leader in the city and county as city clerk, Mahealani has been an advocate for promoting, preserving, and perpetuating the traditional values that dignify, honor, and respect all life, all of which are reflective of Native Hawaiian values. She is fiercely loyal to this mission and loves her work unconditionally.

Her friend and partner in this effort, Rocky Kaluhiwa, commented, "We are not activists; we are advocates. We advocate for a strong, healthy Native Hawaii." Rocky described Mahealani as "a person who is relentless in her pursuit of preserving Hawaii and is an all-inclusive leader who isn't afraid to tell it like it is. She is fearless. She doesn't pull any punches. She can be tough when it is required and shows great compassion when needed."

As Rocky described her to me, I was reminded of my work in Israel and recalled that an Israeli is referred to as a Sabra, originally in reference to the sabra fruit (the prickly pear), which is tough on the outside but sweet and delicate on the inside. This is a perfect description of Mahealani.

This toughness and compassion has served the people well as

Mahealani fights to preserve the land, crops, and water of Hawaii.

Rocky recounted Mahealani's leadership in dealing with a controversy over a citizens' petition to oppose the building of a rail transit system in Honolulu. Mahealani showed unshakable persistence all the way to the State Supreme Court, which agreed with the Appellate Court that her interpretation of law regarding the petition was correct.

Mahealani has persevered the longest in her opposition to a major highway project that threatened the rural communities on Windward Oahu, on which she spent over 30 years. She is now considered someone to consult with before new transportation initiatives are considered.

Her latest successful venture was leading the effort to restore wetlands for the planting of taro, the traditional Hawaiian root crop that is considered by Native Hawaiians as "the staff of life."

She has been confirmed as the newest member of the Board of Water Supply by the city council. She works to preserve another precious gift of Hawaii: water.

Mahealani is quick to say that she has done nothing alone but that is what makes a good leader. She partners with others and leads very effectively.

I admire her purposeful efforts to preserve the environment, the traditions, the people, and the Aloha spirit. She is a very strong woman with a great heart and a love for the island and its Natives that is unsurpassed. Her love for this work is tangible and immediately apparent.

I consider her as one of the top five leaders that I have worked with in Hawaii. Mahealani is a learner and a doer. Over a ten-year period she participated in just about all of the leadership and management courses I led. She also sent all of her managers through the trainings.

When she became the city clerk, she hired me to do a series of workshops for her staff. While all of her staff attended these sessions, Mahealani took on the roles of receptionist, office manager, greeter, and virtually ran the entire office. She ordered us lunch and, when it arrived, she served it. She is a great example of a servant leader, while she is preserving the spirit of Aloha

As a PhB herself, she honored my Professional Human Being workshop by saying the following at the end of the course. "Becoming a Professional Human Being is our life's journey toward 'pono,' the Native Hawaiian term meaning 'That perfect balance within ourselves and between each other and all around us.'"

YOUR EMOTIONAL SIGNATURE

A few years ago I went with my wife Sais to Trinidad to attend a family reunion. Trinidad and Tobago is a Caribbean island nation just off the coast of Venezuela. This is where calypso, the limbo, and steel-pan music originated. Trinidad, the bigger island, feels like India to me because so many Indians live there, and the sights, sounds, and smells have a real Indian flavor. But the background of rhythm, the lush foliage, and the mosaic of people are distinctly Caribbean.

The reunion was an all-day celebration. Many came attired in traditional Indian clothes—men in kurtas and women in saris. The day was well organized and as guests arrived they were handed a brochure. Printed at the top of the program was the Sanskrit word, *dharohar*, which represented the theme of the reunion. Appearing under that was its English translation, *legacy*. The function was about honoring the legacy of my wife's ancestors.

The day began early in the morning with a religious ceremony honoring family ancestors. In the afternoon we gathered at the village temple. The celebration continued with traditional Indian dance, prayer and song, a review of the family tree originating from the first three immigrants, garlanding of the elders of the family, and finally a guest speaker.

Raviji, a well-respected social activist and good friend of the family, was the speaker. He began his talk with several definitions and explanations of the Sanskrit term *dharohar*. The definition that intrigued me most was *signature*. It crystallized the true meaning of the day's celebration but also gave me insight into the real meaning of *legacy*.

Following Raviji's enlightening remarks we all our made our way to the long tables set up for our Trinidadian banquet. What a delight for the senses! Before us were banana leaves heaped with portions of rice, dhal, various curried vegetables, samosas, roti, chutneys, and desserts. While we ate we were able to spend several hours visiting with relatives and close friends.

As Sais and I drove home and pondered on the significance of the day, I found that what lingered in my mind was the idea of legacy. What was my legacy? Did I have one? Of course I had one, but was I consciously creating it?

A person's legacy is his or her signature, the _real_ signature—the signature impressed on the feeling level of those left behind. I call it the _emotional signature,_ an imprint of you left on those you touched.

We all are in the process of creating a signature that will last after we are gone, like a signature on an important document that has been preserved!

When John Hancock signed the Declaration of Independence in 1776, he had no idea that his would become the most famous signature. Even today, when we want someone to sign a document, we say, "Put your John Hancock on this." But this is a physical signature. What has more significance is your emotional signature. This is your legacy. A signature or legacy is the self-definition you write, or self-portrait you paint in life, that you will be remembered by. It's like a building that stands long after you have gone. Just like John Hancock, you are handwriting your signature on important "documents." Those documents are _everyone in your life!_

SIGNATURES THAT INSPIRE

"My life is my message." These are the well-known words of Mahatma Gandhi. What did Gandhi stand for? What signature did he leave behind? We can think of several dimensions of his life—freedom, leadership, revolution, integrity, courage, and perseverance. However, his fundamental legacy is non-violence. Though Gandhi never held an elected office and never had any formal authority, he was able to use his influence and leadership to manifest his vision of a free India, stamped with his signature of freedom through non-violence.

Gandhi accomplished much with few possessions and little money in his life. By contrast, Andrew Carnegie effected great advancement of society through his wealth. He emigrated to the U.S. from Scotland with an impoverished family at age twelve and went on to become the era's greatest industrialist. At age 65, in 1901, he sold Carnegie Steel Company for $500 million to J. P. Morgan, who later formed U.S. Steel. Carnegie then became a philanthropist, establishing major trusts that distributed more than $350 million dollars worth of his personal fortune. The bulk of it went to colleges, universities, and libraries.

In Carnegie's famous article, "The Gospel of Wealth," he expounds on this philosophy and presents it in two components. The first is to become exceptional by using your natural talents and energies for the advancement of society; the second is, having accumulated wealth, use the surplus for the improvement of mankind in philanthropic causes. "A man who dies rich dies disgraced," he believed. Carnegie lived out his philosophy.

Today, his name is as synonymous with industriousness and social responsibility as non-violence is with Gandhi. These are the signatures of two great men.

Who has the ability to leave a lasting mark? Every member of an organization, every family member, and every citizen of every country. You can and will leave a legacy.

Who can leave a legacy—an emotional signature? Everyone can and does. Why not make yours a positive legacy? Why not make it a memorable, inspiring emotional signature?

You may be inspired by a man who has for his entire career focused on the positive legacy he wanted to leave.

Former chairman of Herman Miller, Inc., a furniture manufacturing company, and author of several books, Max De Pree, operated with a specific vision at his company to create a workplace knowing "that there was a common good that we were all connected to and had a right to."

He acknowledged that everyone has different gifts, and created a community in which "we were able to sort out their gifts and assign tasks according to those gifts." His dream was to "create results that were quite rich."

Max De Pree differentiated between strategic intent and the concept of legacy. He defined a strategic plan as "understanding the value you provide to customers, your competitive strengths." He explained that while this is necessary it does not encompass all that is needed to be a leader; what's missing is your legacy. "Leaving a legacy is articulating and bringing to life the kind of organization or community that you want to be a part of [which] is very different. And is every bit as important."

De Pree clearly raised the bar for company legacies. In a 1997 interview with Frances Hesselbein of *Leader to Leader Journal*, he articulated his views about the importance of leadership, followership, and legacy. Here are a few of his key ideas to consider as you contemplate your legacy:

- What matters? Not just richness as measured by accountants. What's more valuable is the community: "what kind of place we work in, what kind of relationships we have within the workplace, what effect work has on our families we go home to, and what effect the family has on the work we do."

- What role do others play? Recognize that you *need* the people in your life and in your workplace. "So long as a person is in your work community, is a legitimate part of that community, she's indispensable to the group. Then you have to work in such a way that your relationships reflect that belief."

- What's the point? De Pree always felt a sense of moral responsibility to others and transferred that sense to his company. He referred to this as a red thread that ran through everything they were trying to do. "It was a thread of moral purpose. In addition to establishing and nurturing good relationships, we tried to do the right thing in the way we researched and developed products."

As we examine the major tenets of his belief system, three main themes emerge: value to the customer, value of his people, and the company's relationship to the greater good. De Pree pioneered profit sharing, gain sharing, work teams, and other participatory management practices at Herman Miller. He understood the mechanics of leadership and its

227

relationship to legacy. Leading is based on following, following is based on relationship, and relationship is based on trust. He busted the myth that higher management is all-important. Instead he put the focus and attention back on who are really the important ones: the followers.

In 1997, De Pree was honored with the Lifetime Achievement Award by the Business Enterprise Trust in recognition of his efforts "to create a thriving work environment centered around a genuine respect for the skills and contribution of every employee" at Herman Miller. The award acknowledged his distinct efforts to serve his workers and his customers in creative and morally thoughtful ways.

It is amazing to me how often I hear a success formula repeated. In his 1997 book *Businesslike Government: Lessons Learned From America's Best Companies,* Vice President Al Gore consulted with more than 200 federal employees and some of the top business leaders. The advice gleaned from these meetings on how to turn the government into a successful business-like government was summed up in two principles: "Focus on customers and listen to workers."

Do you think the answer has been applied? Do you think the government is focused on the customer? What do you think about the legacy of past and present governments?

I once saw a documentary on Gavin and Joe Maloof, the millionaire brothers and businessmen who own the Sacramento Kings basketball team and other sports franchises. When asked about their success, they said that their formula came from their father, who taught them to *cater to their customers and take care of their employees.* Does this sound familiar?

Mahatma Gandhi, Andrew Carnegie, Max De Pree, and Gavin and Joe Maloof are among countless individuals whose signatures will influence us for many, many lifetimes to act at the highest level.

Here are a few more:

Martin Luther King — Vision and Equality

Jim Thorpe — Excellence and Dignity

Harry Truman — I Am Responsible

Mother Teresa — Joy in Service

César Chávez — Stand for What Is Right

Florence Nightingale — Mother of Healing

Nelson Mandela — Never Give Up

Bob Hope — Laughing Is Life

Rosa Parks — Boldness

Our acts are like brush strokes on the canvas of our own self-portrait. Our signatures—our legacies—are like lights that we shine into the future. How bright would you like your light to be? It's clear that the more we serve our fellow men and women, the more brilliant our light. The more spiritual- or principle-centered we are, the brighter the light. Professional Human Beings bring more light into the world.

BLUEPRINT FOR DESIGNING YOUR OWN SIGNATURE

Learn all you can about the signatures of others. Take in the truth of a person as seen in their good works. Remember, some signatures teach us how *not* to act. Learn from these as well.

Your assignment now is to begin to think about and practice developing your unique emotional signature. Why? If you have been inspired to live your highest and best self by the signatures of those who have come before you, you may want to think about creating the kind of signature you want to pass on to posterity. In choosing an uplifting signature you will also create a positive difference now in making your life more enjoyable, passionate, and fulfilling. Choosing now to have the signature of a Professional Human Being can be your first step in creating a better life for yourself, your family, and your world.

I'm going to share with you a simple tool you can use to begin crafting your signature/legacy at its highest value. It has several elements because your signature should express several aspects of you.

You've heard them all before but let's give them a little twist to serve this exercise. Consider the following questions:

L LOVE: What do you love? What is murmuring in your heart? What do you want to be? Who do you want to be? What do you enjoy doing? What do you dream for yourself? What is the best you can be?

E EMOTIONS: How do you want to feel about yourself? How do you want others to feel about you? What do you want from yourself? What would make you proud of yourself?

G GOAL: What is your goal? What is your mission? What do you value most in life? What values and principles do you stand for? What values did you choose in Lesson Five? What is important to you? What do you want your future to look like? What will you create for yourself? See the highest in yourself—stretch yourself. Use your imagination. You can change it if you don't like it. You can change it until you feel comfortable.

A ACTIONS: What key actions should you take to create your vision and achieve your mission? List two or three major actions that would have the biggest impact on your life. What is your next step?

C CALLING: What is your soul whispering to you? Where have you always felt you would end up? Having a strategic intent fuels, guides, and inspires your thoughts, speech, and action during each day. What is inscribed in you, there from the beginning? Like a mission, this is your purpose for being here. What were you engineered to do?

Y YOU: Refine it. Boil it down. Reduce yourself to the finest you. What word or phrase is synonymous with the highest version of you that you want to create?

Let me share my answers to this exercise as an example. These are the expressions of my signature, and may help you form your own.

L   LOVE: I love to teach people and I nurture the people in my life, who are my greatest assets. I enjoy and create this adventure called life. I choose to be happy. I entertain positivity by choice. I enjoy thinking; always there is a way. I may not be able to think all possibilities in any one moment, but I can always think of new possibilities in the next.

E   EMOTIONS: I feel rewarded when I inspire others to go within, turn their thinking upside down, and become awakened to the reality of their own greatness. I want others to feel trust in me; I try to speak the truth and give honest feedback; I admire myself when my words match reality. I am proud when I am financially self-sufficient because money is the energy source used to evolve.

G   GOAL: My mission is to become a Professional Human Being, an example of excellence. My life is my message and I will be what I teach. I keep the promises I make to myself and to others; I walk my talk but I am patient with myself when I fall short. I continuously learn so that my work reflects the highest knowledge available.

A   ACTIONS: My present goals are to speak once a week on the mind/body connection, write two books (this is the first one; the second will be titled *Leading Is Everybody's Business*), coach one new client per month, and generate three strong, new corporate clients per year. I will continue to meditate regularly; I am successful through meditation. I am vigilant about what I eat, my rest, and my exercise; I will be healthy.

C   CALLING: My mission is to be a teacher and coach. To my customers I impart life-changing knowledge that moves them toward the development of their highest Self in their personal and professional lives. My calling is to motivate, inspire, and teach others to tap into the unique qualities within themselves.

Y   YOU: I am a builder of Professional Human Beings. I am curious, pure in heart and mind, positive.

We define ourselves moment-by-moment, minute-by-minute, and hour-by-hour. In each moment we make choices that create our day. During each day we make choices that create our month. Each month we create our year, our years create our life, and the life we lead creates our signature. The question to ask yourself, then, is this: Am I creating the highest version of who I want to be?

What insignia do you want to leave imprinted on the people whose lives you have touched and will have touched? This is your legacy. Controlling the legacy you leave demands that you make a conscious effort.

Answering all these questions could take eight hours, eight days, or eight years. Whatever the time, it's worth it. It's an investment in you. Moreover, this is a dynamic not static process. Take quiet time to start. Your answers represent a direction, not a destination. You must start somewhere and begin to create. You may find better alternatives along the way. No problem. Change course when appropriate. Recalculate. Life is all about learning and experiencing. I learned long ago from one of my mentors that we must choose something and start making our way in that direction. On the way, you may find something better. If you are going nowhere, you won't find anything.

Shaking all the puzzle pieces and putting them together to form the picture of you that you want to present can be the most difficult task. Let it emerge last.

Best friends are a good source of feedback when you get stuck.

TRUE NORTH

You might be surprised where and when you get clues from Mother Nature about your personal mission.

"Regaining the sense of wonder that you had when you were a child." This was a phrase that Doug was fond of saying on stage and during interviews to explain his purpose. I had always been quite curious about this and on one warm day in Los Angeles, as he and I were hiking along a dry creek bed, I asked him about it and he began to explain.

Once while he was traveling with the CBC (Canadian Broadcasting

Corporation) and performing at Army bases, he was asked to perform for the Inuits. Doug thought it sounded like a great idea.

Little did he know that he would be performing in a small shed, in the middle of a winter wonderland, so cold you could see your breath. A small group of Inuits had been assembled for the show. Doug said he performed close-up magic with cards and with cups and balls. He tore and magically restored a newspaper. He produced a rabbit from a box, doves from thin air, and performed what is called the floating "zombie ball," which is getting a silver ball, to float in mid air, through a hoop, and around the room without anything attached to it. He said he thought he was doing very well but the Inuits weren't reacting at all. No smiling, no laughing, and no astonished looks from the audience—not the usual reaction Doug was used to.

After several more illusions, the show ended to no applause. Disheartened, Doug thought they didn't like his performance. Since the Inuits spoke only Inuktitut, Doug asked one of the members who knew English whether or not they had enjoyed the magic. The English-speaking Inuit asked the group, and they began to talk among themselves. They said they had enjoyed it but it wasn't *real magic*. They said real magic was the magic they witnessed in the world.

Doug said, "What about the rabbits and the doves I produced?"

They smiled at Doug's naïveté and said that real magic is when the walruses, seals, and whales appear out of the depths of nowhere so that they could hunt for food.

Still perplexed, Doug asked about the floating silver ball. He thought that illusion was pretty magical.

They responded, "Every day we see a fiery ball appear in the sky to light the day and bring warmth. The ball comes from nowhere. Every night we watch as a white ball develops from a sliver into a big white ball that floats in the sky and lights the night. It is much bigger than the ball you used. The moon is magical. Everything in the world is magical. Think of snowflakes falling from the sky and fish swimming under water. What *you* did was entertaining, but not magic." They asked him why he did these illusions.

Doug felt at a loss. He couldn't explain it other than to say he was entertaining his audience.

Once again the group spoke in their native tongue to one another. They began to laugh and nod their heads as if they understood. Finally the English-speaking interpreter said, "Now they realize why you do this. It is because *your people have forgotten what real magic is and you are reminding them.* It is very good that you are reminding them!"

Doug said this was a profound moment for him. He thought he was bringing them something when in fact they had a message for him. He was so overcome that he wept. It was as if he had come to these wonderful, innocent people to find out what his mission in doing magic really was. What real magic was all about. He discovered his performance was to help his audiences *regain the sense of wonder that had been lost.* His strategic intent or mission was set for an entire career on this cold night and acted as his rudder for the next thirty years.

Thought Provokers

- *As I grow older, I pay less attention to what men say. I just watch what they do.*
  – Andrew Carnegie, American industrialist and philanthropist

- *As a man thinketh in his heart, so is he.*
  – Proverbs 23:7

- *If you don't know where you're going, any road will take you there.*
  – from the song "Any Road" by George Harrison, former Beatle

- Unless we change direction, we are likely to end up where we are going.
  – Chinese proverb

- To paraphrase American education reformer Horace Mann, we should be ashamed to die without having made a substantial contribution to mankind.

Action Ideas

- For inspiration, read an autobiography or biography of a famous or successful person.

- Watch the movie *Groundhog Day*, starring Bill Murray and Andie MacDowell. Andie models what I call a Professional Human Being and influences Bill to become one.

- Watch the movie *Braveheart*, starring Mel Gibson, to experience authentic leadership. *People don't follow titles—they follow courage.*
  – Sir William Wallace

- Watch the movie *Mr. Holland's Opus*, starring Richard Dreyfuss. This exemplifies the power of relationship building and the "platinum rule": Do unto others as they'd like done unto them.

- Of 1,200 centenarians surveyed by Stanford gerontologist Walter Bortz, M.D., on secrets of long life, 90 percent cited the importance of order. Plan your life with daily to-do lists and a long-term mission statement.

Spotlight
FLOYD HOELTING

I first met Floyd Hoelting in 1977 at Western Illinois University, where he interviewed me and offered me a job. We bonded over our shared love for baseball. I consider Floyd one of the best educators, leaders, and Professional Human Beings I have ever met. If you have the opportunity to meet him you will certainly be attracted to his rare zest for life.

He is currently the Executive Director of the Division of Housing and Food Services (DHFS) at The University of Texas at Austin. He credits many mentors for influencing him; he says the new build on the old. Floyd is inspired not only by the renowned figures Gandhi, Mother Teresa, and Martin Luther King, but also by the people around him: neighboring farmers and ranchers; students and

235

staff he works with; John Webb, his first dean of students; officers and pilots; and by so many other people.

He is a man of strong values and principles, which have driven him throughout his life. These principles also guide him as a leader and form the basis of his Code of the Road. At the start of every year, he delivers his Code of the Road speech and includes it in the handbook for each of his 1200 staff.

After reading and digesting it, you may be inspired to cook up one of your own.

FLOYD'S CODE OF THE ROAD
Part 1: How to Stay on the Right Track at DHFS

1. Customer Satisfaction: Remember who pays your salary. They are not always right, but they always have the right to be heard. Treating our customers with respect will go a long way toward gaining acceptance of an unpopular decision.

2. Credibility: If you tell someone what you are going to do or say, then that's what you are expected to do and to say.

3. Honesty: Don't report what you think your supervisor wants to hear. Tell the exact story.

4. Ethics: Ask yourself how whatever you are doing would make you look if everyone knew about it. Never make staff feel they should do as you say, not as you do. There is no right way to do the wrong thing.

5. Confidentiality: If you have confidential information, you should keep it confidential. However, you are required by law to disclose certain information, such as harassment. You should inform staff of this responsibility before they give you confidential information.

6. Communication: With good information, people can make good decisions. Keep staff and students informed and in the know. Close the loop on all communication.

7. Delegation: You will delegate many tasks and decisions. In return, you must take responsibility and keep your supervisor informed. A rule-of-

thumb is that, if there is anything your boss could hear about from another source, he/she should hear it from you first.

8. No Upward Delegation: Don't ask your supervisor to do things that you should do yourself.

9. Let Managers Manage and Let Supervisors Supervise: Don't get too involved in the day-to-day operations. Let supervisors and staff do the job we hired them to do.

10. Admit Mistakes: Along with delegation will come some mistakes. Admit mistakes and learn from them. Don't wear your feelings on your sleeve. You will be offered constructive advice. Learn to make the most of it and move on.

11. Take Chances: Don't let the fear of making mistakes reduce your ability to take chances and make changes. "If you always do what you always did, you will always be where you have always been."

12. Agree to Disagree: We will not always agree, and you will not always agree with your peers, staff, or supervisor. Disagreement is healthy in the proper setting. Never tell staff/students that you are doing something that "I don't agree with, but my supervisor said to do it."

13. Timely Response: You are expected to meet deadlines and respond to issues as fast as possible. If you are going to need something by a certain time or date, inform others with specifics ahead of time.

Part 2: Things You Need to Know

1. The centerpiece of our mission is constant improvement. You are expected to be a proactive agent of this process.

2. You are expected to be an agent of organizational diversity. This includes using your position and influence to confront, teach, and learn about issues of diversity.

3. Don't involve yourself in gossip while at work. If you have issues with another staff person, talk with that person. Do not talk about that person to someone else.

4. Listen, learn, and anticipate. See what needs to be accomplished before someone tells you to do it.

5. You are expected to be a team player by supporting and assisting efforts of coworkers as you/they work. Remember, "We win and lose as a team."

6. You are expected to communicate across unit lines promoting a friendly community setting within the Division. Anyone at any level is welcome and expected to talk with any one at any level.

7. Know that your work in this organization, regardless of what you do, helps and enables our students to be successful at The University of Texas at Austin.

8. When unsure about something, you are expected to take the lead; ask questions and then take the initiative in determining and reaching a solution.

9. The Director of the DHFS prefers to be called Floyd on all occasions. Don't refer to managers/supervisors as the "bosses." Refer to them as teammates or staff-mates.

10. Never be late for a DHFS meeting. Being late is a selfish behavior.

11. Whining and negativism is not accepted; rather you are expected to study situations and present doable options/solutions.

12. Don't be alarmed by DHFS supervisors and managers talking with customers and staff in your area. Managers are expected to be physically in and around their areas observing and getting feedback to improve the organization.

13. Residence Halls are called "residence halls" and not "dormitories."

14. Wellness lifestyles and programs are strongly encouraged for all staff.

15. Remember, students live and eat here. Keep your area attractive and inviting and don't wait for someone else to pick up trash.

Floyd lets his staff know that he has terminated staff for guideline infractions and that he will do so again. He mentions his uncompromising stand on gossip: "If this is the kind of staff you are, then why don't you just draw your pay and move on down the road."

Does this list make you feel empowered? Floyd says that, when he presents this code to new staff, he gives it with such sincerity and intensity that they are at first taken aback. But they appreciate knowing exactly what is expected of them and knowing they won't be working in an uncertain situation, wondering what is expected and where they stand.

They ultimately support it. And employees have told him they would never forget his code. They understand his underlying reason for the code. It is because he cares for the customer (the students) and for his employees.

When I asked Floyd about his legacy, he said that he would like his gravestone to say, "He cared enough to want to make a difference in people's lives." This is his legacy.

What would you like written on your gravestone? What is your legacy?

15

Lesson 7: Keep Your Mind/Body Battery Charged

*It's not humanly possible to do everything right every day;
however, we can improve our health dramatically by dropping
just one unhealthy habit and adding a healthy one.*

— ANONYMOUS

O nce when I brought up the importance of rest during one of my stress-management workshops, a woman stood up in frustration and verbalized the feelings many in the audience, particularly women, shared. She chronicled the numerous activities going on in her life and in the lives of her husband and children—all of which she was responsible for. How could she find time for herself in her busy day?

This is typical of mothers; they don't make time to take care of themselves. It doesn't even occur to them. My mom is like that. They take care of everybody else, but they're last on the list.

Some men, of course, feel this way as well.

So what can I tell you to inspire you to start taking care of yourself?

I can remind you of what airline flight attendants tell you about using oxygen masks just before takeoff. They say put *your mask on first* and then help others.

That's the formula. You must put your mask on first and then help others, because if you don't take care of yourself, you can't possibly take care of anybody else. Not only in the dictionary does "I" come before "u."

241

Remember PhB Law 2: *The most important relationship you have is the one with yourself.* Keeping your mind/body battery charged is primary.

You have to take good care of yourself first so you can take care of others. You have to take care of yourself so you do not go out of your mind, and can use your magic, serve others, be creative, not compromise what you value most, and define your legacy.

So do you have what it takes? Do you have the horsepower and endurance to achieve what you have envisioned for yourself? Are you always tired? If you are then you won't ever make the grade. You have to think in terms of an athlete who conditions his mind and body for excellence. Think in terms of being a mind/body warrior.

Are you prepared for the future of work/life challenges?

Mind/Body Connection

The World Health Organization foresees more unhealthy workers, predicting that diabetes deaths will rise 50 percent in the next decade and that global obesity levels will skyrocket.

Studies show that working more than 55 hours a week, compared to the standard 40-hour week, can cause stress and weaken mental skills, a sure threat to the productivity of companies that demand long hours from workers. Read more about this in *The Future of Work* by Richard Donkin.

THE BATTERY THAT POWERS YOUR MIND AND BODY

This final lesson is about the battery that powers your mind and body—your personal capacity—and how to keep it fully charged and even increase its potential to meet the challenges ahead. A charged mind/body battery fuels your resolve, energy, and focus and enables you to transform your thoughts and actions from Standard Operating Program (StOP) to Professional Human Being (PhB).

Regard this lesson as a foundation for all previous lessons and try to apply as many of the lifestyle considerations recommended in the following pages. Not only will they boost your ability to become a PhB, but they can also make a huge difference in your stress level, your health, and your longevity.

The question I posed to you at the beginning of this book is how long you want to live. Remember, I proposed five fundamentals that affect the quality and longevity of your life. I have talked about the primary one—thinking—throughout this book. Now in this lesson, I'll elaborate on the other factors: rest, diet, exercise, and moderation. In addition, I will talk about more basics, including laughter, your lung health, and connection with the earth. They are all equally important.

THE VALUE OF REST

In the animal world, creatures function on two cycles: rest and activity. That's how nature designed things. However, we human animals, and particularly those of us in the modern industrialized West, tend to accentuate the activity and minimize the rest. There's always too much to do: too much TV to watch, too many video games to play, too much this, and too much that. And when we lay our heads down on the pillow, sleep often takes a long time to come. That's unfortunate because it is during rest that the body gets to work, doing maintenance and repair. This allows us to recharge the battery so we can charge out the next morning for another round of activity.

How important is rest? I like to give the example of Vince Lombardi, the late and great coach of the Green Bay Packers football team. Lombardi's training-camp rule was that his players had to be in bed—horizontally—by 11:00 p.m. His son tells the story that, one evening, future Hall of Fame defensive back, Emlen Tunnell, walked into the training camp dormitory at 10:59 p.m. He was met by Lombardi, who promptly fined him $50. When Tunnell objected that it wasn't yet 11:00,

Lombardi told him there was no way he could change clothes and be in bed by 11:00. The fine stuck.

Lombardi considered rest absolutely vital for his athletes. In *Hamlet*, Shakespeare wrote, "Conscience doth make cowards of us all." Lombardi altered this quote to fit his sport, "Fatigue doth make cowards of us all."

Long before the age of football, wise men put great value on rest as a balance to activity. In Chinese medicine, for example, we have the "yin and yang" concept in which rest, recovery, and nutrition are yin, while competition and activity are yang. In the *Nei Jing* (300 B.C.), the first known Chinese medical book, it is written: "Physical activity is necessary to harmonize the flow of vital energy and blood to develop strength. Excessive labor, however, can strain the ability of the spleen to produce energy, and this causes deficiencies. The body must rest."

REST: SLEEP

Do you sleep enough at night? If you do not, you will be less effective at work. Often ignored, but absolutely critical to stress management is deep, restful sleep. It's not just rest; it's sleep! Most adults need six to eight hours of sleep. Period. Exclamation point! If you rob the sleep bank, you will pay for your crime by running out of energy and putting yourself in an unenviable deficit called sleep deprivation. Many illnesses and workplace inefficiencies can be traced to lack of sleep or irregular sleep patterns.

The body reaches its deepest point of sleep, as measured by oxygen consumption, after six hours and then the metabolism gradually kicks in to return us to a normal waking state. Research also indicates that sleep between 10:00 p.m. and midnight rests parts of the brain not rested at any other time of the sleep cycle. So sound uninterrupted sleep for at least six hours, with a chunk before midnight, is the basis for dynamic performance.

Drowsy America

Are you drowsy? If so, you're not alone. A 1990 *Time* magazine cover article found that millions of Americans are sleep-deprived, trying to get by on six

244

hours or less, and a third of us have trouble falling asleep or staying asleep. The article also revealed some of the dangers of sleep deprivation:

- Human error, in which lack of sleep is a major factor, causes between 60 and 90 percent of workplace accidents.
- The U.S. Department of Transportation reports that up to 200,000 traffic accidents a year may be sleep related.

The status of sleep-deprived Americans hasn't gotten any better since the 1990 article.

And a sleepy America is costly.

Mind/Body Connection

National Sleep Foundation research indicates that sleep loss costs U.S. employers $18 billion each year in lost productivity. And, according to articles on The National Institute of Health website, the approximate annual cost of insomnia is $100 billion.

The New York Times Magazine, in a 1997 report, informed readers that many sleep researchers believe sleep deprivation is reaching crisis proportions.

This is a problem involving not just serious insomniacs, but the population at large, the article said, and added: "People don't merely *believe* they're sleeping less; they *are in fact* sleeping less—perhaps as much as one and a half hours less each night than humans did at the beginning of the century—often because they choose to do so."

Reasons for Sleep Deprivation

This last fact—that they choose to sleep less—came across loud and clear in a 2007 survey by the National Sleep Foundation of a thousand women, ages 18-64. The results suggest American women are seriously sleepy.

Sixty percent said they get a good night's sleep only a few nights a week. Sixty-seven percent say they frequently experience a sleep problem. And 43 percent say daytime sleepiness interferes with their daily activities. The respondents blamed their sleep problems on things such as hormones, housework, and caring for family members. Work-related issues were also involved since 48 percent of adult women are in the workforce.

The poll also showed, and this is fascinating, that the choices women make have an impact on their sleep. For example, instead of getting more sleep, women spend time on the following activities:

- Eighty-seven percent of women watch television in the hour before bedtime.
- Thirty-six percent are on the Internet.
- Twenty-one percent do job-related work at least a few nights a week.

Results of Sleep Deprivation

Most Americans no longer even know what it feels like to be fully alert. I think this is because we are used to feeling tired and think it's normal. "There is a general failure to recognize the importance of sleep across society," the National Sleep Foundation says. "Most women (80 percent) say that when they experience sleepiness during the day they just accept it and keep going. However, in order to keep going, 65 percent are likely to use caffeinated beverages, with 37 percent of all women consuming three or more caffeinated beverages per day."

Cornell University sleep expert, Dr. James Maas, the author of *Power Sleep: The Revolutionary Program That Prepares Your Mind for Peak Performance*, says, "[O]ften we [as Americans] are totally unaware of our own reduced capabilities because we become habituated to low levels of alertness. Many of us have been sleepy for such a long time that we don't know what it is like to feel wide awake." Let me stress that last part: You have been sleep deprived for so long *you don't know what it is like to feel wide awake.*

So what happens to you when you are sleep deprived? Check out this laundry list: lack of energy; bad moods; trouble handling stress; reduced ability to remember, concentrate, think logically, and handle complex tasks; along with reduced ability to assimilate and analyze new information, make decisions, communicate, and create. Motor and perceptual skills, and coordination are all affected. Ka-boom! That's a huge hit on work performance. If your body were a business, could you afford to lose all these assets?

Fatigue is one of the prime reasons for fear of change and fear of risk.

Mind/Body Connection

Many acute and degenerative illnesses are linked to sleep disorders. According to *The Wall Street Journal* 2009 article, "When Sleep Leaves You Tired," "Chronic, inadequate sleep raises the risk of cardiovascular disease, depression, diabetes, and obesity. It impairs cognitive function, memory, and the immune system and causes more than 100,000 motor vehicle accidents a year. Sleep deprivation also changes the body's metabolism, making people eat more and feel less satisfied."

Rest spawns motivation and wide-awake alertness. Coping skills and immunity to disease are at high levels when we get the proper amount of sleep.

The Sleep Bottom Line—for You and the Corporation

Margaret Thatcher, Europe's first female prime minister, claimed she could get by on five hours and joked, "Sleep is for wimps." The "Iron Lady," as she was called, exemplifies the prevailing 'macho' attitude toward sleep. Sleep is a self-indulgent extravagance for the weak.

Charles Czeisler, M.D., Professor of Sleep Medicine at Harvard Medical School, disagrees with Thatcher's viewpoint and goes as far as chastising those who promote such habits. In an article in *Harvard Business Review* titled "Sleep Deficit: The Performance Killer," he calls it a "culture of sleepless machismo" and warns of the dangers of lack of sleep.

Dr. Czeisler observes that top executives have a critical responsibility to take sleeplessness seriously. He encourages companies to create a sleep policy and not permit anyone to take an overnight flight and then drive to a business meeting somewhere. He says sleep deprivation is not just an individual health hazard; it is a public one, endangering everyone around us.

If you travel a good deal for business, I suggest you read *Hotel Secrets from the Travel Detective,* by Peter Greenberg. In his book, he writes about a study of volunteer business travelers commissioned by Hilton Hotels and Resorts. The findings were extremely significant. Monitoring seven days around a business trip, the study found that the participants had the lowest amount of sleep (five hours) on the night before the trip. "Essentially, travelers are at a decreased productivity level before they even walk out their door," said Mark Rosekind, a former director of NASA's Fatigue Countermeasures Program. By the time they returned home, participants had logged a total sleep loss of almost eight hours, the equivalent of one full night's sleep. Such deficits, the study concluded, have even broader implications than just performance.

Mind/Body Connection

After analyzing 16 studies involving 1.3 million people, a team of researchers from the University of Warwick, U.K., and Federico II University Medical School, Naples, Italy, found that people who sleep less than six hours per night are 12 percent more likely to die before age 65. The May 2010 study also found that sleeping longer than 9 hours is an indicator of serious illness. According to Professor Francesco Cappuccio, leader of the Sleep, Health and Society Programme at the University of Warwick, "whilst short sleep may represent a cause of ill-health, long sleep is believed to represent more an indicator of ill-health.

Bill Gates, founder of Microsoft, has said he gets seven hours of sleep a night because "that's what I need to stay sharp and creative and upbeat." Marc Andreesen, co-founder of Netscape, also values a good night's rest: "I can get by with 7 ½ [hours] without too much trouble. Seven and I start to degrade. Six is suboptimal. Five is a big problem. Four means I am a zombie." And he likes to get extra sleep on the weekends—over twelve hours sometimes. Jeff Bezos, CEO of Amazon.com, talked to *The Wall Street Journal* about his full night's sleep. "I'm more alert and I think more clearly. I just feel so much better all day long if I've had eight hours," he said.

Dr. Czeisler's message for corporate leaders is simple. To raise performance, both your own and your organization's, you need to pay attention to this fundamental biological issue: We need adequate sleep!

How to Get a Good Night's Sleep

First, medication is not the best way to put yourself to sleep. The pharmaceutical industry pushes its sleep products in ads and TV commercials and, while effective, such aids are addictive and potentially deadly (the deaths of entertainment greats Judy Garland and Marilyn Monroe were both reportedly linked to sleeping pills). In his e-book, *The Dark Side of Sleeping Pills*, Daniel F. Kripke, professor of psychiatry at the University of California, San Diego, who has been studying sleep disorders since 1973, reports that the use of sleeping pills shortens lives by increasing the risk of suicide and other causes of death. They are "unsafe in any amount," he says.

Here are some much safer options:

- Don't nap during the day if you have trouble sleeping at night.

- Avoid caffeine and alcohol late in the evening.
  For some, even after lunch is too late. Caffeine is a mild stimulant that forces your brain to be more alert when it doesn't particularly want to be so alert. Caffeine has a half-life of 6 hours. So half of the caffeine in your coffee at dinner is still there at midnight. Alcohol causes fragmented sleep and worsens the symptoms of sleep deprivation.

- Eat only light snacks after 7:30 p.m., but no sweets.
  A heavy meal before sleep can make it difficult to fall asleep and may even cause indigestion. Have your biggest meal at lunch. Refined sugar before sleep can keep you up by causing your blood sugar to rise and then drop.

- Have a glass of warm milk spiced with a bit of cardamom or nutmeg. This may help calm your body for sleep. Bring the milk to a boil and let it cool down a bit. Milk contains tryptophan, an amino acid used by the body to make the neurotransmitter serotonin and the hormone melatonin, both of which are involved in better sleep. Also, milk contains calcium which helps the brain use tryptophan.

- Try some herbal teas.
  Herbs and herbal teas can help you fall asleep. They come singly, such as valerian root and chamomile, or in combinations. The website, mapi.com, offers a product called "Blissful Sleep" that works very well for me on the road.

- Try nutritional supplements with sleep-inducing properties.
  Melatonin, also excellent for combating jet lag, is the hormone that's the key to deep, restful sleep. Your melatonin level rises with darkness and declines at dawn. Supplemental melatonin works well for many people, but not all. Magnesium is a great muscle relaxant. The forms that absorb the best are magnesium citrate, glycinate, or orotate. 5-HTP, an amino acid, is a precursor to the neurotransmitter serotonin which helps regulate mood and sleep. You can find most of these products in health food stores. You'll have to experiment to see which one works best for you.

- Exercise regularly, but not within two hours of bedtime.
  Think of sleep like parking your car. You have to slow down to do it. Physical activity too close to bedtime leaves your motor running in high gear.

- Practice a simple set of yoga postures.
  Yoga can calm the body down right before sleep.

- Don't watch the news or a sports event on TV before bedtime.
  The news is full of negativity that can cause stress. Sports events rev up the excitation level of your mind. Connecticut cardiologist, Stephen Sinatra, tells about one of his heart patients who suffered an

angina attack and a sleepless night after watching a seesaw basketball game involving his beloved University of Connecticut Huskies.

- Establish a relaxing bedtime routine.
  Perhaps incorporate some meditation, prayer, light reading, soft music, or some aromatherapy—lavender is a good scent to help you fall asleep.

- Keep your bedroom cool and dark.
  Darkness tells your body to make melatonin.

- Don't use your bed for anything other than sleep or sex.
  In other words, don't work in your bed or do other activities that keep your mind active.

- Go to bed at the same time each night, ideally before 10 p.m.
  This puts you in line with your body's natural sleep/wake cycle. For practically all of past human existence, we went to sleep early and arose early.

For more information on sleep and sleep disorders, check out the following websites: sleepnet.com and sleepfoundation.org.

TRANSCENDENTAL MEDITATION

After graduating from college I embarked on an exciting but difficult adventure. My full-time job at The University of Akron coupled with beginning graduate school was a heavy load to bear. I began to feel a lot of anxiety and stress in attempting to handle both; I even thought I was developing symptoms of an ulcer. So I went in for a checkup at the university clinic, drank the barium, and had an x-ray taken of my stomach. The doctor found I had an irritated duodenal cap, and explained that, if I didn't take care of it, the problem could ulcerate. She prescribed phenobarbital, a common sedative drug, to help me relax. She also told me to take the antacid Maalox before and after each meal and to eat a strict, bland diet. I took the phenobarbital for two days. Did it work for me? Oh yes! In

251

fact, it worked too well. I was so relaxed that all I could do was smile. I did nothing at work for those two days. I could not function. I went back to the doctor and told her I couldn't handle the drug. She actually suggested I try Transcendental Meditation (TM).

I didn't know where to learn about TM. But one day, after the stress became overwhelming, I walked out of class, looking for a sign; I crossed the quad and wandered to the auditorium. Outside the door was the sign: "Transcendental Meditation." I walked in and heard a man lecturing with an English accent. His name was Guy Hatchard, a certified instructor of TM from London, England, now living in New Zealand. I sat down and listened to my first lecture on TM.

A week later, I traveled 10 miles to Kent State University to learn the technique. This day was a turning point in my life. From then on, I began practicing TM regularly. Not only was I feeling more rested and fresh, my mind was clearer. I was relaxed, but not overly relaxed. I felt much less tension. I experienced a very natural state of physical rest, and that released a lot of the accumulated deep stress and fatigue—I felt revitalized almost immediately. Within three months of practicing TM with no phenobarbital, my symptoms disappeared.

I went back to the doctor and told her I had started the meditation practice and I felt better.

She said, "Well, let's take another x-ray to see what's happening." So I drank the barium again. She was amazed at the results of the x-ray: there was no sign of an irritated duodenal cap. While she had recommended this technique to several of her patients, I was the only one to try it. We were both thrilled with the result.

That was forty years ago and, to this day, what I look forward to most is the time I spend in meditation. My experience has encouraged me to recommend this technique to many others, including workshop participants, colleagues, and friends. I've received nothing but great feedback.

It may seem as though I am selling TM. I am. It is the best part of my day, and it reinvigorates me especially after a long, exhausting day. After 20 minutes of meditation, I feel as though I have just gotten up from a full night's sleep.

Although it is easy to put off a health routine, I learned from Doug Henning that keeping the mind/body battery charged is critical—in fact, primary—for success. This is the launchpad for all activities and endeavors.

Patricia Aburdene, in her book *Megatrends 2010: The Rise of Conscious Capitalism*, projects seven super trends for the future. One of them is what she calls "the wave of conscious solutions" in business. This can be readily attained through meditation as a business standard operating procedure. Businesses can promote meditation practice and allow time and space for the practice.

What Is TM?

TM is a non-religious meditation technique, introduced to the Western World by Maharishi Mahesh Yogi around 1959, that allows the practitioner to gain a unique state of restful alertness. Maharishi describes the TM technique as "a natural procedure, [through which] by itself the mind settles down." TM is practiced for 20 minutes morning and evening while sitting comfortably with the eyes closed. Those who practice it will tell you that it is easy to learn, effortless, and does not require specific beliefs, behaviors, or lifestyle changes. Around the world, more than five million people of all ages, cultures, religions, and educational backgrounds practice the technique.

Maharishi Mahesh Yogi brought TM out of India and showed that it is a powerful technique that eliminates suffering and stress, lowers blood pressure, improves heart health, and makes you happier, more creative, more productive, and more intelligent. TM even has the most pronounced effect on self-actualization compared to any other meditation or relaxation technique.

Transcendence: Total Brain Functioning

What makes TM different than the many forms of meditation available today? It is the "Transcendental" in Transcendental Meditation. Transcendence is what differentiates this technique from others. The

253

experience of transcendence or transcending is a unique state of consciousness called "restful alertness." This serene, tranquil, yet crystal-clear awareness gained during TM is actually a fourth state of consciousness, separate from waking, dreaming, and sleeping. This is a natural state we all can access, one which spontaneously dissolves physical stress and reorganizes mental clutter. We just need the proper technique. During TM, the body gains a unique state of deep rest along with heightened awareness that dissolves accumulated stress and revitalizes the nervous system, as well as enlivening more coherent brain functioning and improving health.

Electroencephalographic (EEG) studies have actually shown, using subjects fitted with electrodes wired up to measuring devices, that during TM, the different parts of the brain work in concert. This is one of the key features of attaining transcendence. Brain-wave coherence has been studied by brain and meditation expert, Dr. Fred Travis, who has been the director of the Center for Brain, Consciousness, and Cognition at Maharishi University of Management in Fairfield, Iowa, for the past twenty years (drfredtravis.com). Brain waves are patterns of electrical activity arising largely from the cerebral cortex.

Alpha EEG is a slow frequency, usually indicating restfulness. Generally we don't generate much alpha in the front of the brain just sitting with the eyes closed. But during TM we see significant increase of frontal alpha EEG along with beta, which indicates alertness and focus resulting in what is called "restful alertness." More interesting though is the coherence factor. All the various parts of the brain usually generate different frequencies, but during TM the waves of a given frequency from different parts of the brain fall into coherent step with one another.

Dr. Travis' EEG research has revealed that during transcendence there is increased coherence in alpha frequency (relaxation and inner reflection) and the lower part of beta frequency (focus and decision-making) in the prefrontal cortex. This part of the brain is known as the CEO of the brain. It is known as the chief executive officer because it is responsible for the regulation of emotions, evaluation of the importance of things, and plays a vital role in the decision-making process.

The CEO is not the only part of the brain enlivened though. The EEG readouts of subjects practicing TM show that waves from different parts of the brain become highly correlated with one another. This indicates that different regions of the brain are working together more cooperatively. They all line up indicating a global coherence across the entire brain. The waves of coherence and calmness spread across the whole brain, while simultaneously organizing the prefrontal areas (CEO) in preparation for improved focus and decision-making.

I once heard a neuroscientist use an analogy to describe this process. He asked if we had ever heard a symphony orchestra warming up. Most of us had. It is a chaotic, discordant mixture of sounds. This is the normal brain-wave signature (readout) of a person under stress. He then reminded us of what happens when the conductor raises his baton and the orchestra begins. Concordant music flows from the instruments of the musicians. This is analogous to a person beginning to meditate.

Dr. Travis' research demonstrates that after regular exposure to the transcendence experienced during TM, the EEG patterns become more and more coherent throughout the day after meditation. The profound result is that the individual has the potential to have spontaneous utilization of the total brain in every thought, speech, and action.

Brain-Wave Coherence

The more synchronized your brain, the more of your mental potential becomes available to you. Research indicates that brain-wave coherence fosters:

- Self-development
- Learning ability
- Intelligence
- Emotional stability
- Concept learning
- Moral reasoning
- Calmness

- Creativity
- Self-awareness

These elements, along with better long- and short-term memory and an improved ability to focus, correlate brain-wave coherence with high levels of competence and capacity.

How does brain-wave coherence translate into competence and increased capacity? Dr. Fred Travis and his team have the answer. They studied twenty top-level managers in Norway. These twenty veteran managers had proven their expertise over a long period of time by either expanding a business or turning around a business that was failing.

They compared these twenty successful managers to twenty knowledge workers who had limited management experience or responsibility. They were only matched by age and gender. They found that the managers showed greater coherence during tasks than the control managers. In a similar research project they studied thirty-three athletes and found that the elite athletes showed greater EEG coherence during tasks than those who weren't as successful. The conclusion is that EEG coherence reflects brain efficiency.

Brain Integration Scale

Dr. Travis and his team have created what is called the Brain Integration Scale (BIS). The BIS may measure in a more complete manner than any other assessment, the managerial capacity of the person being evaluated. It measures a combination of three brain functions. It measures the power of alpha waves in the frontal part of the brain, the part that functions as the CEO. Secondly, it measures alpha-wave coherence or alpha-wave patterns in different parts of the brain, and how correlated they are with one another. Thirdly, it measures what is called task-to-brain response, that is, within the tests how the brain adapts to and responds to different types of computer tasks.

TM meditators demonstrate more alpha density in the frontal lobes; they show greater alpha coherence between different parts of the brain. The meditator's brain becomes better adapted to respond to different computer tasks.

This is significant because high scores on the BIS are associated with higher levels of emotional stability; moral reasoning; and inner directedness, a term referring to a personality acting independently and according to one's own personal moral code as opposed to a person seeking approval and acceptance from others known as outer-directedness. High scores also indicate lower anxiety.

Dr. Travis has co-authored a paper that is in press in *Cognitive Processing* that reports significantly higher levels of brain integration in top managers compared to middle managers. This connecting of managing and leading to measurable brain functioning is a major breakthrough for training new leaders. The BIS is well on its way to becoming a staple in the battery of tests used by businesses to determine who is right for what position, and what personality is right for the management role.

Through the development of the mind and body resulting from the experience of this coherent state of transcendence, you enjoy increasing satisfaction in life and in work. TM recharges your battery. But more accurately we should say that it rewires it and increases your physical and mental capacity, enlivening and enabling total brain functioning. This is experienced as bliss and harmony. This is what you can expect from investing in practicing TM twice a day for 20 minutes. You can learn more about the TM technique at www.tm.org or tmwomenprofessionals.org

TM's Primary Goal: Self-Actualization

Among all the technologies that I have recommended over my 25 years of coaching executives, TM is the most comprehensive and holistic technique for self-development.

Peter Drucker, the father of the discipline of management, highlighted the importance of self-development: "The manager must acquire today the skills that will be effective tomorrow. He also needs an opportunity to reflect on the meaning of his own experience and—above all—he needs an opportunity to reflect on himself and learn to make his strengths count.

And then he needs *development as a person* even more than he needs development as a manager." [Italics added.] Drucker devoted three chapters to self-development in his legendary, groundbreaking book, *Management, Tasks, Responsibilities, and Practices.*

What is self-development? For twenty years Abraham Maslow studied what he considered to be people who had full use of and were capable of capitalizing on their potentialities, capacities, and talents. Maslow's definition of the highest form of self-development he called self-actualization. *"Self Actualization is the intrinsic growth of what is already in the organism, or more accurately, of what the organism is."*

During my graduate program in Psychology my favorite psychologist was the renowned Carl Rogers. He agreed with Maslow and simplified the concept by saying that, *"Every person has one basic motive and that is to self-actualize, to fulfill one's potential and achieve the highest level of 'humanbeingness.'"*

Since hearing about self-actualization in my first year of college, it has been difficult for me to understand how to achieve it. Research on TM and the practice of TM have helped me to understand how to make progress in realizing this goal.

There are several inventories to measure self-actualization; that is, assessments to establish how actualized one is. The most popular is the Personal Orientation Inventory (POI), which measures attitudes and values relating to the construct of self-actualization.

E.L. Shostrum developed the POI with the input of psychotherapists who studied individuals considered to be mentally healthy like the subjects studied by Maslow. Its absolute accuracy has been challenged, but it is the most utilized and the most validated assessment of its kind to date.

The editor and contributing author of the seminal book, *Higher Stages of Human Development,* and an adept TM researcher, Charles Alexander, Ph.D., and his colleagues conducted a meta-analysis of eighteen studies on the effects of TM on self-actualization. Fourteen of these studies used the POI. The results, published in the *Journal of Social Behavior and Personality,* were highly significant and found that the beneficial effects of TM on self-actualization increased over time.

In order to compare the results of TM on self-actualization with other types of meditation, Alexander's team found forty-two studies to analyze, including studies on Zen, the Relaxation Response, and fifteen others. The results were remarkable. TM's effect on self-actualization, as measured by written tests, was about **four times** as great as that of any other meditation and relaxation procedure. Why? The study suggested that TM was far superior because it provides the experience of the *transcendence* that allows for brain transformation through brain-wave coherence.

Here are some of the many components of self-actualization that the practice of TM develops more of: emotional maturity, a resilient sense of self, a positive and integrated perspective of ourselves and the world, ability to live in the present, increased flexibility, increased spontaneity, increased self-acceptance and self-regard, perception of men and women as essentially good, increased acceptance of feelings, increased capacity for warm interpersonal relationships, and a greater ability to embody the values of self-actualization.

These improvements in the measured components of self-actualization through TM describe the person I want to be. They describe the true Professional Human Being. The great professional baseball player, Larry Bowa, now a major league baseball analyst, when asked about his TM practice, said, "TM is allowing me to be the person I've always wanted to be." I agree with Larry. My practice of TM allows me to be the kind of person I really want to be.

Enlightenment

These components of self-actualization sound much like the definition of enlightenment.

In 1982, as I mentioned previously, we were in rehearsal for the Broadway play *Merlin* in which Doug Henning played Merlin. He also co-wrote the original story. In one of the rehearsals a Columbia Pictures' executive heard one of the lines in the play where Merlin's master gestures towards young Merlin, played by Doug, and says the words, "Become enlightened!" Following that, Merlin is capable of commanding all the laws of nature and using all of his potential.

Columbia Pictures, owner of the rights to *Merlin,* informed Doug that they would have to eliminate these words from the play because no one would understand what enlightenment meant. Doug, of course, responded indignantly by saying that he wouldn't act in the play if they removed this line and that scene. The line and scene remained.

Just like Doug, I cannot leave the word "enlightenment" out of this book when speaking of TM. Today the most recent scientific research on TM and self-actualization, transcendence, and brainwave coherence allows us to understand what this word means in very practical terms.

Robert Keith Wallace, a physiologist; Lawrence Domash, a physicist; and Maharishi Mahesh Yogi, a Vedic scientist, collaborated to define the term. They concluded, that scientific research on TM "has revealed several important features of the nature of enlightenment and the process through which it is gained. Enlightenment is not a hypnotic state of self-delusion or self-denial. The state of enlightenment represents the ultimate development of what we ordinarily consider to be the most valuable qualities of human life. It is something real, natural, and tangible, and develops systematically in a continuous and progressive manner..." (They are referring to the regular practice of TM that exposes one to transcendence and its profound state of transformation in the brain physiology.) They go on to say that the process of gaining enlightenment is "open to anyone starting from any level of consciousness, without requiring any special lifestyle or system of belief. The ability of gaining enlightenment is innate in the physiology of every human being..."

This definition closely reflects the definitions of self-actualization by Maslow and Rogers, but also gives us a procedure to hasten its development.

David Houle is a renowned futurist and has dubbed the years 2010 to 2020 as the decade of transformation. What we have within our reach is a technology, TM, which will allow us to keep pace with this global transformation.

TM in the Mainstream

Dr. Mehmet Oz, well-known surgeon, author, and host of *The Dr. Oz Show,* also recommends and practices TM. His daily routine was noted in a cover story in the May/June 2010 issue of *AARP The Magazine,* titled, "Dr. Oz: America's Hardest-Working Doctor":

> The doctor follows his own orders for healthy living, and it shows, both in the slender frame he reveals in close-fitting surgical scrubs and in his seemingly boundless energy— "electrifying vitality," as Diane Sawyer puts it. His diet features fruits and veggies, grains, and lean protein. (Raw nuts soaked in water, in the Turkish style, are a staple.) He does transcendental meditation regularly and says his 20-year habit of daily yoga is "the most important health practice I have adopted."

On Wednesday, December 7, 2011, Oprah Winfrey was featured in a candid, one-on-one interview on *The Dr. Oz Show.* During the interview, she discussed her life after *The Oprah Winfrey Show,* including the impact her practice of the Transcendental Meditation technique is having in her own life, and in the lives of her 400 meditating employees. For more details you can go to an article by Oprah on her practice of the TM technique at www.tm.org/oprah-on-tm.

In Jay Marcus' book, *Success From Within: Discovering the Inner State That Creates Personal Fulfillment and Business Success,* Monty Guild, the Los Angeles investment manager, acknowledges how critical to success the technique really is. He says, "There is an ad I often see for *The Wall Street Journal.* It says that, 'you need *The Wall Street Journal* to be faster, tougher, and smarter and to effectively compete in today's business world.' What I would say is that you can't effectively compete in today's business world without TM."

The book also quotes Walter Eisenberg, vice president in charge of production at an East Coast wholesaler/retailer, who saw a substantial difference in his employees' attitudes toward their jobs. He found that people who practice TM enjoy life more and have a marked difference in their attitude towards life and work. "It is very hard to convert it to dollars and cents directly, but your business is made up of people and, if your people function better and produce better, the business is way ahead."

Stephen Covey, business guru and bestselling author of *The Seven Habits of Highly Effective People,* was asked about the value of the TM practice in his life. He answered that he believes in TM and values his twenty minutes twice daily. He said it allows one to tap into the four unique human endowments: self-awareness, conscience, independent will, and creative imagination.

Several companies I have personally worked with, including Doug Henning Magic, had many of its employees practicing TM. Another was Jake's Crane & Rigging International, a family-owned firm that has provided much of the heavy construction equipment used in the building of Las Vegas. Many employees, as well as the president of the company, Bob Dieleman, practiced the TM technique. I have also worked with Monty Guild, CIO of Guild Investment Management, in Malibu, California, where almost all employees practice TM. Marshal Belden, the owner of MB Operating, an oil company based in my hometown of Canton, Ohio, is a meditator and offered TM to every employee who wanted to learn it. Patricia Aburdene, the author of *Megatrends 2010: The Rise of Conscious Capitalism,* envisages, "If meditation were a machine, every CEO in America would buy one." I agree, but only if they knew what scientific results this machine produces.

TM: Science-Based Program

I focus my emphasis on the TM technique, not only because it is the best *"transcending"* meditation technique on the market today, but also because it is the technique I have over 40 years of personal experience with and which is the most thoroughly validated by science. It is a science-based program.

Since the 1970s, there have been 357 published, peer-reviewed research studies. If you are not familiar with the rigorous process involved in scientific publishing, peer-reviewed studies are required to be scrutinized by independent reviewers who are authorities in their fields. The experts then suggest changes and recommendations and only after these changes are made are the studies published. The research has appeared in many prestigious journals: *Hypertension; The American Journal of Cardiology; Anxiety, Stress and Coping; Social Behavior and Personality; American Journal of Health Promotion; Journal of Clinical Psychology;* and *American Psychologist.*

Robert Roth, author of *TM: Transcendental Meditation,* says, "Tens of thousands of business professionals and hundreds of companies have begun the practice of TM." In the book he cites a Fortune 100 company that found—through surveys of their employees—less anxiety, tension, insomnia, and fatigue, reduced use of hard liquor and tobacco, greater effectiveness in job satisfaction, improved health, and fewer health complaints. These results occurred after only three months. For sure, no pharmaceutical can do that!

Patricia Aburdene (*Megatrends 2010*) cites R.W. "Buck" Montgomery, who introduced TM in 1983 to his Detroit chemical-manufacturing company, H.A. Montgomery. "Results were dramatic," he said. Fifty-two of the company's 70 workers meditated at home before work, and then again in the afternoon on company time at the plant—20 minutes each time. The results were astounding: Absenteeism fell 85%, injuries fell 70%, sick days dropped 76%, productivity soared 120%, quality control rose 240%, and profits skyrocketed an amazing 520%! "Admittedly," Patricia added, "this is an old study, but I report these findings rather than dismiss them because, as amazing as these numbers sound, they're consistent with the results meditation practitioners report."

Mind/Body Connection

A review of 32 physiological studies found that the TM technique produces deeper rest than ordinary relaxation, and also shows that meditators have lower baseline levels of stress.

Another review of 146 independent study outcomes found that the TM

---

technique produces greater reductions in anxiety than other relaxation and meditation techniques.

A review of 42 studies found that the TM technique produces greater self-actualization—developing one's potential—than other meditation and relaxation techniques. The regular practice of TM effectively reduces blood pressure. According to studies funded by the National Institutes of Health, one review indicated a reduction of 4.7 mm Hg in systolic, and 3.2 mm Hg diastolic blood pressure, clinically meaningful changes that can reduce cardiovascular disease risk.

TM and Business

Such glowing assertions, backed up by some interesting workplace research, have major implications for productivity, worker satisfaction, and health care. They are summarized as follows:

- Researchers at the National Institute of Industrial Health of the Japanese Ministry of Labor compared 447 industrial workers who were taught the TM technique with 321 workers who did not learn the practice. According to the findings cited in *Japanese Journal of Industrial Health*, the meditators showed significant decreases in: physical complaints, impulsiveness, emotional instability, anxiety, and also insomnia.

  The study was done at Sumitomo Heavy Industries, Ltd., a diverse international company that develops heavy machinery for science and industry. As part of their self-improvement program, Sumitomo also introduced the program to its executives and managers at their head office in Tokyo. More than 600 managers, including the company's chairman, learned TM. Since then the health insurance division of the company recommends TM to workers as a means of disease prevention and control, and for creating a harmonious work environment. Presently more than a hundred Japanese companies have implemented TM programs for managers and executives.

- Two studies found that employees practicing the TM programs on an average of 11 months showed significant improvements at work, compared with a group of non-meditators. Relationships with coworkers and supervisors improved, as did job performance and satisfaction, while the desire to change jobs decreased.

- One study analyzed health insurance usage for more than two-thousand people practicing TM over a five-year period. It was found that the meditators had less than half the doctor visits and hospitalization, and less medical treatment in seventeen disease categories, compared to other groups of comparable age, gender, and profession. Another study showed decreased hospital admission in all categories of disease.

I wrote earlier about brain capacity. Instead of pursuing the usual strategy of education by just filling up the brain, the container-of-knowledge, with information, we need to expand it! The question is then, how does TM help to expand capacity? We need to know, based on what Arie De Geus of Royal Dutch Shell said, "The ability to learn faster than our competitors may be the only sustainable competitive advantage."

TM significantly produces increased fluency of verbal creativity, efficiency of learning new concepts, more principled moral reasoning, higher verbal IQ, and decreased neuroticism. In addition, the technique actually increases IQ, according to a study, which found that over a two-year period, those who regularly practiced TM increased significantly in intelligence and the ability to make rapid-choice decisions compared to the control subjects. Both indicate an increase of mental capacity. Learn more about TM in business by going to www.tmbusiness.org/.

TM and Aging

Scientific research has demonstrated the detrimental effects of the aging process can be slowed down or neutralized through TM, as the chart below indicates.

Mind/Body Aspect	With Aging	Through Practice of TM
Cardiovascular efficiency	Decreases	Increases
Cerebral blood flow	Decreases	Increases
Vital capacity	Decreases	Increases
Neuromuscular coordination	Decreases	Increases
Fluid intelligence	Decreases	Increases
Creativity	Decreases	Increases
Learning ability	Decreases	Increases
Memory	Decreases	Increases
Organization of memory	Decreases	Increases
Self evaluation of health/well-being	Decreases	Increases
Insomnia	Increases	Decreases
Susceptibility to stress	Increases	Decreases
Depression	Increases	Decreases

In 2011 the number of people learning Transcendental Meditation was again on the rise in the United States due to a best-selling book, *Transcendence: Healing and Transformation Through Transcendental Meditation,* by renowned psychiatrist and medical researcher, Dr. Norman Rosenthal. He says that the experience during meditation of "transcendence, is a powerful antidote for many of our modern woes, a way to help overcome stress and stress-related disorders while opening a new window to the potentialities of the human brain."

The book explores the scientific documentation of healing and transformation through the TM practice and also features case studies and interviews with meditators including Paul McCartney, Russell Brand, Martin Scorsese, Moby, Laura Dern, and David Lynch.

Dr. Rosenthal says, "If TM were a new prescription drug, conferring this many benefits, it would be a billion-dollar blockbuster."

DIET

So far in this lesson, I've covered the importance of sleep and meditation, two springboards for better health, energy, and performance.

Let's jump into six more basic areas of lifestyle that contribute as well to our health, energy, and performance, and which many people often tend to treat thoughtlessly.

Water: The Silver Medicine

Let's start with how much water you should drink. One current estimate is based on body weight. Divide your weight in half and that is on average the number of ounces you should drink in a day. Of course, if you are an athlete and sweat a lot, you need more water to compensate.

Why should we drink plenty of water? Simply put, you can't be energetic without it. Lack of water is a primary cause of daytime fatigue. Be moderate, however. Drinking too much water is also not healthy.

We all know that water is essential for life; yet, when people are thirsty or tired, they are so programmed by advertising they often reach instead for a soda, beer, juice, cup of coffee, or a candy bar. This makes no sense. Such products contain too much sugar, alcohol, or artificial this-and-

267

that. Moreover, alcohol and caffeine actually dehydrate your body. You end up needing *more* water.

When you ask people if they are drinking enough, they usually say they are, but that's only because they include all that other stuff, not the basic fluid that the human body evolved on. Studies indicate that perhaps three-quarters of Americans are chronically dehydrated. Your body needs water— good, clean water, as nature made it.

We can't go more than a few days without it. Physiologically, water plays a big role in maintaining health. To know just how much, you should read *Your Body's Many Cries For Water: You Are Not Sick, You Are Thirsty! Don't Treat Thirst with Medications!* This eye-opening book, by an Iranian-American named F. Batmanghelidj, M.D., is the only one I know written specifically about health and water.

Dr. Batman, as he is generally called for obvious reasons, did extensive clinical and scientific research showing how the body naturally generates different thirst signals that can be mistaken for symptoms and signs of illness. Recognizing them for what they really are, you can avoid costly mistakes, he said: "Humans seem to lose their thirst sensation and the critical perception of needing water. Not recognizing their water need, they become gradually, increasingly, and chronically dehydrated with progress in age." He continues, "Chronic dehydration causes symptoms that equal disease when the variety of emergency signals of dehydration are not understood—as they are until now not understood."

Do you have a glass of water next to you? If not, go get one. I'll wait!

Mind/Body Connection

When people become sick or vulnerable to illness, it's often due to dehydrated cell membranes, inhibiting the ability to properly take in nutrients and expel wastes. Your brain cannot function without water. Research says a mere 2 percent drop in body water can trigger fuzzy short-term memory, trouble with basic math, and difficulty focusing on a

---

computer screen or printed page. Drinking five glasses of water daily decreases the risk of colon cancer by 45 percent, breast cancer by 79 percent, and bladder cancer by 50 percent.

According to the journal, *Cancer Epidemiology, Biomarkers & Prevention*, "Water intake alone…was significantly associated with a reduced risk of colon cancer among women."

James Martung, a Doctor of Chinese medicine who lived on the island of Trinidad, had patients from all over the world, including me, until he died at age 100 plus. He recommended hot water in tandem with Chinese herbs to heal the body and to activate the intelligence of the herbs he prescribed. He told me that it kept blood pressure normal, cleansed the system, and helped the body to assimilate nutrients from foods and herbs.

His secret was to fill up a thermos in the morning so that your water is with you all day. When you are thirsty reach and drink. If you don't have it, you won't drink it. Dr. Martung advised that hot water, warm water, or water at room temperature are much better than cold. Cold water dampens digestive fire and dampens the functioning of the internal systems. You may want to heed his advice; he was healthy until age 100 plus.

Dr. Martung's star pupil and protégé, Dr. David Lee Sheng Tin (psychedonlife.net) is one of the best holistic health coaches. He dubbed water "the silver medicine," elevating water to its rightful status in the realm of health care. Water is absolutely necessary to heal the body.

Prior to the implementation of new airport restrictions, I boiled my own water and carried two Thermos-fuls on planes. Now I carry empty flasks into the airport and, after passing through security, I fill them up with hot water at the airline clubrooms. I prefer hot water to cold water; my body metabolizes it better. And I use Thermoses so I know what amount I'm drinking. I recommend you find a way to measure your intake so you meet a minimum.

Have you ever experienced dehydration? I have, as a result of taking long flights and not putting enough water in my body before and during the flight. You lose one cup of water per hour on a plane; to stay even, you need to drink one cup per hour.

Headaches are one major sign of dehydration for me. As an international professional speaker, I really need my daily supply of water. I never fly into a city on the day I'm scheduled to speak, but I usually speak the very next day. It is important I have a good flight—I don't need a headache. I need to be clear and energetic. I've learned to drink plenty of water on flights.

Try this experiment: During your next afternoon at work, as soon as fatigue hits, drink a glass of water and then another one over the next half-hour. Monitor your energy level.

You'd better take care of yourself because science will keep you alive.

— DANA CARVEY
Comedian

If I had known I was going to live this long, I would have taken better care of myself.

— MICKEY MANTLE
The late baseball great

Good Eating

I'm not going to nag you about eating well. You've heard it all a million times and you're smart enough to know what to eat and what not to eat.

Dr. Stephen Sinatra, a metabolic cardiologist who practices integrative medicine using the best of both conventional and alternative approaches, has a fabulous monthly newsletter that opens your understanding of how cardiovascular disease can be prevented, minimized, and treated with nutrition, supplements, and stress-reduction techniques. If you are interested in tapping into this refreshing source of information, go to drsinatra.com.

Dr. Sinatra says, as your own doctor would tell you, a good diet is essential to cardiovascular health.

He recommends a diet that avoids sugar, sodas, sweets, refined carbohydrates, and trans fats. "They are, without a doubt, the biggest enemies of a healthy cardio-vascular system because they ramp up the level of inflammation in your body."

"Limit beef and dairy and eliminate processed foods. Instead, eat a varied diet filled with fresh vegetables, whole grains, fruits, fish (wild, not farm-raised), nuts and seeds, and healthy oils such as olive, walnut, and almond." A survey of Chinese centenarians in the early 1980s found that beans and green vegetables form a major part of their diets. The British Medical Association refers to research that vegetarians live longer than meat-eaters. Vegetarians have a 28 percent lower risk of heart disease and a 39 percent reduced chance from dying of cancer.

EXERCISE

What you also can't do without is exercise. You've got to move. Some of you, I am sure, are exercise devotees. But most of us are slackers. More than 75 percent of American adults are sedentary.

But there is hope for slackers, as I learned in the book *Move Yourself,* written by two experts from the Cooper Clinic in Dallas, Texas, the leading fitness research center in the world. Yes, we all know we should exercise moderately at least thirty minutes a day on five or more days a week. That will reduce your risk of many common diseases.

However, according to Tedd Mitchell, M.D., and Tim Church, M.D., Ph.D., the authors, you can do much less than that and still make a big impact on your health. Something is better than nothing, they say. Based on cutting-edge research and results from 85,000 patients at the clinic, they have found amazing life-changing benefits from low-dose physical activity. Just a few minutes each day, much less than is generally recommended, immediately generates major health and quality-of-life improvements, including more energy, better mood, memory, sleep, and sex life. This itself should motivate you right now to go take that five-minute walk.

The book provides great ideas for sedentary folks and even gives you a plan for incorporating physical activity into your workday, including how to use a step counter, a terrific gadget for getting you off the dime and staying with it.

Walking

How about taking a brisk, two-minute walk five-to-ten times a day, even in your office building, or a ten-minute walk three times a day after meals? It works, say doctors.

You can also take a brisk morning walk. Ayurveda, the oldest form of medical science, prescribes a morning walk to eliminate depression. Sunrise is the best time for a walk. Recent studies suggest that exercise improves more than just your physical health; it also improves your mental outlook.

Get moving. Exercise maintains and increases your mental acuity. Mental acuity is not sharp without physical and mental exercise. You have to exercise the mind and you have to exercise the body. For me, taking a walk before a presentation is an excellent way to keep my mind sharp. Before some of my best talks I have gone for a brisk walk. I recently did this in San Marcos, Texas, where I presented for the Department of Aging and Disability. They were running behind schedule, so I went outside and walked around the building several times. Like a boxer hopping in place before the bell dings, I had a lot of energy that I had to keep pumped up. When I started the lecture, I was amazed at my clarity and energy level.

Both physical and mental exercise gives me a sense of self-esteem, strength, and a boldness to do things that I may not feel capable of doing. This book will elevate you past excuses and lift you to a new level of vitality.

Stretching and Yoga

Move Yourself also teaches some simple stretching exercises you can do in a few minutes. Of course, yoga is wonderful for that as well, and a practice I do every day. Among their many benefits, stretching and yoga increase circulation, stimulate the movement of cerebral fluid in the spine, and activate all of the glands in the body.

If you're not already doing yoga, I recommend you try it. If you are already practicing it, I encourage you to do it regularly. Yoga maintains muscle tone and flexibility despite your age and is excellent for the nervous system and the brain. It allows for better circulation to the entire body, especially to the brain. The Center of Integrative Medicine at Thomas Jefferson University recently discovered that, after a single session of yoga, levels of the stress hormone cortisol dropped, even in first-time participants.

MODERATION

Finally, moderation. The dictionary tells us that moderation means restraint, temperance, and the avoidance of extremes or excesses. A simple intention might be to meet the midpoint between excess and deficiency in your approach to life. At the start of this book I referred to Bill Cosby's book *I Am What I Ate and I'm Frightened*. I mentioned that he left his chapter on moderation blank. I will also say very little about moderation. Instead I will leave you with these two quotes:

> *If taken in excess, even nectar (amrita) is poison.*
>
> — HINDU PROVERB

> *Enough is as good as a feast.*
>
> — ENGLISH PROVERB

MORE BASICS

Your Lung Health

Smoking is a major risk factor for Alzheimer's, heart disease, and cancer, among other serious illnesses. Cigarettes cause at least 30 percent of all cancer deaths and contribute to tumors of the lungs, larynx, mouth, throat, esophagus, bladder, liver, and pancreas. Smoking is bad for you. Need I say more?

Even if, like me, you don't smoke, there are still hazards. I used to be tolerant of friends and clients who smoke especially in Europe but now, after reading several studies on the dangers of secondhand smoke, I am leaving my tolerance behind and avoiding smoke at all costs.

The National Cancer Institute, one of the 27 institutes that make up the National Institutes of Health (NIH) in the U.S., summarizes, "You don't have to be a smoker for smoking to harm you. You can also have health problems from breathing in other people's smoke. Secondhand smoke is the combination of smoke that comes from the burning end of a cigarette, cigar, or pipe and the smoke exhaled by the smoker. Secondhand smoke contains more than 50 substances that can cause cancer. Health effects of exposure to secondhand smoke include lung cancer, nasal sinus cancer, respiratory tract infections, and heart disease. There is no safe amount of secondhand smoke."

As of January 2011, according to the American Nonsmokers' Rights Foundation, 35 states in the U.S. have laws requiring 100 percent smoke-free workplaces and/or restaurants and/or bars. This is important because, according to Tobacco Smoke Pollution in Oklahoma Workplaces, the February 2010 report by Oklahoma Tobacco Research Center (OTRC), "The exhaust required by statutes for smoking rooms is intended to help speed clearance of smoke...but concentrations of smokers in the confines of these smoking rooms produce very unhealthy levels of toxic smoke." And "non-smoking dining areas in restaurants with smoking rooms had three times as much [of the toxic substance] as restaurants that were entirely smoke free." There is no safe amount of smoke and, if you're in a smoking establishment, you can't get away from it!

Sir, Laugh a Lot

Laughter is serious stuff. Laugh as much as you can. Studies show laughter helps keep blood vessels dilated, protects against heart attacks, strengthens the immune system, lowers stress hormones, and lifts your mood!

In Norman Cousin's 1979 bestseller, *Anatomy of an Illness,* the famous literary editor described how he healed himself from a debilitating disease with megadoses of *Candid Camera* and old Marx Brothers films. Cousins regarded laughter as "a form of jogging for the innards."

Mind/Body Connection

The American Journal of Medicine tells us that laughter increases the secretion of catecholemines and endorphins, subsequently increasing the oxygenation of the blood, relaxing the arteries, speeding up the heart and decreasing blood pressure (which has a positive effect on all cardiovascular and respiratory ailments) as well as overall increasing the immune system response.

In the mid-1980s, he inspired Lee Berk, a young researcher, to explore the physiology of laughter. At the time Berk was investigating how exercise produces endorphins. He was the first researcher to demonstrate how exercise-induced endorphins relate to *runners' high* and that exercise could benefit the immune system.

Berk's subsequent research showed that laughter, similar to exercise, produces a high tide of endorphins, in addition to lowering stress hormones.

Cousins felt strongly that laughter acted as a metaphor and mobilization of one's full range of spiritual, emotional, and physical resources in the striving for wellness and the battle against illness. Berk's work validated Cousins' on this point as well. In numerous experiments he proved laughter impacts the physiology in specific ways to bolster the healing potential of mind, body, and spirit. Detrimental stress hormones decrease. Beneficial hormones increase.

Their work mirrored that simple line in the Bible: "A merry heart doeth good like a medicine."

So go see a funny movie, watch Comedy Central, tell a joke, share some laughs. I once read that children laugh 400 times a day and adults only 15-20 times. So get with it! "He who laughs," said Mary Pettibone Poole, "lasts."

Earthing: A Natural Stress-Buster

One of the most fascinating, and natural, forms of stress-busting I've come across was introduced to me by my good friend and health writer, Martin Zucker. His book, *Earthing: The Most Important Health Discovery Ever?* was co-written with Clint Ober, and Stephen Sinatra, M.D. It describes the discovery of significant health benefits resulting from contact with the planet's gentle electric energy. Earthing involves making direct contact with the earth while you sleep and even while you work.

You can, of course, make contact by going barefoot outside, and many of you reading this book may remember a time when you walked on a sandy beach or dew-moistened grass and felt some subtle warmth or tingling in your feet and legs. This is the earth's electrical energy you were feeling.

However, most people won't or can't go barefoot long enough to experience the benefits that the earth's surface provides. Zucker, and his co-authors, one a cardiologist and the other a fascinating gentleman who first made the discovery, describe how people can sleep or work indoors on specially conductive sheets and mats connected via a wire to a ground rod outside the window or to a properly grounded wall socket in their bedroom or office.

The book chronicles the scientific research, along with many testimonials, showing major benefits such as improved sleep, more energy, reduced inflammation and pain, accelerated healing from injury or surgery, and a shift in the nervous system away from a stressed (sympathetic) mode to a more calming (parasympathetic) mode. Personally, I have found Earthing extremely practical and beneficial in my busy life of traveling and speaking all over the world. It eliminates jet lag, helps relieve travel fatigue, and contributes to clear thinking.

Throughout history, humans walked barefoot and slept on the ground, largely oblivious to the fact that the surface of the earth contains this limitless healing energy. Science has now discovered that this energy promotes health, harmonizes and stabilizes the body's basic biological rhythms, and neutralizes inflammation.

Modern lifestyle, including the widespread use of insulating rubber- or plastic-soled shoes, has disconnected us from this energy and, of course, we no longer sleep on the ground as we did in times past. Zucker's book describes how this physical disconnect from the earth creates abnormal physiology and contributes to inflammation, pain, fatigue, stress, and poor sleep; and how by reconnecting to the earth, symptoms are rapidly relieved and even eliminated. People sleep better. They are more energized. And they have less stress.

Earthing is a powerful and amazing tool, easily incorporated into the busiest of lives. After you read this book you will never look at the ground beneath your feet the same way. Visit www.earthing.com for more information on how you can make a big difference in the quality of your life.

HOW CAN YOUR ORGANIZATION GET WITH IT AND ASSIST YOU IN YOUR PURSUIT OF HEALTH?

If the organization will follow some of these simple recommendations, they will be laughing their way to the bank with health-care savings.

Mind/Body Connection

Companies can save millions by proactively caring for workers. British Telecom launched health initiatives in 2005, leading to a 33 percent decline in workers using sick days, saving $48 million annually.

—*The Future of Work* by Richard Donkin.

277

Is your organization prepared for the future? The future is now. Many companies are taking on the social responsibility of creating a healthy workplace for their employees.

Several of my clients have removed all vending machines that do not encourage healthy habits and have replaced them with those that do. One example is in replacing soda with natural juices.

A CEO in Romania has his security people make sure everyone is out of their office and the building by 6:00 p.m. He says if you can't do your job in the allotted time, then he has you in the wrong job.

Talent Plus, Inc., a company in Nebraska, has a kitchen and a professional chef on board to make its employees fresh and healthy meals.

Ashton Service Group near Vancouver, B.C., Canada offers $1,000 dollars to employees who quit smoking. So far, three have been successful and have collected on the offer. The company also declared all areas of the company, including trucks, non-smoking areas. In addition, the organization allows for a certain number of paid hours per week to their employees who volunteer in the community.

Another company in England encourages employees to wear pedometers which mark the number of steps taken per day. If 10,000 steps are taken, rewards are given. This company also gives bonuses for not taking sick days; in other words, for staying healthy.

David Ali, M.D., and Patsy Ali, owners of Gulf View Medical Centre, Ltd., on the Caribbean island of Trinidad, have built and equipped a beautiful, spacious gym on the top floor of their four-story medical center. From here they can enjoy the view of the Gulf of Paria as they exercise. A fitness enthusiast himself, Dr. Ali encourages employees and staff to use the gym daily. This is provided as a service to the 100 plus employees and staff and their families. Surrounding neighbors are also welcome.

Many companies are paying for their employees to meditate 20 minutes twice daily on company time, following many Japanese companies who are aware of the prevention it offers.

Nutritionist and exercise guru, Covert Bailey, says in his book *Fit or Fat*, "If I were offering a pill to decrease the tendency of the body to make fat, fat people would be lining up to buy it. I am offering such a pill; it takes just 12 minutes a day to swallow it!'"

Thought Provokers

- Most medical and scientific experts agree that here are three major killers in our society today: coronary disease, cancer, and stroke. These conditions are all linked to what we eat and drink.

- What heals the body is motion and movement. If you sit around and don't move, then healing doesn't take place. You get old.
  Nothing happens until something moves.
  – Albert Einstein.

- *Work harder on yourself than you do at your job. Working hard on your job will earn you a living, but working hard on yourself will earn you a fortune.*
  – Jim Rohn, American author and speaker

- God speaks through silence. Everything else is a poor translation.

- *Men do not quit playing because they grow old; they grow old because they quit playing.*
  – Oliver Wendell Holmes, American jurist

Action Ideas

- Eat less—and get used to it! The longest-lived populations in the world have a couple of things in common. One is that they consume only one-half to two-thirds of what the average American does, a quarter of the fat and half of the protein. Their carbohydrate intake is about the same, but it is unprocessed. The latest research says lowering your caloric intake leads to fewer toxins and less stress on the digestive system.

- Read labels on food products before buying. The more ingredients in a product, the more unnatural it is. Ideally, purchase as much organic as possible.

- Read *YOU The Owner's Manual: An Insider's Guide to the Body That Will Make You Healthier and Younger* by Michael F. Roizen, M.D. and Mehmet

C. Oz, M.D. In this Diet-Activity Crib Sheet (page 344) they capture the basics of exercise.

Diet-Activity Plan Crib Sheet

Walking	30 minutes every day (or other general physical activity like swimming, if you cannot walk)
Stamina training (biking, swimming)	3 times a week, at a rate at which you are sweating for 20 minutes or are out of breath by the end
Resistance training	3 times a week, 10 minutes a day
Stretching or yoga	Every day, after a walk
Deep breathing	Take 10 deep breaths every morning and night (refer to Chapter 5 of their book to learn how)
Sleep	Plan time for 7 to 8 hours daily.

- Visit The Raj, a preeminent hotel and health spa. The Raj Health Spa programs have been featured on CBS, NBC, ABC, CNN, *Newsweek*, *Time*, *New York Times*, *Wall Street Journal*, *Elle*, *Los Angeles Times*, *Town & Country*, *Body+Soul*, and travel.msn.com. What is Ayurveda? "Ayurveda is a health system that has been successfully used for prevention and healing for over 5000 years." www.theraj.com

- Read *When the Body Says No* by Gabor Maté, M.D. The author delves into the cost of hidden stress and its consequences on the body. He is a strong believer in the mind/body connection.

Spotlight
THE GODFATHER OF FITNESS

Some years ago, I was privileged to meet Jack LaLanne in the Admirals Club at the Los Angeles airport. I introduced myself and one of the first things I said to him was, "You know Jack, you are one of my heroes. I've got your juicer!"

He laughed. Then he made a fist, tensed his bicep, held it up, and said, "Feel that, Jim!"

I squeezed his bicep and it was hard as rock. This guy is strong!

Next he patted his abs and instructed me, "Feel this."

His stomach muscles were like the proverbial washboard. I believe that he was around 93 years of age at that time. Really, he looked 30 years younger.

I also chatted with his wife Elaine, who was a delightful person. Jack told me she was the power beneath his muscle. "We are partners and friends and lovers, everything." You could even see this on their television program, which I was a big fan of.

LaLanne is known as the "Godfather of Fitness" and, though gone now, he's been inspiring us to stay fit since 1936. We can transform our lives by following his mandates: "Eat fresh fruits and vegetables. If man made it, avoid it. Eat whole grains, lean meat, and fish; avoid processed foods; no white flour, no white sugar, and no snacking. Get off your seat and onto your feet. Exercise hard for 30 minutes a day, three to four times a week. You gotta eat right, exercise, and have goals and challenges."

LaLanne's most famous mantra was, "Exercise is king; nutrition is queen. Put 'em together and you've got a kingdom!"

He walked his talk. His day consisted of a two-hour workout from 6:00 to 8:00 a.m.; breakfast of a power drink with 50 grams of soy protein and a whole-grain cereal; lunch of fruit, four egg whites, and soup; and dinner of a raw, ten-vegetable salad, soup, whole-wheat pita bread, three to four ounces of fish, and a glass or two of wine. So there you have it, from the Godfather of Fitness!

You may not have known that LaLanne grew up weak and sickly. As a young boy in Berkeley, California, he filled up on cakes and pies and stayed inside his house. He credits his change at age 15 to going to a lecture by nutritionist Paul Bragg, who pounded up and down the stage and talked about nutrition. LaLanne said, "He had all this energy I wanted." He remembers Bragg saying, "If you obey nature's laws, you'll be born again." Bragg meant eating only natural unprocessed foods, a message that fell on LaLanne's young ears and created a lifelong mission.

LaLanne was ahead of his time. An enterprising young man, he had his own health-food bakery by age 18, and at age 21 started his own gym in downtown Oakland. One person who has followed LaLanne's career is Charlie McCarl, who began working out at LaLanne's gym when it first opened and has been his friend ever since. McCarl believes that LaLanne has made a difference in a lot of people's lives: "He wasn't in it to make a lot of money; he just wanted to make people look better, feel better, and stay healthy."

So let me shine the spotlight on Jack LaLanne, America's exercise guru. I still love to watch reruns on ESPN Classic of old episodes of *The Jack LaLanne Show*; they introduce new generations to LaLanne's fitness regime and high energy.

Jack LaLanne is someone I would like to be like. He had all the energy and vitality I would like to have now and into my 90s.

This lesson contains within it the fundamentals of health. I find that, if we become enamored with complicated strategies, we lose sight of fundamentals and no strategy will work. I believe that the PhB does the fundamentals well and uses them as the foundation for successful living. Work at living, not dying; have goals and challenges that make you get up in the morning. Jack LaLanne was an incredible inspiration for these very ideals.

PART III

COMMENCEMENT

16

Conclusion:
Requirements for Graduation

*Sometimes our light goes out but it's blown again into flame by
an encounter with another human being.
Each of us owes the deepest thanks to those who have
rekindled this inner light.*

— ALBERT SCHWEITZER
humanitarian

Michael Jordan was once asked by an interviewer, "What's it like to be called the best basketball player ever?" Michael replied, "Don't believe everything you read, especially about yourself. I will never be the best ever, but I will never stop *working toward* being the best ever."

Becoming a Professional Human Being is a way of living rather than a destination. One doesn't go to the symphony to listen to the applause at the end. One enjoys the exquisitely played music throughout the whole piece. It is the process that matters.

A Professional Human Being is much like a Ph.D. Once you receive a Ph.D., you do not instantly know everything on the topic. Instead, having a Ph.D. opens you up to a field of investigation that is lifelong. The more you know, the more you know you don't know. You become acutely aware of the immense amount of knowledge that lies ahead. Becoming a PhB is also a work-in-progress.

Getting your PhB means recommitting to living one day at a time. Not all days will go as smoothly as planned. Still, there is perfection within the seemingly imperfect—and this is one of the joys of being human. We may get off-balance at times, but now we have learned ways to recover and move forward.

Reflect on these questions and thoughtful quotes as we review the seven lessons of becoming a PhB:

Lesson 1: Perform Your Magic
A PhB uses his magic in performing whatever activities he's involved in.

> *There are only two ways to live your life. One is as though nothing is a miracle. The other is as though everything is a miracle.*
> — ALBERT EINSTEIN

What do you want to create through your magic, through your specific and unique abilities?

Lesson 2: From Here I Am to There You Are
A PhB defines herself by the difference she makes in other people's lives. She cherishes her ability to be of such high service to her fellow men and women that there is joy, even ecstasy in that experience of giving.

> *I've learned that people will forget what you said, people will forget what you did, but people will never forget how you made them feel.*
> — MAYA ANGELOU

What helps you make a difference in your life as well as in the lives of others?

Lesson 3: Stop Going Out of Your Mind
A PhB takes responsibility for her life, becoming the master of her own destiny—to the greatest degree possible. She is sovereign of her world and is not found playing the role of victim. She is in control of her responses to even the most undesirable circumstances given to her by life—as well as to the most desirable. How we respond to success is just as crucial to our health and well being and future success as failure.

Life can either be accepted or changed. If it is not accepted, it must be changed. If it cannot be changed, then it must be accepted.
— ANONYMOUS

How do you choose to move through the changes that you will face and not go out of your mind?

Lesson 4: See Yourself on Broadway

A PhB is brimming with a creative force. He sees possibilities where others see problems. He envisions what he desires for his life with a refined imagination. He doesn't misuse his imaginative power with toxic thinking.

Imagination is more important than knowledge. Knowledge is limited. Imagination encircles the world.
— ALBERT EINSTEIN

How do you stay in that calm space of creativity so that your problem-solving and idea generation capability grows?

Lesson 5: Stand Up for What You Value Most

A PhB is one who knows what she values most and lives those values. She doesn't fight with herself by compromising what she believes in.

Character isn't something you were born with and can't change, like your fingerprints. It's something you weren't born with and must take responsibility for forming.
— JIM ROHN

What do you value the most?

Lesson 6: If You Don't Know Where You're Going, Speeding Up Won't Help

A PhB is invigorated by focus, direction, mission, and purpose.

Once you make a decision, the universe conspires to make it happen.
— RALPH WALDO EMERSON

What is it that you want to create? What is the future you envision?

Lesson 7: Keep Your Mind/Body Battery Charged

A PhB has high voltage-energy running through his system, not only pumping him with good vitality for a better life, but giving him energy overflow, which can be given out and shared with the world.

The best six doctors anywhere,
And no one can deny it—
Are Sunshine, Water, Rest, and Air,
Exercise and Diet.
These six will gladly you attend
If only you are willing,
Your mind they'll cheer, your ills they'll mend,
And charge you not one shilling.
— AN OLD RHYME

Do you feel ready to take on the world?

Meet someone who is doing just that.

17

Valedictorian:
The Saint of Colombia

Nobody cares if you can't dance well. Just get up and dance.
Great dancers are not great because of their technique,
they are great because of their passion.

— MARTHA GRAHAM
teacher and choreographer of modern dance

Father Gabriel Mejía is a man who is saving lives, one van-full at a time. In the introduction of this book I introduced you to Leroy Grant, the leather technician, and now I want to end the book by introducing you to someone else. I am honored to call friend and someone I admire immensely, Father Gabriel.

I first heard about Father Gabriel from my niece Angela while she was a student at Maharishi School in Fairfield, Iowa. Father visited her class and spoke to them about his programs. Angela gushed about how kind, loving, and sweet the priest was. She was inspired by him. As am I—and as you will be!

Father Gabriel lives in Colombia. He was born in beautiful Cali, a city I've had the pleasure of visiting recently when I presented at Pontificia Universidad Javeriana, the prestigious Jesuit University. Father—himself a practitioner of Transcendental Meditation for the deep rest, stress relief, alertness, and expansion of awareness it offers—was at the Maharishi School to learn more about the technique's applications in education and child development.

Father Gabriel is from a community of Roman Catholic priests and brothers founded in 1849 by Saint Anthony Mary Claret called the Claretian Order. Their aim is to see life through the eyes of the poor and respond to their greatest need. For Father Gabriel, that translates into saving the street children of Colombia—children dropped off in large cities to fend for themselves, by their poor, desperate families no longer able to support them. Many of these street children turn to sniffing glue and taking other substances to escape their pain. They often end up turning to theft and prostitution just to survive. It makes me sad even to type these words. These poor children are at risk of drug addiction, starvation, and early death.

Father Gabriel established Centers to help these children. Scouring the city, he and his staff drive vans searching the streets relentlessly for them. The children willing to accept help are picked up and taken to one of the Centers.

About the homeless Father says, "when we bring them from the street, many have no money in their pockets. We provide them with hot water, soap, shampoo, a shower; we give them a towel and new clothes. We give them breakfast. The child eats eggs for the first time in a long time. The educator then asks. Why don't you stay here and get help? If the answer is yes, the transformation begins. It is hard work!" One of Father's favorite sayings is "there is no such thing as a free lunch."

In fact, May 2011 marked the 27-year anniversary of when Father began responding to these tragedies in his homeland. He now has 54 programs with a staff of more than 700 operating around Colombia and the rest of South America. To date, Father and his staff have served more than 43,000 young adults. What a contribution! Imagine saving that many lives. And, as he explained to me, he does it all using his Catholic faith, Transcendental Meditation, yoga, group counseling, the Boy Scouts and Girl Scouts concepts and practices and above all, love. Father himself was a Boy Scout and now wants the children to learn what he learned from the Scout experience. There are campouts and very practical lessons to be learned from scouting.

Father's foundation is successful because it is a complete program attending to the whole child. It addresses many aspects.

1. Psychological: group counseling

2. Spiritual: Catholic faith
3. Physical: yoga postures
4. Practical Application: practices and principles of the Boy Scouts and Girl Scouts
5. Emotional: the imperial medicine of love
6. Brain Transformation: consciousness-based education / Transcendental Meditation

The basic therapy he uses is love. He describes love as "the imperial medicine for any illness or disorder." Father clarifies, "The heart doesn't have any language. We hug our children. We look at them with love. We heal them with love." When I spoke with him on the phone recently, he told me the story of that morning's Mass, when he read from the Book of Matthew, telling the children of how Jesus healed two blind men through touch. The blind men came to Jesus, crying for help. He touched their eyes and brought them sight. Jesus healed them through touch. Father Gabriel and his staff use love to touch and heal the hearts of the children.

Father told me that he begins his day with a three-hour personal program, which includes an hour of exercise, an ayurvedic health massage, and his practice of Transcendental Meditation. He completes his session by saying Mass. He takes care of mind, body, and spirit. He explained that he gives these three hours to himself and, besides sleep, the rest to others.

I visited Father Mejia and his foundation and volunteered my time for one week by speaking at several of his program locations in Bucaramanga and Medellin. I watched him in action with the children; I saw the joy on his face. I saw the profound dedication to and affection for the children from Father, of course, but also equally from the staff. I saw a lot of hugging and genuine love there. I did a lot of hugging and fell in love with Father and the children myself.

All children have the opportunity to learn Transcendental Meditation while in his programs. Actually, his five full-time TM teachers have taught over 7,000 children to meditate. Father says that TM takes away the stress in the children's lives and, when the children begin to meditate, they open themselves up to the infinite. The world opens up for the child. The child discovers his inner nature, which is love. He said that every time he looks into the eyes of a child he is inspired to help. Whenever a child in need is standing in front of you there exists an opportunity to help. His philosophy is that "the child is not a problem; she is an opportunity. She has infinite potential."

Like any great leader, Father Gabriel could not do this work alone. When I asked him what makes him successful, he responded, "The people I work with. My 700 staff along with another 700 volunteers inspire me as they work with the kids every day. They listen, they love, and they have a profound feeling of compassion for the kids. This inspires me every day. This makes me successful."

Father's success is immeasurable, but I was especially impressed by the fact that about 35 percent of his staff had actually come from the streets, gone through his program, and now are the most devoted of his staff members. Some have even gone on to become his best, most compassionate directors.

One of the wonderful, dedicated volunteers of Father Gabriel's organization is Sonia Vera. I met Sonia at Maharishi University of Management while I was completing my master's program. She introduced me to Father and acquainted me with his work and foundation. With tears in her eyes, Sonia began to tell me about Juan Camilo Estrada-Parra. Juan is just one example of the many successes of Father's programs.

Born in Medellin, Colombia, his biological parents never raised Juan; his godparents took him in. His godparents, however, threw him out of their home when he was 14 because he was not attending school and was taking drugs. He ended up living on the streets, feeling completely lost. He was introduced to Father Gabriel and his Center. He had meals there off and on but didn't move in right away. When he would visit the Center he began to feel "at home" for the first time in his life. After Juan made the decision to stop using drugs, he was placed in Libertad, the Center for boys ages 14 through 18.

During his time at this Center, he finished high school and then decided that he wanted to join the staff and become an "educator"—to help the new arrivals in the same way that he had been helped. This position cares for the children entering the program. Like Juan, about one third of the educators in Father Gabriel's program were once on the streets and addicted to drugs and are now assisting others to become drug-free and get on track to a successful life. Father says "he considers working with the educators one of his richest experiences. They are so compassionate!"

In order to qualify as an educator, Juan had to participate in a one-and-a-half-year training program. He received a certificate from La Federación Latinoamericana de Comunidades Terapéuticas (Federation of Latin American Therapeutic Communities), which is an exclusive program sponsored by the United Nations.

Today Juan is 20 years old and is attending Maharishi University of Management. He is taking classes in English as a second language while pursuing a degree in Physiology and Health. With this specialized knowledge, his goal is to return to the Center and establish more natural Ayurvedic-based detox programs. Juan told me that he believes "he was born to help these kids in need." You'll be happy to know that Juan has been reunited with his godparents who are proud of his academic pursuits.

Father Gabriel's overall mission is revealed when he says, "We are all committed to transforming the world we are living in. We should leave the world a better place than we have found it." His philosophy to meet the many challenges and resistance he faces is that, "Drop by drop, water can break a stone." He has broken many stones!

Father Gabriel's important work has been recognized worldwide, including by an award from the World Federation of Therapeutic Communities, an award from the Queen of Spain for his humanitarian work, and by the Catholic Men of Austria Foundation in Salzburg. He has served as president of the Latin American Federation of Therapeutic Communities. In 2009, the pinnacle of recognition occurred when Father Gabriel was nominated for the Nobel Peace Prize—which, in my opinion, he should have won!

To see Father interacting with the children, search online for *Saving the Disposable Ones,* a documentary about Father Gabriel made by the David Lynch Foundation. You can support Father Gabriel's extraordinary work by purchasing the documentary. Visit Father Gabriel's site at foundationclaret.org to find out how you can help.

Thousands of children who have passed through the doors of Father Gabriel's Centers are dramatically transformed through love, caring, and meditation. He says that the children in his care leave as "professionals."

I love that one Professional Human Being is transforming others into Professional Human Beings!

To call Father Gabriel a Professional Human Being may even be trivializing his status because he has been referred to as the "Saint of Colombia," but with permission I will add yet another title to this wonderful human being. I would like to follow his example by changing and saving one life, as he is saving many. While being with him, I feel his extraordinary love and compassion. I experience a "contact high." I walk away wanting to do only right in the world. I feel the reality that we can really change lives. When I reflect on the time I spent with Father Gabriel and his children I cannot remember fully the contribution I may have made, but I can tell you that the visit transformed me in a dramatic way. It contributed to my growth in a dramatic way by having direct contact with a man and a mission that represent purity and nobility.

How does Father Gabriel personify the qualities of a Professional Human Being?

Lesson 1 Do you think he performs his magic?

Lesson 2 Has Father Gabriel helped make a difference in his own life and in the lives of others?

Lesson 3 Would you consider Father Gabriel a sovereign or prisoner of his life?

Lesson 4 Does he see possibilities in his life instead of seeing problems?

Lesson 5 Does he know what he values and live by those values?

Lesson 6 Does he have a clear view of where he's going?

Lesson 7 Does he keep his mind/body battery charged?

It is a laudable goal for us all as we strive to become PhBs to have the kind of influence Father Gabriel has in the world—whether we are priests, teachers, nurses, plumbers, mothers, bus drivers, students, magicians, politicians, or leather technicians.

In the stories in this book, we have seen people making choices that brought them health and happiness, choices that actualized their potential and enabled them to spread their magic in the world.

Becoming a Professional Human Being is not a destination; it's a lifelong journey. It is a unique experience. Committing to living as a Professional Human Being on a daily basis is the goal.

And now, my friends, you are ready.

GODSPEED ON YOUR JOURNEY!

Acknowledgements

As you can imagine, I could not have accomplished this by myself. I am very grateful to all of you who have contributed in your own way to the creation of this book. The names are many.

Bob Larson: You recruited me to attend The University of Akron in 1967, were instrumental in getting me a scholarship, gave me my first professional job in 1971, believed in me enough to send me out to speak for the university, and told me at the end of our work together that my two greatest strengths were my ability to speak and to write. I have made a profession out of speaking, and now I am writing. Thank you for pointing out what was possible and walking with me down this path. I am deeply indebted to you.

Marci Shimoff: You helped me to outline my first presentation on this topic in 1985, organized my first public speech, and outlined this book, which you thought should be written. You inspire me with your best-selling books and by being who you are.

Dr. Warren Blank: Thank you for introducing me to my profession and for your encouragement to write this book. You did the first reading and, when you liked it, inspired me to continue. You have always been the best of partners in business and on the path to enlightenment.

Aaron Brown: As my first agent, you gave me a chance with this topic in a very conservative venue almost twenty years ago. You also gave me great guidance on the development of this book, which was formed during that 18-year run at the Western Management Development Center. Your encouragement and at times prodding to write were essential.

Marty Zucker: You spent months with me structuring and writing our book proposal, which in turn was the blueprint for this book. You then, as the great wordsmith you are, did a thorough edit of my writing and got rid of a

296

lot of the fat in my first attempt at book writing. You have provided a lot of guidance and knowledge to refine this text. You also added your enormous experience as a medical writer. More than that, you and Rosita are dear friends of mine from India to California and I cherish our friendship. Also, I send a special thanks to our literary agent, Jack Scovil, for believing in the project when there are innumerable projects to consider.

Dr. Kim Payton and Valerie Payton: I appreciate your friendship and diligent work on the assessment that will be a companion to this book. Also, Kim, thank you for your support in getting the presentation of this material to our clients in Hawaii.

John Bagnola: Your videos were the essence of this book's manifestation. Capturing my presentations for the past 20 years provided the foundation for this book. Thanks for being a good business partner, a fantastic brother, and a Professional Human Being.

Steve Katz: Thank you for being a great friend and for videotaping my PhB presentations in Hawaii. They were later transcribed for this book.

Judy Kew: Your hard work doing the very first transcription of the videos and audios shaped this book. Your ideas and wisdom have made their way into my book and into my world.

Naomi and Ryan Abe: Your speedy, accurate, and thorough transcriptions created my master's thesis of this topic and then evolved into this book. I'm indebted to the Hawaii Prince Hotel for allowing me to borrow your talents.

Mary Mathew: Every story in this book comes alive with your vivid creativity and amazing command of the English language. Your incredibly sharp editing eye and attention to detail have fine-tuned and enhanced the entire book. I appreciate your giving this book high priority over the last couple of years. Thank you for your assistance and cleverness on this and many other projects over the years.

Jeanette Delmar: The last ten yards are the hardest to cover. Without you, my dear, I would not have traversed these ten yards and scored. You are tireless in your support, unselfish with your skill in writing, boundless with patience, and generous with your enlightened vision. You have given me your steady stream of consciousness that has made the book coherent and special, just like you.

Jan Sickler: I'm lucky to have you as my brother-in-law; you have such a sharp intellect and creative nature. My book got infected with it. Thank you, Jan!

Brad Fregger: You have been a great friend and resource in this book writing process. Thank you for sharing your knowledge of book publishing and design so freely. Thanks also for the time you invested in bringing my book to completion.

Barbara Foley: Thank you for your keen editing and the many hours of attention you gave to the book. I also appreciate all your great suggestions and contributions.

To all of you in the fields of health, management, and workplace environment whom I have quoted and consulted: You have made the book what it is. I thank you all.

To all of you who allowed me to use your personal stories: I am deeply indebted.

To the thousands of workshop participants over the last 25 years: Thank you so much for all the wisdom you have brought to me about this topic and life.

To all of you who previewed my book and graciously wrote the comments that I quoted at the front of the book and on the back cover: Thank you!

To my editors: I am eternally grateful for your commitment to excellence. Thank you Marty Zucker, Jeanette Delmar, Barbara Foley, Mary Mathew, Jan Sickler, and Sais Bagnola.

Dr. Fred Travis, Lee Moczygemba, Candace Badgett, Dr. Ron Hulnick, and Lindsay Oliver: Thank you for the time you spent reading this book and giving me valuable feedback.

Dr. Veronica Butler: You generously and brilliantly wrote the Foreword to this book. Thanks for taking the time. I am very grateful to you.

George Foster: Your clients told me that your covers are award winning and now I know why. Thank you for my superior cover design.

Thank you to many others who gave me the opportunity to develop and present the content of this book over the last twenty years: Mike Durbin, John Hale, Rich Liebl, Phil Evans, Jimie Ramirez, Brigadier General Michael L. Cunniff, Lt. Col. Steven Rothstein, Ernest Norte, Lina Savkar, Sharon Senecal, Joe Riddle, Andy Jardine, Phyllis O'Meara, Tonie Campa, Robert Stevens, Bob Zincke, Barney Asato, Steve Kamaura, Jane Uyetake, Davis Yogi, Mahealani Cypher (Denise DeCosta), Babs McGuffin, Lee Moczygemba, Petru Pacuraru, Ovidiu Bujorean, Marshal Belden, Ben Thomas, Jan Kemp, Kathy Matayoshi, Brooks Yuen, Peggy Hong, Pat Hamamoto, Wynette Nagai, Manny Nevis, Christian Douglas, Dr. David Biemer, Garry Foster, Susan O'Donnell, Bill Ennis, and Freda "Sunshine" Borden-Ealy. Thanks for your continuing support.

And to you, my dear Saismatie, what can I say? Thanks for being my true magician!

About Jim Bagnola

For over twenty-five years, Jim has been speaking, coaching, and educating worldwide on the topics of leadership, stress management, customer service, coaching, and change—all in relation to the secrets of the mind-body connection. He is an expert in the field of leadership and mind-body management, with emphasis on the influence of thinking patterns on health, happiness, success, and the capacity to lead. His focus is on building Professional Human Beings.

Jim studied Political Science at The University of Akron (Ohio), Vedic Science (Human Development) at Maharishi European Research University in Switzerland, and Spiritual Psychology at University of Santa Monica (California). He completed his master's degree in Vedic Science at Maharishi University of Management (Iowa). A certified stress-management instructor since 1975, he is also an executive coach to Fortune 500 company leaders. Jim has had various professions. He has held corporate VP positions, served as Assistant Director of Financial Aid at The University of Akron, Director of Conferences at Western Illinois University, and in Hollywood worked as business manager for world-famous magician Doug Henning.

In 2002, Jim earned the designation of Certified Speaking Professional (CSP), a recognition conferred by the National Speakers Association and the International Federation for Professional Speakers. This designation has been awarded to only about six hundred professional speakers worldwide. This qualifies him as one of North America's top-rated speakers. Leadership Gurus International listed him among the "World's Top 30 Leadership Professionals" from 2007 through 2010. This honor is given to select professionals who have distinguished themselves for their originality, practicality of ideas, presentation style, and proven ability to assist organizations to achieve superior results.

He is President of The Leadership Group International, a visiting faculty member of Western Management Development Center in Denver, the Chairman of the Board of Leaders Romania, and a member of the Board of Trustees of Olive Branch Foundation in Ohio. He also gives much of his time as a frequent lecturer for Association Internationale des Étudiants en Sciences Économiques et Commerciales (AIESEC), an international student organization that enables young people to explore and develop their leadership potential with the intention for them to have a positive impact on society.

Jim values his ongoing opportunity of influencing and interacting meaningfully with both private- and public-sector organizations, including Shell Oil Company, The Kroger Company, U.S. Secret Service, U.S. Department of State, U.S. Air Force, United Nations Development Programme, Marriott Hotels, Siemens, Motorola, Scotiabank (Canada), McEnearney Alstons Ltd. (Trinidad), PT. Ispat Indo (Indonesia), Hella (Romania), Ecolab (Romania), Castle & Cooke (Hawaii), The University of Texas, Continental Airlines, Air France, Talent Plus, Inc., Pontificia Universidad Javeriana (Colombia), and Radisson Hotels.

Born and raised in Canton, Ohio, Jim is a voracious reader and learner, health enthusiast, world traveler, and ardent sports fan. When he isn't living in a hotel, Jim spends time at his home in Austin, Texas.

Jim would love to hear how this book has inspired you!

Email: Jim@JimBagnola.com
Website: www.jimbagnola.com
Tel: 512-419-4139